To
Sheryn and Anthony
and
Helen and Salome

who exemplify the
"meaning of life: the act of living itself"
(Erich Fromm)

A time there was – as one may guess
And as, indeed, earth's testimonies tell –
Before the birth of consciousness,
When all went well.

Thomas Hardy, "Before Life and After" (1928),
from *Winter Words* (Gibson (2001))

GOD, FREUD AND RELIGION

The origins of faith, fear and fundamentalism

Dianna T. Kenny

Routledge
Taylor & Francis Group

LONDON AND NEW YORK

First published 2015
by Routledge
27 Church Road, Hove, East Sussex, BN3 2FA

and by Routledge
711 Third Avenue, New York, NY 10017

Routledge is an imprint of the Taylor & Francis Group, an informa business

British Library Cataloguing in Publication Data
A catalogue record for this book is available from the British Library

Library of Congress Cataloguing in Publication data
Kenny, Dianna T.
    God, Freud and religion : the origins of faith, fear and fundamentalism / Dianna T. Kenny.
       pages   cm
    Includes bibliographical references.
    1. Freud, Sigmund, 1856–1939.   2. Psychology and religion.   3. Violence–
    Religious aspects. 4. Psychoanalysis.   I. Title.
    BF173.F85K46 2015
    200.1'9–dc23
    2014039671

ISBN: 978-1-138-79132-9 (hbk)
ISBN: 978-1-138-79133-6 (pbk)
ISBN: 978-1-315-76289-0 (ebk)

Typeset in Bembo
by Out of House Publishing

GOD, FREUD AND RELIGION

Does God exist? Was Freud right to view religion as a residue of infantile wish-fulfillment? Can modern science and spirituality be reconciled? Not afraid to tackle the big questions, Kenny's prodigious combination of clarity and scholarship are exceptional. If Freud is the Bach of modern psychology, reading her – uniquely a Professor of Music as well as Psychology – is to encounter classic psychoanalytic scores interpreted in the light of contemporary understanding. A must-read for all students of psychoanalysis, psychology, philosophy and religion, and all who seek illumination in a post-modern world of chaos and confusion.

Professor Jeremy Holmes, MD, FRCPsych, University of Exeter, UK

This is a remarkable work of analysis and integration of perspectives. Dianna Kenny addresses crucial questions: can science and religion pull together as a team instead of pulling apart? Should we blame religious fanatics or religion itself for violence? Does religion have a monopoly on values? The author canvasses questions of faith, extremism and violence in Christian and Islamic religions and evokes parallels with nationalistic ideologies and dictatorial regimes from earlier and more recent history. This work should help us understand how fundamentalist beliefs are formed and why they are difficult to modify, and how religious beliefs can be employed in the service of perverting human nature for political and other secular purposes. Professor Kenny's discussion of the formation of fundamentalist beliefs can contribute towards understanding some of the underlying roots of current conflicts, for example in the Middle East, and assist in conflict resolution and the achievement of peace in our troubled world. As such it is particularly timely.

Ahmad Shboul, AM, Former Chair of the Department of Arabic and Islamic Studies, The University of Sydney

Religious fundamentalism – what Kenny aptly characterizes as terror theology – has been a major source of violence, both large scale and small, over the course of human history. The terrorist attack on the World Trade Center and the "holy" crusades are just two of a multitude of examples of atrocities committed in the name of God. Thus Kenny's penetrating, exhaustive, multidisciplinary examination of the genesis of religious belief and how it has been exploited for political purposes is no mere academic exercise. It is an attempt to locate significant roots of what philosopher Hannah Arendt aptly terms radical evil.

Robert D. Stolorow, PhD, author, World, Affectivity, Trauma: Heidegger and Post-Cartesian Psychoanalysis (Routledge, 2011)

Did God create man or did man create God? In this book, Dianna Kenny examines religious belief through a variety of perspectives – psychoanalytic, cognitive, neuropsychological, sociological, historical and psychiatric – to provide a coherent account of why people might believe in God. She argues that psychoanalytic theory provides a fertile and creative approach to the study of religion that attempts to integrate religious belief with our innate human nature and developmental histories that have unfolded in the context of our socialization and cultural experiences. Freud argued that religion is so compelling because it solves the problems of our existence. It explains the origin of the universe, offers solace and protection from evil, and provides a blueprint about how we should live our lives, with just rewards for the righteous and due punishments for sinners and transgressors. Science, on the other hand, offers no such explanations about the universe or the meaning of our lives and no comfort for the unanswered longings of the human race.

Is religion a form of wish-fulfilment, a collective delusion to which we cling as we try to fathom our place and purpose in the drama of cosmology? Can there be morality without faith? Are science and religion radically incompatible? What are the roots of fundamentalism and terror theology?

These are some of the questions addressed in *God, Freud and Religion*, a book that will be of interest to psychoanalysts, psychologists and psychotherapists, students of psychology, psychoanalysis, philosophy and theology and all those with an interest in religion and human behaviour.

Dianna T. Kenny is Professor of Psychology at the University of Sydney, Australia. She is the author of over 200 publications, including six books.

CONTENTS

TABLES

1

SCIENCE, GOD AND RELIGION

Introduction

> *Le doute n'est pas une condition agréable, mais la certitude est absurde.*
> (Doubt is not a pleasant condition, but certainty is absurd)
> > Voltaire, in a letter to Frederick II of Prussia (6 April 1767)

Historically, enlivened debate on religion and the existence of God has been prompted by scientific advances. Examples include Copernicus's heliocentrism (i.e., discovery that the earth was not the centre of the universe) and Galileo's telescope that allowed us to see further into the galaxy than ever before, and which supported Copernicus's view that the sun was the centre of the cosmos. In 1632, Galileo published *The Dialogue Concerning the Two Chief World Systems* in which he was charged with the task of presenting the arguments for and against the thesis that the sun or the earth was at the centre of the universe. The book infuriated Pope Urban VIII because Galileo argued that science (and not religion) could better answer questions about the universe. In 1633, he was brought to trial for heresy. What was really on trial was the question of who owned the truth about the cosmos. Sadly, it wasn't Galileo, who was found guilty, condemned to life imprisonment and died a broken man.

Isaac Newton's masterpiece, *Principia* (1687), which explained how the force of gravity held the planets on course, crystallized a new vision of the universe. More than 200 years later, Edwin Hubble, an American astronomer, burst the bubble of Newton's concept of a 'mechanistic universe'. He created the next radical shift in our understanding of the universe, demonstrating that the earth is but one small planet in one galaxy amongst a vast number of galaxies. In between came Darwin's (1876) evolutionary theory, which prompted panicked calls for a return to the familiar doctrines of creationism and intelligent design.

More recently, quantum physics, the multiverse hypothesis (i.e., there may be many other universes apart from our own) and MRI imaging of the brain are challenging the concept of a non-physical 'soul', and explaining the possible neurochemical bases of religious hallucinations, near-death experiences and ecstatic states. Unsurprisingly, these lines of enquiry have also spawned both reactionary and revolutionary calls for or against religious doctrine. Notwithstanding tremendous advances in the brain mapping of human emotion, memory, cognition and movement, there are many unsolved mysteries in human subjectivity that are not (yet) accessible to the neurosciences. For example, Pribram (2004) has rightly observed that brain imaging has not (yet) revealed the locus of subjective states such consciousness, meditation or inspiration. However, science is rapidly advancing in its capacity to understand previously puzzling phenomena like out-of-body experiences and other disturbed self-perceptions (Heydrich & Blanke, 2013), issues that I will take up later in the chapter.

Recent scholarship on the relationship between science and religion falls into three main groups: the first group argues that science and religion are not mutually exclusive. Exemplars include Joan Roughgarden (2006), Francis Collins (2006) and Peter Todd (2012). The second group comprises atheists such as Christopher Hitchens (2007), Daniel Dennett (2006), Richard Dawkins (2006) and Sam Harris (2004, 2006), whom Gorski and Türkmen-Dervişoğlu (2013) described as "the four horsemen of the new atheism" (p. 197) and reductionist materialists like Lewis Wolpert (2006). They view science and religion as incompatible and not only argue forcefully against the existence of God but assert that religion is conducive to violence. See, for example, Dawkins's (2006) statement, "We should blame religion itself [for violence], not religious extremism as though that were some kind of terrible perversion of real, decent religion" (p. 345).

The third is a 'middle' group, exemplified in the journal *Zygon* (from the Greek 'to yoke'), who attempt to resolve the schism between science and religion, to get them to pull together as a team rather than act as adversaries, because it "is essential for a viable dynamics of human culture" (Peters, 2010, p. 431). According to Zygonists, neither science nor religion is an end in itself, nor is the project of integrating or uniting science and religion. The ultimate aim is the advancement of life on earth; science and religion take their places alongside technology and political and social structures to form a sustainable socio-cultural system that honours life. Peters (2010) argues that the purposes of science and religion are different – the goal of religion is to transmit life's values, aims and motivations, while science is charged with the acquisition and transmission of knowledge. The split between knowledge (science) and values (religion) is problematic because they are naturally interdependent. Older forms of religion cease to be credible in the wake of new sciences and technologies and must therefore change and adapt in light of new knowledge, just as the world of Copernicus, Galileo and Newton had to adapt, however reluctantly, to their scientific insights about the nature of the universe. Science transforms man's worldview about the "nature of the forces and realities that shape his destiny" (Peters, 2010, p. 432), which in turn transforms our way of life, and with it our responsibilities and moral obligations. For example, the advent of the atomic bomb created enormous moral and philosophical dilemmas for humanity. In 1945, during World War II, the United States government had to balance its actions for the common good in deciding to drop the atomic bomb on Hiroshima, the site of large military supply depots, in order to end the war, knowing that such as an action would kill 80,000 Japanese citizens.

Zygonism is an idealistic but implausible vision. It takes for granted that religion is the only vehicle for the development and dissemination of morals and values. Yet, it is possible to exist in a humanistic society that espouses fundamental values such as the right to liberty, justice and equality without shrouding these values in the cloak of religious doctrine. Fromm (1964) offered a humanistic interpretation of Christian religion, arguing that "the fundamental concept of humanity is embodied in Christ" (p. 70) because Christ was both God and man. Several philosophers, including Hume, Goethe, Kierkegaard, Russell and Einstein, have extolled similar humanistic values that could potentially unite the human race, obviate the need for religion and prevent the "total bureaucratization of man" (Fromm, 1964, p. 71). This may be true for the project of developing universal human values, but humanism does not offer redemption or eternal life, features that that make religion so attractive.

Conservative religions appear to conflate religion with the cultural worldview in which it is practised. Although religions are expressed within the worldview of a wider culture, the worldview is more than the religion. Religious conservatives attempt to maintain the faith status quo as it is expressed within pre-scientific worldviews, believing that the worldview is essential to the expression of their religious faith. Religious conservatism has been a significant problem for the Roman Catholic Church, which, at all stages of its history has been slow to adapt to the insights of science and changing worldviews. In fact, the Catholic Church was so opposed to progress that it spearheaded the Counter-Reformation in the sixteenth century, which spawned a number of Catholic Inquisitions – Roman, Spanish, Portuguese and Maltese – whose remit was to prosecute those accused of heresy, that is, beliefs or opinions contrary to official Church doctrine. I will have more to say about the Inquisitions in the final chapter.

A more contemporary example of the confusion of religion with worldview is the bitter debate that erupted in several states of the USA about whether schools should be permitted to teach the doctrine of creationism as part of their science curriculum, which, among other content, tells students that the earth is 6,000 years old, that the Bible is the written word of God and therefore incapable of error or contradiction, that the resurrection of Jesus was a physical and historical fact and that the world has a pre-ordained end at which time God will gather His people to Him. Eventually, the Supreme Court of the United States ruled in 1987 that teaching creationism as science in public schools was unconstitutional and banned the practice, declaring that teaching science must have a secular purpose, whose primary aim is neither to advance nor inhibit religion. Further, the ruling upheld the doctrine of the separation of church and state. This was a courageous ruling given that 53 per cent Americans are creationists (Harris, 2008).

> Those with the power to elect our presidents … believe … that the first members of our species were fashioned out of dirt and divine breath, in a garden with a talking snake, by the hand of an invisible God.
>
> (Harris, 2008, p. xi)

These brief examples show how the conflation of religion with worldviews gives rise to problematic expressions of religion, including literalism and fundamentalism, phenomena that are the subject of the last chapter.

Freud, science and religion

> For the Jews require a sign, and the Greeks seek after wisdom; but we preach Christ crucified.
>
> (1 Corinthians 1:22–23)

Freud (1935) explained in the "Postscript" to his *Autobiographical Study* that he had retained an abiding interest in the question of religion and "cultural problems" for the whole of his life, which, he said, "had fascinated me … when I was a youth scarcely old enough for thinking" (p. 72). Despite his keen interest, Freud, although Jewish and married to a Jew whose grandfather (Isaac Bernays) was a Chief Rabbi, decided early in his life that he did not believe in God or immortality, although he professed respect for the ethical demands facing human civilization, and the importance of conduct consistent with the values of social justice.

Freud's family were non-observant Jews who celebrated Christian holy days, such as Easter and Christmas, rather than Jewish feast days. However, he was well instructed in the Jewish faith, knowledge which no doubt was immensely helpful to him in the writing of *Moses and Monotheism* (1939), a work devoted to tracing the origin of the Jewish religion. Freud valued science and reason above religion and superstition and located his work within the determinist-scientific tradition of Copernicus, Galileo, Kepler, Newton and Darwin (Palmer, 1997), which viewed science and religion as radically incompatible. Freud's position on this relationship is elaborated in "The question of a *Weltanschauung*" [worldview], in *New Introductory Lectures on Psycho-Analysis* (1933).

"Obsessive actions and religious practices" (Freud, 1907) represented Freud's first attempt to codify his thoughts on culture and religion. This was followed by *Totem and Taboo* (Freud, 1913a) and *The Future of an Illusion* (Freud, 1927). The opening paragraphs of this work presage *Civilization and its Discontents* (Freud, 1930a). Then followed "The question of a *Weltanschauung*" in *New Introductory Lectures* (Freud, 1933a); "Why war?" (Freud, 1933b); and *Moses and Monotheism* (Freud, 1939), Freud's erudite examination of the origins of belief in a singular deity.

Judging by the large number of books written on religion, by both protagonists and antagonists (Barbour, 2000), Freud was certainly not alone in his fascination to understand "the human quest for the experience of the numinous and for trans-personal meaning in life" (Todd, 2012, p. 23). Most recent books on religion have variously been written from historical, philosophical, theological, scientific (biological) or personal perspectives and employ evolutionary, empirical, rationalist, positivist or critical approaches. Freud (1918) and Jung (1933) argued that theology and the concept of God must be understood from a psychological perspective, a call echoed by Todd (2012), who opined that without reference to post-quantum physics, cognitive neuroscience and depth psychology, much of the scholarship on God will fail to satisfy our deepest longings for resolution of the psychophysical (mind/matter) problem, the problem of metaphysical materialism (i.e., the doctrine of mortality as extinction of the self) and our place in the "drama of cosmology" (p. 1). Psychoanalytic theory has provided a fertile and creative approach to the psychological study of religion that continues to reverberate in most current texts on the subject. Freud's work is distinctive, if not unique, in his attempts to integrate religious belief with our innate human nature (comprising our temperament and instinctual drives) and developmental histories that have unfolded in the context of our socialization and cultural experiences (Beit-Hallahmi & Argyle, 1997).

Although Freud had great faith in science's ability to solve the riddles of our existence, he was also aware that "it is not easy to deal scientifically with feelings" (Freud, 1930, p. 64) and that feelings on matters of religion run very deep. The same is true for religious experience. In "The question of a *Weltanschauung*" (in 1933a), Freud stated that religion is so compelling because it 'solves' all of the problems of our existence. It answers questions about the origin of the universe, it offers comfort and solace in life and protection against evil and provides a blueprint about how we should live our lives, with just rewards for the righteous and due punishments for sinners and transgressors. Would that we could all embrace the bountiful and beneficent Father God of the nineteenth century, as expressed in this extract:

> Contemplating the endowments of man, the provision made in nature for his happiness, and the order of God's providence for encouraging him to work out his own improvement and elevation, the intelligent mind thrills with vivid emotions of love, gratitude, and admiration of their great Author. A "present Deity" is felt to be no longer a figure of speech or a flight of poetry, but a positive and operating reality. "We not only feel that we live, and move, and have our being" in God, but become acquainted with the means through which His power, wisdom, and goodness affect us, and discover that we are invited, as His moral and intelligent creatures, to co-operate in the fulfilment of His designs. The beautiful exclamations of King David, "If I climb up into heaven, Thou art there; if I go down to hell, Thou art there also; if I take the wings of the morning, and remain in the uttermost parts of the sea; even there also shall Thy hand lead me, and Thy right hand shall hold me", are felt to be expressions of a living truth; and man takes his true station as the interpreter and administrator of nature under the guidance of nature's God.
>
> (Combe, 1857, p. 253)

Science, on the other hand, offers no such explanations about the universe or the meaning of our lives and no comfort for the unanswered longings of the human race to know. Melanie Klein (1975) believed that the need to know was so strong that it took on the quality of a drive that she called the "epistemophilic instinct", which Bollas (1998) believed represented "an essential part of one's encounter with the mysteries of life" (p. 29) in contrast to the acceptance of theological explanations, which constitute a symptom of "strain of trying to know more than one does" (p. 29).

Science can only derive from observation and reasoned argument about those observations; it eschews divine revelation and faith as sources of knowledge. Nonetheless, human beings cling wistfully to religious belief, an edifice, according to Freud, constructed of their own fantasies that originated from feelings of helplessness in infancy and early childhood and which transmute into adulthood as a belief in a beneficent deity, a remnant of the Father God of childhood. Freud discussed the differences between science and religion in the following terms:

> *Scientific thinking does not differ in its nature from the normal activity of thought, which all of us, believers and unbelievers, employ in looking after our affairs in ordinary life.* ... [I]t takes an interest in things even if they have no immediate, tangible use; it is concerned carefully to avoid individual factors and affective influences; it examines more strictly the trustworthiness of the sense-perceptions on which it bases its conclusions; it provides itself with new perceptions which cannot be obtained by everyday means and it isolates the determinants of these new experiences in experiments which are deliberately varied. Its endeavour is to arrive at correspondence with reality ... with what exists outside us and independently of us and ... is decisive for the fulfilment or disappointment of our wishes. This correspondence with the real external world we call "truth". It remains the aim of scientific work even if we leave the practical value of that work out of account. *When, therefore, religion asserts that it can take the place of science, that, because it is beneficent and elevating, it must also be true, that is in fact an invasion which must be repulsed.* ... It is asking a great deal of a person who has learnt to conduct his ordinary affairs in accordance with the rules of experience and with a regard to reality, to suggest that he shall hand over the care of what are precisely his most intimate interests to an agency which claims as its privilege freedom from the precepts of rational thinking. And as regards the protection which religion promises its believers, I think none of us would be so much as prepared to enter a motor-car if its driver announced that he drove, unperturbed by traffic regulations, in accordance with the impulses of his soaring imagination. [My italics]
>
> (Freud, 1933a, pp. 170–1)

Freud (1935) concluded that "the events of human history, the interactions between human nature, cultural development and the precipitates of primeval experiences (the most prominent example of which is religion) are no more than a reflection of the dynamic conflicts between the ego, the id and the superego" (p. 72), and that the best hope for mankind is intellect as opposed to "religion's prohibition against thought" (Freud, 1933a, p. 171). I will take these matters up again in Chapter 6, where I critique Freud's theory of religion.

In an early paper, Zilboorg (1939) attempted to account for the prevalent hostility directed towards psychoanalysis.

> Every scientific system begins as a *revolutionary idea*. Opposed at first, it grad-ually crystallizes into a set of accepted *dogmatic principles*; an *orthodoxy* is then established which creates a rapidly growing harvest of *heterodoxies*. These het-erodoxies, for the most part eclectic compromises, give *violent battle to the prevailing system of thought*. On the other hand, the *established dogma defends itself with considerable vehemence but ultimately degenerates into a set of authori-tarian, lifeless postulates* which prove very brittle in the hands of an objective investigator. In the wake of this débris, there is left as a permanent heritage of knowledge the few data which are truths and therefore able to withstand the storm of events. Hippocratic medicine and its offspring, the Galenic system, went through this series of developmental stages until they finally yielded, *not without bloodshed and passionate stultification*, to modern scientific principles. [My italics]
>
> (Zilboorg, 1939, p. 481)

I wonder whether this argument holds true if we replace the concept 'scientific' with 'religious'. In the following pages, you will be intrigued to find that the history of psychoanalysis and indeed all new knowledge, religions and 'movements' demonstrate uncanny parallels with the processes described by Zilboorg.

Aims

The Bible tells us that God created man in his own image. Freud argued in the reverse – that man created God in his image (Freud, 1901) and that these images were derived from "revivals and restorations" (Freud, 1910, p. 123) of children's early images, later called object representations, of their parents (Klein, 1948; Winnicott, 1953). Put otherwise, Freud believed that one's God-concept represents and expresses one's internal psychic reality. This book interrogates these two prop-ositions. From an examination of religious belief through multiple lenses – psycho-analytic, cognitive, neuropsychological, sociological, historical and psychiatric – I hope to provide a coherent account of why people might believe in God. I will argue that the psychoanalytic perspective and Freud's works on religion offer the theoretical scaffolding upon which some of the timeless questions concerning the genesis of religious belief can be understood and how it is employed in the service of perverting human nature for secular or political purposes.

Through the application of knowledge derived from cognitive and developmental psychology, social psychology and neuroscience, together with a close reading of Freud's works on religion and subsequent psychoanalytic scholarship on that body of work, this book applies a number of theoretical perspectives to help us to understand the origins of religion, and its relationship to human nature, madness, fundamentalism and terror theology. I propose that reason and philosophical argumentation alone cannot advance our understanding beyond a certain point. While there is a body of work on the relationship between psychoanalytic theory and religion (e.g., Black, 2006; Meissner, 1984, 2009; Rizzuto, 1979), there are few studies that review the psychoanalytic perspective in the context of other disciplines within psychology (e.g., neuroscience, cognitive, developmental and social psychology) or apply this theorizing to understanding fundamentalism and terror theology in a systematic way. In this book, I hope to integrate knowledge from all of these disciplines in order to provide a richer and more nuanced understanding of religion, how people behave with respect to their religious beliefs and perhaps how we can understand and prevent the 'holy' wars that are destroying our planet.

Structure of the book

In this chapter, I have presented a brief outline of the course of religion and science, and their periodic, very public collisions at times of scientific advancements. I have situated Freud in the science/religion debate.

In Chapter 2, I explore the major arguments for and against the existence of God and note that neither group of arguments is likely to result in religious conversion in the reader. I then discuss the problem of morality – whether there can be morality without religion – and the primacy of subjective experience in religious belief. An exploration of advances in neuroscience that can inform the debate follows, including a review of the evidence that may explain out-of-body experiences, near-death experiences and other spiritual and numinous events. I conclude this chapter with a discussion of the role of 'ordinary' cognition in the formation of religious beliefs.

Chapters 3, 4 and 5 examine Freud's seminal works pertaining to religion. We begin with *Totem and Taboo* (Chapter 3) and examine Freud's argument that religion may have developed from totemic practices in primitive tribes. I examine the practices and beliefs of totemism from the perspective of pre-logical thinking, obsessional neurosis and the notion of conscience. I conclude this chapter with a comparison of Durkheim's and Freud's theories of religion.

In Chapter 4, I provide a close reading of *The Future of an Illusion, Civilization and its Discontents* and *Moses and Monotheism* – in order to examine the intersection of religion, culture and philosophy from a psychoanalytic (Freudian) perspective.

In Chapter 5, we begin with a discussion of the demonic and its relation to madness. I consider the context embeddedness of both the form of religious belief and madness citing two case studies graphically portrayed by Freud – those of

Christoph Haizmann, a medieval monk, and Daniel Schreber, a prominent German judge – who both presented with demonic religious delusions as the central feature of their mental illnesses. There follows a brief discussion of the psychodynamics of myths, legends and fairy tales that keep such beliefs alive, how such beliefs arose in the course of human evolution and why so many people are able to believe in a set of propositions that not only cannot be verified, but for which there is vast evidence to the contrary. I conclude this chapter with an examination of the auto-biographical nature of faith, illustrating it with four short biographies of philosophers – Kierkegaard, Nietzsche, Wittgenstein and Heidegger – whose philosophical theories encompassed religion. I also explore the possible motivation, from a psychoanalytic perspective, underpinning Richard Dawkins's stance that God does not exist.

In Chapter 6, I review Freud's theories related to religion and the critiques of these theories offered by contemporary psychoanalysis.

In Chapter 7, I examine group processes, the origins of interpersonal violence and contributions to our understanding of group behaviour, including religious-nationalist violence and cult membership from the perspective of the psychology and psychoanalysis of violence and social psychology, referencing the work of Milgram, Bandura and Zimbardo.

I conclude, in Chapter 8, with a discussion of fundamentalist religious beliefs in both Christian and Islamic religions, how they are formed and why they are so difficult to modify. I finish with some thoughts about how the ideas presented in this book may assist conflict resolution and the attainment of peace.

2

DOES GOD EXIST?

The affirmative argument

> In the beginning God created the heavens and the earth. Now the earth was formless and empty, darkness was over the surface of the deep, and the Spirit of God was hovering over the waters.
>
> (Genesis 1:1–2)

In this chapter, I will tackle the numerous arguments for and against the existence of God. It is not intended to be an exhaustive review of the very large popular and scholarly literature on the subject. Rather, it is intended as an overview to assist readers to situate their own thoughts, beliefs and questions about the existence of God and to provide an anchor for what is to come. We will start by summarizing the arguments for the existence of God. This will be followed by the counter-arguments from the atheists and agnostics. First, we need to understand what we mean by the word 'God'. Below is a working definition that I will use throughout this book:

> Western concepts of God ... [encompass the characteristics] of a creator and sustainer of the universe ... [who is] unlimited with regard to knowledge (omniscience), power (omnipotence), extension (omnipresence), and moral perfection. Though regarded as sexless, God has traditionally been referred to by the masculine pronoun.
>
> (Internet Encyclopaedia of Philosophy (IEP), 2013)

Does God exist, and if He does, how do we know and what is His nature? In a now famous paper, the philosopher Thomas Nagel (1979) asked "What is it like to be a bat?" Nagel concluded that we have no idea and no way of finding out what it is like to be a bat. We may very well ponder the same question in relation to God, but we will press on regardless. We will begin with one of the oldest arguments for the existence of God from the modern era.

[Anselm's] ontological argument

Anselm, a Christian thinker who lived in the eleventh century, was the first to formulate an ontological argument that God exists, which he set out in his *Proslogium* (*Discourse on the Existence of God*) (1962, 2013). Anselm argued that a fool, like the one described in Psalms 14:1 ("The fool hath said in his heart, There is no God", KJV), whom today we would call a rational atheist, understands the claim that God exists but does not himself believe in God. According to Anselm, to hold both of these propositions to be true is internally inconsistent, thereby making any man who held them a fool. The ontological argument constitutes an attempt to deduce through logic that our concept of God proves that God exists. It makes no empirical claims of proof, as do other arguments to be discussed below. Rather, ontological arguments try to show that we can deduce the existence of God from the definition of God. In other words, Anselm argued that God cannot exist in understanding alone. It is a tortuous argument that states that if we can conceive of two identical 'things', one of which exists only in understanding and the other of which also exists in reality, then the thing that exists in reality is greater than the thing that exists only in understanding. This being the case, the 'God' that exists in understanding can be conceived as greater than it actually is, which is absurd because the definition of God is one who cannot be greater. Hence, God must exist in reality. Put another way, if God existed only in the mind and that mind is limited and finite, then a greater being than one who exists in understanding must be possible. The corollary is that if the concept of the greatest possible being exists in the mind, it must also exist in reality.

Anselm developed a set of propositions based on this argument to demonstrate that God exists. God is defined in Anselm's argument as "the being than which nothing greater can be conceived". These propositions have subsequently been expressed in various ways, of which two are given below. The first is Plantinga's (1965, 1974) version based on modal logic, which is the logic of the modal, the possible, the contingent and the necessary (Garson, 2013).

1. God exists in the understanding but not in reality. (*reductio* assumption)
2. Existence in reality is greater than existence in the understanding alone. (premise)
3. God's existence in reality is conceivable. (premise)
4. If God did exist in reality, then He would be greater than He is. (from (1) and (2))
5. It is conceivable that there is a being greater than God is. ((3) and (4))

6.   It is conceivable that there be a being greater than the being than which noth-
     ing greater can be conceived. ((5) by the definition of 'God')
7.   It is false that God exists in the understanding but not in reality.

A more recent version (Craig, 1994) states the ontological argument as follows:

1.   It is possible that a maximally great being exists.
2.   If it is possible that a maximally great being exists, then a maximally great being
     exists in some possible world.
3.   If a maximally great being exists in some possible world, then it exists in every
     possible world.
4.   If a maximally great being exists in every possible world, then it exists in the
     actual world.
5.   If a maximally great being exists in the actual world, then a maximally great
     being exists.
6.   Therefore a maximally great being exists.

The arguments proceed from a comparison of what exists in understanding (I
would also add imagination) and what exists in reality. For example, we may have
some understanding (imagination) of extra-terrestrial beings but we may not
believe they exist. It is therefore possible for things to exist in understanding but
not in reality (e.g., vampires); to exist in both understanding and reality (e.g., the
sun); and to exist in reality, but not (as yet) understood (e.g., other solar systems).
There have been many critiques of the ontological argument, among which Kant's
is pertinent.

> If … I annihilate the predicate in thought, and retain the subject, a contradiction
> is the result; and hence I say, the former belongs necessarily to the latter. But
> if I suppress both subject and predicate in thought, no contradiction arises; for
> there is nothing at all, and therefore no means of forming a contradiction. To
> suppose the existence of a triangle and not that of its three angles is self-contra-
> dictory; but to suppose the non-existence of both triangle and angles is perfectly
> admissible. And so is it with the conception of an absolutely necessary being.
> Annihilate its existence in thought, and you annihilate the thing itself with all its
> predicates; how then can there be any room for contradiction? Externally, there
> is nothing to give rise to a contradiction, for a thing cannot be necessary exter-
> nally; nor internally, for, by the annihilation or suppression of the thing itself, its
> internal properties are also annihilated. God is omnipotent – that is a necessary
> judgement. His omnipotence cannot be denied, if the existence of a Deity is
> posited – the existence, that is, of an infinite being, the two conceptions being
> identical. But when you say, God does not exist, neither omnipotence nor any
> other predicate is affirmed; they must all disappear with the subject, and in this
> judgement there cannot exist the least self-contradiction.
>
>   (Kant, 1781, trans. Meiklejohn)

Kant is saying that worlds are possible without God and that a godless world contains no contradictions. Kant also argued that both the ontological and cosmological arguments are not sustainable because both attempt to establish the existence of God empirically. Kant proposed that no argument from human experience can be brought to bear on the question of the existence of a super- or supra-human entity like God. However, Kant then engages in some fancy footwork by stating that the very limitations of human knowledge actually raise the question of faith, not on the basis of any rational proof that may be offered but on the basis that the very limitations of man indicate that he needs moral guidance from a higher being. Carl Jung subsequently developed a similar thesis: first, that "the psyche cannot leap beyond itself. It cannot set up absolute truths" (Jung, cited in Dembski, 2003, p. 299); second, because of man's propensity to develop images of God, these images always contain a moral dimension. Jung (1963) equated God with the Unconscious, and through humanity God became conscious of His creation. Jung (1977) further argued that if God is a psychic reality, and if psychic reality is the only experience that we can know, then the claim that God exists is psychologically true. Jung distinguished between psychic experience, which we 'know', and metaphysical assertions, which we believe. Belief implies uncertainty – I believe that God exists but I cannot know with certainty. Jung (1979) is concerned only with what we know, and if we know that God exists, we have no need of belief.

For my own part, I agree with the propositions of Kant and Jung that a human mind cannot apprehend the transcendental, just as we cannot apprehend what it is like to be a bat. The propositions contained in the ontological argument are constructed with a human mind, necessarily using concepts available to the human mind and therefore delimited by our finite cognitive capacities. How then does a finite mind apprehend the concept 'maximally great'? Maximum on what scale of measurement? Great with respect to what capacities? If we return to our definition of God, the scales of measurement appear to be omniscience, omnipotence, omnipresence and moral perfection. What are the extreme or maximal endpoints of these dimensions and how can we recognize them as maximal endpoints? For example, morality is a social construction, and perfection in morality does not comprise a universally agreed set of precepts across culture and history, so by what standard can we know the moral perfection of God? Further, is it not possible for an anti-God, for example, a demon or Satan, to be conjured into existence using the same set of logical propositions that Anselm, Plantinga and others have used to demonstrate that God exists? We can imagine a demon as well as a god and show similar 'understanding' of these entities. If we can imagine that God (a maximally 'good' being) exists, surely we can imagine that Satan (a maximally 'bad' being) exists. The apprehension of the concept 'maximally' is equally problematic for both 'good' and 'bad'. St Thomas Aquinas (1224–74) expressed a similar objection to the ontological argument. He believed that the existence of God was self-evident and could not be deduced from arguments about the nature or character of God. Because we are finite humans with finite capacities for understanding, Aquinas argued that we can only understand finite concepts. Claiming that God is the greatest being that we can imagine or that exists does not clarify the nature or character of God.

In other words, if we conclude that God exists using the ontological argument, then Satan has an equal probability of existing. But what are the scales of measurement that should be applied to Satan? On what dimensions do God and Satan differ? Moral perfection is the obvious candidate. God is (purportedly) morally perfect and Satan morally imperfect. As humans are morally imperfect, are we more likely to have been created in Satan's image than God's? What are the other characteristics of Satan? Is he also omniscient, omnipotent and omnipresent? If he is not, God should be able to defeat and banish Satan from soul and mind and to end all evil in the world. Clearly, this has not been achievable, so Satan must be God's equal on all dimensions save for morality. How, then, can we deduce who created us, or rather, in whose image we have been created?

Further, Anselm and Jung appear guilty of the 'sin' of psychic equivalence, that is, the error of equating the contents of one's internal mental states or mind with external reality (Fonagy & Target, 1996a). In fact, Gaunilo of Marmoutier, a monk and contemporary of Anselm's, was quick to alert Anselm to the problem of defining an idea into existence. This cognitive error explains why children are afraid of the monsters of their nightmares (Siegel, 2005). Anselm makes a similar error. He moves from the idea of God, which is an internal mental state, to asserting the existence of that idea as substantive in external reality. It is the equivalent of saying "I had a nightmare about a monster that came to eat me. Therefore, there must be a monster out there in the world of which I must be afraid lest he does eat me." I will later show how frequently the cognitive errors of children appear in religious thinking.

A similar problem of psychic equivalence arises with the leap from possible worlds to actual worlds. The possible worlds are the worlds that I imagine and actual worlds are substantially real worlds. The argument stating "If a maximally great being exists in some possible world, then it exists in every possible world" does not allow for the possibility that the maximal beings who created these worlds are indeed one and the same. Humans in our world worship and understand God in different ways, particularly with respect to moral perfection; it is therefore likely that the gods in other possible worlds would be 'different' from the god in our world – that is, they may have different dimensions of maxima, some of which we may not yet know or understand. (For a detailed and authoritative discussion of the ontological argument, see the Internet Encyclopedia of Philosophy.)

It is ironic that so many philosophers have spent so much time discussing this argument for God's existence even though it is unlikely to be a stimulus leading to belief or religious conversion. A number of other arguments for the existence of God have been proposed and they will be briefly summarized in the next session.

Cosmological argument

The cosmological argument (also known as the First Cause argument) addresses one of the most fundamental questions in our quest for understanding ourselves and our place in the universe, if indeed we have one! Why does anything exist at all?

Why is there a universe rather than nothing? Why do we humans populate this universe? Swinburne (1996) argues that it is natural for humans to seek "the ultimate explanation of everything observable" upon which the existence and explanation for existence of all other entities depend. The simplest explanation is God; theism claims that God is the First Cause; that every object is caused to exist by this First Cause.

Aquinas's *Summa theologica* contained the first modern treatise on the cosmological argument, although its arguments were influenced by both Plato's (428–327 BCE) *Timaeus* (Plato, 1949) and Aristotle's (384–322 BCE) *Metaphysics* (Aristotle, 1956). Modern supporters include Craig (1993, 1994), Copan and Craig (2004) and Swinburne (1996). Critics include David Hume (1757), Immanuel Kant (1781), Bertrand Russell (1957) and Kenny (1979). This argument is a seemingly simple and elegant solution to the cosmological question. Simple is good, but it is usually the case that the issue is not so simple. Albert Einstein once quipped, "We should make everything as simple as possible, but not simpler." The problem with the cosmological argument is easy to grasp – who or what created the First Cause? Although the First Cause theory attempts to explain everything that exists in the universe, we cannot explain the existence of the First Cause. This is known as the problem of infinite regression.

Atheists address this fundamental flaw with the cosmological argument by stating that the universe was not created – it is eternal and uncaused. As Russell (1957) stated "If there can be anything without a cause, it may just as well be the world as God" (p. 2). However, both of these arguments suffer from the problem of infinite regression. If the universe never began to exist but just existed for all eternity, then there would be an infinite number of past events, which implies a regression to infinity. In response to the question, who or what created the First Cause? Theists respond that God was uncreated, that is He is an uncaused cause, but this is essentially the same unsatisfactory argument given by atheists about the universe. The idea of an infinite past is not sustainable. Infinity is a man-made construct that does not exist in reality. It cannot be found in nature nor can it provide a basis for rational thought. So both theists and atheists are in trouble with the cosmological argument (Harris, 2008).

Most scientists believe that the universe is not uncaused and that the earth came into being approximately 13 billion years ago as a result of the Big Bang (Behe, 1996; Meyer, 2013). It follows that anything that has a beginning has a cause, and at some point in the causal chain, we must inevitably arrive at an uncaused cause. Aquinas (2012) appeals to two principles in science, namely, that (i) every effect requires a cause, and (ii) nothing in the world can be the cause of its own existence. For Aquinas, the uncaused cause is God; for the materialist, the uncaused cause is a singularity that we cannot explain. David Hume (1779) and Bertrand Russell (1957) agree that we need to accept the existence of the universe as a 'brute fact', that is, the universe just is and we cannot expect to know otherwise (Ash, 2001). If we reject God as the uncaused cause, equally we cannot accept that physical entities like our universe materialized out of nothingness (Copan & Craig, 2004).

Christian cosmologists argue that the cause that brought the universe into being also created time and space. To achieve this bringing of time and space into being, the cause (God) must not only be causeless, but timeless, spaceless and immaterial (non-physical); hence, a transcendent, omnipotent, omniscient, intelligent mind created the universe (Moreland & Craig, 2003). This view has received support from the declared scientist-Christian Francis Collins (2006), of mapping the genome fame. In *The Language of God: A Scientist Presents Evidence for Belief*, Collins argues that the existence of God is not a scientific question and can therefore not be answered by appeals to science. God, he says, 'exists' outside of nature, space and time, and would necessarily have had to be 'outside' in order to create the universe. This kind of reasoning is also applied to explain the inexplicable in Christian doctrine, for example, the 'facts' regarding the resurrection of Jesus after his crucifixion and purported miracles, including raising Lazarus from the dead, exorcising demons and turning water into wine. All defy natural laws. However, Collins sees no problem because (a) God operates outside of natural laws; and (b) Christ himself was divine, and therefore not beholden to the laws of nature.

In glaring contrast to his scientific writing, Collins's writing on evangelical Christianity appears, in the words of Sam Harris, to be "intellectual suicide" yet he has garnered the reverence and support of those in high places, including the editors of the prestigious scientific journal *Nature*, who cannot see that the emperor has no clothes (Harris, 2009). Collins actually subscribes to the view that "after evolution had prepared a sufficiently advanced 'house' (the human brain), God gifted humanity with the knowledge of good and evil (the Moral Law), with free will, and with an immortal soul" (Collins, 2008). Collins came to faith from a 'God-revealed-in-nature' moment in the shape of a frozen waterfall. He appears to be imbued with pre-modern, indeed medieval notions of God's will and purpose as mystery, and resorts to such explanations whenever confronted with theological and philosophical inconsistencies. Of all his beliefs and assertions, the prize for the one producing the most astonishment is his account, borrowed from John Polkinghorne, also a scientist, of the human soul.

> If we regard human beings as psychosomatic unities, as I believe both the Bible and contemporary experience of the intimate connection between mind and brain encourage us to do, then the soul will have to be understood in an Aristotelian sense as the "form", or information-bearing pattern, of the body. Though this pattern is dissolved at death it seems *perfectly rational* to believe that it will be remembered by God and reconstituted in a divine act of resurrection. [My italics]
>
> (Polkinghorne, 2003, pp. 22–3)

Perfectly rational? Cursory reading of any of Collins's works on religion will reveal a form of magical, pre-operational, non-logical thinking that is found in young children, which I discuss at length at the end of this chapter and again in Chapter 3. May I respectfully suggest that the cosmological Christians consult Kant (1781), who, in a series of brilliant *Antinomies*, argued persuasively both for and against the existence of God, freedom and immortality? He concluded, consistent with the thesis of this book, that philosophy is incapable of reconciling reason and religion.

Teleological argument

> The brain is just the weight of God,
>   For, lift them, pound for pound,
>   And they will differ, if they do,
>   As syllable from sound.
>
> (Dickinson, 1924)

The principal thesis of the teleological argument (also known as the natural law argument) is that the 'conditions' or circumstances under which the Big Bang brought our universe into being were fine-tuned with such precision to support intelligent life that only a transcendent, intelligent mind would be capable of such a feat. An early proponent was Sir Isaac Newton. Today's creationists, such as Joan Roughgarden (2006) in *Evolution and Christian Faith: Reflections of an Evolutionary Biologist* and Francis Collins (2006) in *The Language of God: A Scientist Presents Evidence for Belief*, assert that their work in science has convinced them that the hand of God is at play. Collins (2006) claims that the simultaneous occurrence of the precise conditions, called the six constants, required to create life as we know it are so improbable as to require God to explain it. In other words, the odds against the occurrence of these six constants by chance are so great as to be almost impossible. Thus enters the theory of Intelligent Design (Behe, 1996; Meyer, 2013), which is argued to be the best explanation for the simultaneous confluence of so many complex systems and laws that permit the development of life, such that only an intelligent designer who stands outside of his creation could have masterminded such a masterpiece. The counter-argument is, of course, the Darwinian notion of adaptation to the environment – living creatures who adapt to their environment are more likely to survive than those who do not adapt. The notion of adaptation does not require the notion of intelligent design to sustain it.

> The old argument of design in nature … which formerly seemed to me so conclusive, fails, now that the law of natural selection has been discovered. We can no longer argue that, for instance, the beautiful hinge of a bivalve shell must have been made by an intelligent being, like the hinge of a door by man. There seems to be no more design in the variability of organic beings and in the action of natural selection, than in the course which the wind blows. Everything in nature is the result of fixed laws.
>
> (Darwin, in Barlow, 1958, p. 87)

Russell was similarly singularly unimpressed with the quality of design, if such design existed.

Do you think that, if you were granted omnipotence and omniscience and millions of years in which to perfect your world, you could produce nothing better than the Ku Klux Klan or the Fascists? Moreover, if you accept the ordinary laws of science, you have to suppose that human life and life in general on this planet will die out in due course: it is a stage in the decay of the solar system; at a certain stage of decay you get the ... conditions of temperature and so forth which are suitable to protoplasm, and there is life for a short time in the life of the whole solar system. You see in the moon the sort of thing to which the earth is tending (something dead, cold, and lifeless).

(Russell, 1957, p. 4)

Atheists and rationalists counter-argue in favour of the multiverse hypothesis (Carr, 2007). Because there is a very narrow band of conditions in the universe that make life possible, life-prohibiting universes are therefore more probable than life-permitting universes. Recent advances in astronomy have confirmed the existence of planets outside our solar system. Astronomers have also discovered that these planets behave quite differently to the planets familiar to us. Some of these planets appear to be made of ice and water, others of gas, yet others of rock. Just as Copernicus radically changed our thinking with his discovery that the earth was not the centre of our universe, now we know that our solar system is neither unique nor central in the multi-planet systems beyond our own universe (Marcy et al., 2005). There may be an infinite number of randomly ordered, undetectable universes of which our universe is a very small part. Because the odds of a life-permitting universe are so small, such a universe can only appear by chance. Bertrand Russell (1957) explained "The laws of nature are ... statistical averages such as would emerge from the laws of chance ... the whole idea that natural laws imply a lawgiver is due to a confusion between natural and human laws" (p. 3). Richard Dawkins (2006) argued that God is even more improbable than the conditions required to create life; that the six constants happened to be in an invariable relationship with each other; and if there is no life in other universes, perhaps it is due to the fact that these constants were not aligned in the same way as they were in our universe.

Moral argument

Simply stated, the moral argument claims that if God does not exist, then objective moral values that are universally valid and binding are not possible. The case is presented in terms of the tendency for humans to adopt a normative moral code; that is, humans are intrinsically aware of the difference between right and wrong, what their moral obligations are and which behaviours are forbidden or taboo (see Chapter 3). They also understand that moral obligations are binding and must be

TABLE 2.1 Percentages of Muslims who believe in God (Q1), that God is necessary for human morality (Q2) and that religion is very important in my life (Q3)

Country	Q1 (percentage)	Q2 (percentage)	Q3 (percentage)
Afghanistan	>99	86	92
Palestinian territories	–	–	85
Egypt	99	94	72
Thailand	99	94	95
Indonesia	98	95	93
Malaysia	98	–	–
Pakistan	98	85	94
Turkey	97	70	67
Bangladesh	96	89	80
Nigeria	93	68	87
Democratic Republic of Congo	90	63	82
Russia	89	56	44
Kazakhstan	83	41	–

Source: Pew Research Center - Templeton Global Religious Futures Project, www.globalreligiousfutures.org/.

fulfilled. These moral imperatives seem to have a universal quality. For example, a promise is a promise in every culture and the correct behaviour with respect to having made a promise is to fulfil it, regardless of other contingencies cohering to that promise. The moral argument is simply stated as follows:

1. It appears to human beings that moral normativity exists.
2. The best explanation of moral normativity is that it is grounded in God.
3. Therefore God exists. (Byrne, 2013)

It seems that a large majority of Muslims agree with this proposition. Researchers at the Pew Research Center asked them three questions: (Q1) "Do you believe in one God, Allah, and his prophet Muhammad?";[1] (Q2) "Is it necessary to believe in God to be moral and have good values?"; (Q3) "How important is religion in your life?". Replies from Muslims from countries around the world are collated in Table 2.1.

The practical theistic approach to morality states that we would become discouraged and despairing if there were no moral order. Demoralization of the human race is undesirable because we need to believe in a moral order. Belief in God makes it easier to accept that there is a universal moral order in the world. Striving to be good – that is, to act according to the universal moral code – allows us to reap rewards from the divine arbiter (Adams, 1987; Drabkin, 1994). I will discuss the alternative to theistic morality in the next section. For a detailed treatment of the moral argument, the interested reader is referred to Byrne (2013).

The immediate experience of God

> For now we see only a reflection as in a mirror; then we shall see face to face.
> Now I know in part; then I shall know fully, even as I am fully known.
>
> (1 Corinthians 13:12)

This 'proof' states that God's existence does not rely on logic, science or evidentiary facts. We know as a matter of faith that God exists; we know through our direct and immediate experience of God. Knowing that God exists is a "properly basic belief" (Craig, 1994) like the belief in the reality of the external world, the existence of the past and the presence of other minds. There are many 'basic beliefs' or 'brute facts' that we cannot prove but which we accept and believe intuitively to be true. These beliefs are grounded in experience, not reason. Craig (1994) further asserts that those who know God have a properly basic belief in the existence of God. In fact, engaging in arguments to prove God's existence can distract us from seeking God. So concerned was the Catholic Church about the many attempts to prove that God existed through reason and logic that they published an edict that stated that "God can be proved by the unaided reason" (Russell, 1957, p. 2). If we are genuinely seeking God, then God will make His existence known to us. The inner voice of God will speak to us directly, thereby becoming an immediate reality in our lives.

If someone asserts that he believes in God, what he actually means is that God is a psychic reality, an immediate, almost self-evident fact of his subjective experience. We cannot progress, however, to draw the conclusion that God exists apart from this psychic experience. This is not to argue that God does not exist, simply to state that this 'proof' of God is proof of nothing but my subjective experience. However, since the concept of God has arisen in human consciousness and language, it follows that without man and his psychic (and cognitive) experience, God does not exist. This was in fact the argument put forward by Friedrich Nietzsche which resulted in his pronouncement that "God is dead". Jung (1976) concluded that pursuing the question as to whether or not God exists is futile; one either has numinous or divine experiences or not. Erik Erikson (1959), a developmental psychologist, proposed an appealing but flawed alternative. He devised a theory with eight stages of development, in each of which certain psychological tasks had to be achieved if children were to grow to be autonomous adults. The first developmental task is the development of basic trust – in themselves, their caregivers and the world in general. Erikson links this stage with religion – parents who are religious derive a faith in themselves and the world that they communicate to their infant as basic trust. Parents who don't have religion must derive such faith and trust from another source because we know that children of atheists are capable of basic trust, so the immediate experience of God or the transmission of this immediate experience to offspring are not necessary or sufficient conditions for either development of belief in God or basic trust in ourselves and others.

In a more recent treatment of this 'proof', Peter Todd (2012), in his book *The Individuation of God*, describes the immediate experience of God as a fundamental search for a numinous experience, for which he believes we all yearn. Todd attempts to construct a mystical, holistic vision of the numinous that embraces all people, transcending the barriers of culture and ethnicity to gather mankind under the mantle of the unified Jungian archetype of the collective unconscious. Todd argues that the evolution of God and man are coextensive. Necessarily then, the human vision of God has transformed in the course of human evolution from a primitive, animistic entity into the terrifying deities of mythology and the Old Testament, to a benign and beneficent Father God of the New Testament, to the vengeful God of the Middle Ages and finally to a bifurcated view of God in the modern era – the first a "demythologized and annihilated god" (Cruz, 2013) and the other the fundamentalist god of literalist religions. Todd is highly critical of the god defiers and deniers like Richard Dawkins and Christopher Hitchens, whom he argues prosecute an anachronistic case against a now defunct conception of an anthropomorphic and patriarchal God, an intelligent designer of a mechanistic universe. Rather, he endorses a return to the Jungian conception of God as a timeless cosmic archetype (Jung, 1970). Todd entertains the notion that if God through Christ, as a symbol of the Self, can become human, then humanity can become divine, thereby reaching an "omega point" at which humanity attains the apex of cosmic consciousness, a transcendent reality far beyond ego consciousness. Jung's concept of mind goes even further, beyond the collective unconscious of humanity – it becomes coextensive with the cosmos itself as it approaches the infinite. These are complex ideas not readily accessible to the majority of struggling humanity. Reduced to its minima, the fundamental issue for this approach is "to ponder Jung's question as to whether we are connected to the infinite or not" (Kenny, 2012, p. viii).

The negative argument

> Atheism that consists entirely in vacuous arguments afloat on oceans of historical ignorance, made turbulent by storms of strident self-righteousness, is as contemptible as any other form of dreary fundamentalism.
>
> (Hart, 2009, p. 3)

Hart (2009) is here making the point that the 'new atheism' is itself fundamentalist or in danger of becoming so. I will be arguing later in this book that fundamentalism of all colours – Christian, Islamic, atheistic, national socialist, communist – has its origins in the personal experiences of its exponents, in particular those early, often preverbal, experiences that have long been obscured by language and so-called rational, sometimes strident argument. On the surface, these forms of fundamentalism appear very different, but if we peel away their historical, social, cultural and political vestments, we may come to common ground in their multifarious formation – human nature. First, though, we need to hear from the new atheists themselves.

Sam Harris (2004, 2006) presents the most common objections to the doctrines of Western (Christian) theology. Put simply, religion is a bad but entrenched idea, just as the idea of witchcraft was a bad idea, and bad ideas must be challenged with logical argument. Harris views the Christian religion as an ugly doctrine that has ugly consequences because the Bible promotes division and inequality – *inter alia* it demands the execution of 'witches', supports slavery, endorses mass killing of infidels and condemns homosexuality. God lets bad things happen; for example, despite the earnest supplication of their parents, millions of children die each year from preventable causes, often in terror and agony. Harris believes that a god who would allow children to die in this way and do nothing is either impotent or evil. Harris also rails against the narcissism of a religion that claims that God has counted the hairs on the heads of believers, signifying His close involvement with and care of His flock, yet does not seem to care about the unrelenting suffering of more than half of the world's population, who are caught in wars, poverty and natural disasters. Christianity is therefore a religion for the 'chosen few' even though God purportedly made all of humankind in His own image.

As for non-believers or those who have non-Christian religious beliefs, such as the world's billion Hindus, they are, according to Christian doctrine, consigned to the torment of hell for all eternity. The place of forgiveness in Christian doctrine is inconsistent. On the one hand, it is an exacting and unforgiving doctrine that makes extreme demands on its adherents: "If your hand causes you to stumble, cut it off. It is better for you to enter life maimed than with two hands to go into hell, where the fire never goes out. And if your foot causes you to stumble, cut it off. It is better for you to enter life crippled than to have two feet and be thrown into hell" (Matthew 9:44–47). On the other hand, a sinner or a criminal need only come to God in the moment before death to be saved and to enter the kingdom of heaven. In a Note to the Reader of his book *Letter to a Christian Nation*, Harris (2008) states:

> Since the publication of my first book, *The End of Faith*, thousands of people have written to tell me that I am wrong not to believe in God. The most hostile of these communications have come from Christians. This is ironic, as Christians generally imagine that no faith imparts the virtues of love and forgiveness more effectively than their own. The truth is that *many who claim to be transformed by Christ's love are deeply, even murderously, intolerant of criticism.* [My italics]
>
> (p. vii)

Harris's observation of the murderous intolerance of believers is enacted daily around the globe in suicide bombings, assassinations, random shootings, massacres, civil wars and genocide. I will try to help us understand the reason why in the final chapter of this book.

Daniel Dennett (2006), in *Breaking the Spell: Religion as a Natural Phenomenon*, hypothesizes five possible futures for religion. (i) The Enlightenment is over and religion is again sweeping the planet; in due course one religion will take over, but which one is not clear, since all religions are minority religions: Christianity (31–33%), Islam (18–23%), Hinduism (13–16%), no religious belief (12–16%), Buddhism (6–7%), Chinese traditional (6%), primal-indigenous (4–6%) (ii) religion is in its death throes; (iii) religions will transform themselves into creedless moral 'teams'; (iv) religion will diminish in prestige and visibility, like smoking; and (v) Judgement Day will arrive and there will be a new world order or the end of the world (57% of Americans believe this!).

Dennett presents an evolutionary argument for the origin of religion. Just as all life forms have evolved through processes of both natural selection and, more recently, methodical selection by biologists, so too did religion evolve through the same processes. So well designed are religions that they have survived through the millennia, unlike some animal species that failed to adapt or that succumbed to catastrophic environmental conditions. What factors have ensured the survival of religion? At the heart of most of the world's religions is the precept of surrender. In fact, the word 'Islam' means 'surrender' (to the will of Allah). When evangelical Christian pastor Rick Warren lost his 27-year-old son to suicide, he told his congregation: "God knows what it's like to lose a son. … Satan picked the wrong team to pick on. … God wants to take your greatest sorrow and turn it into your life's greatest message. … Thy will be done on earth as it is in heaven, since in heaven God's Will is done always" (Dalton, 2013). Warren's (1997) book *The Purpose-Driven Life: What on Earth am I Here For?* preaches the message of surrender, in which he urges us to seek not our own desires and dreams, but rather God's purpose for us here on earth. If the promotional material is to be believed, this book has sold 32 million copies, suggesting that Warren was peddling a very popular message. These kinds of doctrines share the concept of self-sacrifice and surrender with ideologies like communism and Nazism, which both preach selflessness and subjugation to the state. Why do we, who are purportedly intentional and agentic beings, seek surrender and subjugation?

Dennett offers a radical evolutionary explanation as to why man may be so willing to surrender his agency to an unseen, unknown entity or to an ideology that is clearly in conflict with man's nature. He argued that when people congregated into larger groups that eventually became cities, decision-making became more onerous than it had been in the more primitive and smaller tribes from which they evolved – the larger the group, the more difficult the decision-making process. People therefore sought exo-psychic means of decision-making – rituals, sacrificing animals and looking at their entrails, reading tea leaves, contact with the spirit world, and so on. These were simply variations of flipping a coin to aid in decision-making. Eventually, in most societies, one of the main strategies to aid decision-making was to consult the gods. If things went well, the gods were praised; if not, it was the will of the gods, which exempts us from responsibility. Such practices can spread without anyone understanding the rationale for them. I believe that the process is more complicated, as did Freud. I will explore an alternative explanation that has a psychological dimension for the origin of the need to surrender in Chapter 3.

Richard Dawkins (1989) coined the term 'meme' to describe the smallest replicating unit of human cultural evolution, that is, a 'cultural gene', which is a metaphor for the psychological process that transmits cultural information through cultural means, such as talking, writing, engagement in rituals, various art forms and through conditioning, modelling, imitation and social reinforcement (Barkway & Kenny, 2009) in much the same way as a gene transmits biological information. Both memes and genes self-replicate, mutate and respond to selective pressures. Both memes and genes are selfish in the sense that they are designed to foster their own replication in greater numbers than their competition, just as viruses and bacteria seek means of surviving and replicating in their host organisms. In the same way that viruses and bacteria compete for the resources of their host organisms, so too do ideas compete for 'brain space' and collective mind space. Ideas can be replicated *en masse* in the medium of human culture, just as viruses can be replicated within cells. "If 'survival of the fittest' has any validity as a slogan, then the Bible seems a fair candidate for the accolade of the fittest of texts" (Pyper, 1997). There have been dozens of versions and hundreds of translations. At one time there was a Gideon bible in every hotel room globally. Dawkins considers the Bible as one of the great cultural 'replicators'.

Freud once quipped that wherever he had been in his exploration of the human psyche, a poet had been there before him. The same might be said of Freud. I am hard pressed to find a 'new' idea about the human psyche for which I cannot find a similar or related comment by Freud. For example, I believe the following passage expresses very similar sentiments to those of Dawkins and his memes about the generational transmission of human culture.

> Without the assumption of a collective mind, which makes it possible to neglect the interruptions of mental acts caused by the extinction of the individual, social psychology in general cannot exist. Unless psychical processes were continued from one generation to another, if each generation were obliged to acquire its attitude to life anew, there would be no progress in this field and next to no development. This gives rise to two further questions: how much can we attribute to *psychical continuity in the sequence of generations* and *what are the ways and means employed by one generation in order to **hand on its mental states** to the next one*? [My italics]
>
> (Freud, 1913a, p. 158)

However, it is important that we don't disappear down a rabbit hole trying to strictly define the exact nature of a meme or to reify it with the status of a biological gene. Its place in our understanding remains as a colourful, heuristic metaphor that applied Darwinian insights into biological evolution to cultural reproduction. If we extend the metaphor, it is possible to see that memetic ideas are akin to Lamarck's belief in the inheritance of acquired characteristics. Although Lamarck was referring to physical characteristics, if we apply the notion to psychological characteristics, it becomes more plausible. We now understand that what is acquired psychologically is the nature of object relations or internal working models of caregivers, which are 'inherited' (i.e., internalized) by their offspring. Securely attached mothers have securely attached children; insecurely attached mothers have insecurely attached children (Bowlby, 1958, 1960, 1969). These processes are now understood to explain the generational transmission of culture (Schönpflug, 2009), attachment quality (Fearon et al., 2006) and trauma (Leen-Feldner et al., 2013).

In reviewing the body of work of the new atheists, Hart (2009) is unilaterally critical of most of the current discourse on the subject. In the most colourful language, he systematically demolishes the members of the "devoutly undevout": Richard Dawkins, "with his embarrassing incapacity for philosophical reasoning"; Christopher Hitchens, "whose talent for intellectual caricature … exceeds his mastery of consecutive logic"; Sam Harris, with his "extravagantly callow attack on all religious belief", whose book is "a concatenation of shrill, petulant assertions" (Hart, 2009, p. 8) and Daniel Dennett's "attempts to wean a credulous humanity from its reliance on the preposterous fantasies of religion" (p. 3). In sum, laments Hart, current argumentation lacks the "fierce elegance and moral acuity" (Hart, 2009, p. 5) of earlier philosophers; current commentators are "gadflies" who lack insight, subtlety or refinement, who are ethically complacent and offer only "facile simplifications of history" (p. 6). I wonder how my book will fare under his uncompromising gaze! Woe to him or her who makes assertions with which Hart does not agree …

The challenge of natural religion

> As a substitute for the longing for the father, the superego contains the germ from which all religions have evolved.
>
> (Freud, 1923b, p. 37)

Man has, from earliest times, searched for the numinous and mystical in human experience. Two main paths emerged from this search to understand God. The first, the theological approach, believed that God was revealed to man through the Holy Scriptures, which are apprehended through faith. The second, the philosophical or naturalistic approach, makes no assumptions about the existence or nature of God and seeks to understand reality through reliance on the capacities of the human mind, as opposed to faith and revelation. As Aquinas stated:

> [T]he believer and the philosopher consider creatures differently. The philosopher considers what belongs to their proper natures, while the believer considers only what is true of creatures insofar as they are related to God, for example, that they are created by God and are subject to him.
>
> (1992, bk II, ch. 4)

Natural religion (natural theology) is grounded in ordinary experience, in contrast to revealed religion, which is based in the study of the scriptures and religious (numinous) experience such as revelation and miracles (Hume, 1779). In contrast to the Abrahamic religions that are suffused with dogma, scripture and revelation, Buddhism is more akin to a natural religion with its focus on subjective experience and understanding, its embrace of doubt rather than retreat to scripture in times of uncertainty and acceptance of 'hindrances' along the path to enlightenment.

The concept of natural religion, also known as deism, has long traditions in both Western and Muslim religions. We know this from examining the sacralizing of totems in primitive tribes, the earliest burial rituals that reached the height of complexity in the pyramids in ancient Egypt and the attribution of supernatural qualities to natural phenomena. Natural religion – that is, the religion of God-in-nature – subscribes to the animistic belief that everything that exists, including the supernatural (God, soul, spirits), is an integral part of nature. Expressed otherwise, Nature is God's 'ordinary miracle'. Aristotle believed that God was the "soul of the universe". Galileo understood the universe as a "book of Nature" which was a sign of God. Bill Lauritzen (2006) proposed an interesting theory about the natural origins of religion, which, he argued, derived from three groups of natural phenomena: (i) the 'heavens', that is, astronomical phenomena; (ii) the earth, that is, geological phenomena, especially volcanos; and (iii) the air that we breathe, which has been variously called spirit, psyche, *ba*, *prana*, *reiki*, *qi* and *tao*. It is a bold proposal but not too far-fetched, given our discussion to date.

According to adherents of natural religion, accounts of religion based on the extraordinary, including revelation, were really a misunderstanding of natural phenomena, which are themselves marvellous but not extraordinary, in the sense that the extraordinary needs super- and supra-natural explanations, such as the invocation of gods, demons and other imaginings to be explained or understood. The social anthropologist Alfred Radcliffe-Brown (1952) captured the fundamental differences in worldview between those with naturalistic and those with mythological, spiritualistic or theological conceptions of reality. These vastly incompatible and indeed irreconcilable conceptions are at the heart of the debate about whether God exists.

> In every human society there inevitably exist two different and in a certain sense conflicting conceptions of nature. One of them, the *naturalistic*, is implicit everywhere in technology, and, in our twentieth-century European culture, has become explicit. . . . The other which might be called the mythological or *spiritualistic* conception, is implicit in myth and in religion, and often becomes implicit in philosophy.
>
> (Radcliffe-Brown, 1952, p. 130)

Hicks (2006) observed that "primal religion" continues to be a "living substrate" (p. 4) upon which world faiths have been superimposed, making a similar argument to Freud's – that we need the immature as a substrate of the mature.

Natural religion flourished as a result of the scientific advances in physics and cosmology in the seventeenth century, revulsion at the pessimistic view of human nature proclaimed in the Old Testament and Church orthodoxy (e.g., Pope Innocent III, in *De Miseriae Conditionis Humane Vitae* (On the misery of human life), propagated the view that "man is dirt; he is weak and unstable, and hence he must be directed by strong authorities") and resistance to the idea of "revealed" knowledge, which the Age of Reason demanded be obtained through experience, reason and observation (Greene, 1959). With the application of the methodology of the natural sciences to the study of man and nature, questions inevitably arose as to the truth and infallibility of the Bible. One of the most cogent criticisms of the Bible and the concept of revealed religion came from Charles Darwin. In his autobiography he stated:

> I had gradually come ... to see that the Old Testament from its manifestly false history of the world, with the Tower of Babel, the rainbow as a sign ... and from its attributing to God the feelings of a revengeful tyrant, was no more to be trusted than the sacred books of the Hindoos [*sic*], or the beliefs of any barbarian ... the clearest evidence would be requisite to make any sane man believe in the miracles by which Christianity is supported ... the more we know of the fixed laws of nature the more incredible do miracles become ... men at that time were ignorant and credulous to a degree almost incomprehensible by us. ... [T]he Gospels cannot be proved to have been written simultaneously with the events. ... [T]hey differ in many important details, far too important as it seemed to me to be admitted as the usual inaccuracies of eye-witnesses. [B]y such reflections as these ... I gradually came to disbelieve in Christianity as a divine revelation. ... I was very unwilling to give up my belief ... [b]ut I found it more and more difficult, with free scope given to my imagination, to invent evidence which would suffice to convince me. Thus disbelief crept over me at a very slow rate, but was at last complete. The rate was so slow that I felt no distress and have never since doubted even for a single second that my conclusion was correct. I can indeed hardly see how anyone ought to wish Christianity to be true; for if so the plain language of the text seems to show that the men who do not believe and this would include my Father, Brother and almost all my best friends, will be everlastingly punished. ... [T]his is a damnable doctrine.
>
> (Darwin, in Barlow, 1958, pp. 85–7)

Both Darwin and Freud subscribed to the view that religion(s) developed by natural selection, as one of many domains of human culture that has been shaped by its evolutionary history (Hinde, 1999).

[P]assing over the endless beautiful adaptations which we everywhere meet with, it may be asked how can the generally beneficent arrangement of the world be accounted for? Some writers indeed are so much impressed with the amount of suffering in the world, that they doubt if we look to all sentient beings, whether there is more of misery or of happiness; – whether the world as a whole is a good or a bad one. According to my judgment happiness decidedly prevails, though this would be very difficult to prove. If the truth of this conclusion be granted, it harmonises well with the effects which we might expect from natural selection. If all the individuals of any species were habitually to suffer to an extreme degree they would neglect to propagate their kind; but we have no reason to believe that this has ever or at least often occurred. Some other considerations, moreover, lead to the belief that all sentient beings have been formed so as to enjoy, as a general rule, happiness.

(Darwin, in Barlow, 1958, p. 88)

Darwin had an ardent supporter in Thomas Huxley (1913), who wrote about his frustration and astonishment that his colleagues "shut their eyes to the obstacles which clericalism raises ... against scientific ways of thinking. ... I desire that the next generation be less fettered by the gross and stupid superstitions of orthodoxy" (pp. 123–4).

Boyer and Bergstrom (2008) have offered a set of seven "natural" parameters belonging to ordinary experience that mark out the contents of the religious domain. I reproduce them below.

(i)   mental representations of nonphysical agents, including ghosts, ancestors, spirits, gods, ghouls, witches, etc., and beliefs about the existence and features of these agents;

(ii) artefacts associated with those mental representations, such as statues, amulets, or other visual representations or symbols;

(iii) ritual practices associated with stipulated nonphysical agents;

(iv) moral intuitions as well as explicit moral understandings that people in a particular group connect to nonphysical agency;

(v)   specific forms of experience intended to either bring about some proximity to nonphysical agents or communicate with them;

(vi) ethnic affiliation and coalitional processes linked to nonphysical agents;

(vii) cross-cultural commonalities in each of these domains of thought and behaviour.

(p. 112)

Archaeological evidence indicates that religious practices (e.g., elaborate burial procedures, rock art) existed as early as the Palaeolithic era (Trinkaus & Shipman, 1993). The evolution of tribal instincts supported adherence and loyalty to the specific norms of the tribe as did punishment for norm violations (Nichols, 2002). Humans' natural propensity for reciprocity and cooperation within groups that share cultural (religious) norms further supported the survival and dissemination of the tribe's cultural (religious) practices (Gintis, 2000). However, religious rituals, such as initiation rites, human and animal sacrifice, unfocused exertion such as frenetic dancing and falling into trances, do not appear to support survival. So what is their purpose? They, too, appear to support the norms of the tribe; these behaviours were always performed publicly and everyone was expected to attend to show their support for the tribe and its practices (Sosis, 2003). This view of religion points to its social and communicative roles; there was little emphasis on the internal beliefs of its individual members.

As a counterpoint to the concepts of natural religion, let us briefly examine how the very unnatural (revealed) religion of the Catholic Church became established in Medieval England and across Europe in the Middle Ages. At this time, the country was organized according to a feudal system, in which serfs worked the land of their masters for very little recompense and were thus maintained in a condition of poverty and slavery. To win the hearts of this population, who were unimpressed with promises of eternal life, given the miseries of their earthly lives, the Church needed to find a way to break the hold of paganism and the attraction of more proximal promises of a better life. The Church cleverly began to appropriate pagan practices into their own by incorporating non-Christian holidays into the Christian calendar and conducting them at the same time as scheduled pagan festivities. A clear example is the replacement of the festival of Saturnalia (a pre-medieval Roman feast), a celebration on 25 December of the birth of the sun, with Christmas, the celebration of Christ's birth. Hence, this date was arbitrarily decreed to be the birthday of Christ. Similarly, the period of Lent culminating in Easter was originally a pagan celebration of the renewal of life in spring; the Church appropriated this celebration to signify Christ's resurrection from the dead. The Church also appropriated pagan symbols and practices into their own rituals. Atkinson (1891) captures the ploy perfectly:

> Christianity turned the nature deities into devils, spells into magic, and spaewives into witches – but could not banish the ideas from the imagination of men. So adopted stones and wells turned spells into exorcism and benedictions and charms into prayers.

> (p. 255)

The Church, in this quest to win hearts and pockets for the faith, met all seven criteria for a natural religion, thereby ensuring its growth and survival!

However, the advent of evolutionary biology and the inherent refutation of biblical teaching contained in its theorizing produced extreme opposing reactions – that of the modernists and that of the fundamentalists. Modernism discarded revealed religious concepts of creationism, inspiration and revelation, while the fundamentalists clung tenaciously and rigidly to these sentiments, rejecting all aspects of the natural sciences that could not be reconciled with scriptural teaching (Greene, 1959).

Morality: evolutionary and psychological perspectives

A challenge similar to that posed by natural religion is inherent in our understanding of morality. Do we need religion to be moral? What is morality and how is it expressed in action? The moral sense is a complex mental phenomenon comprising thoughts and feelings about rights and duties, good and bad, and right and wrong motives and behaviour. It is underpinned by a set of standards of conduct that have been socially derived because they are necessary for the smooth functioning of the collective. These include notions of distributive, contractual, restorative, retributive and procedural justice (Krebs, 2008). Although for a large number of people conceptions of morality are embedded in religious beliefs, as we shall see in the last chapter with data from Muslim populations, evolutionary and psychological accounts do not perceive religion to be either a necessary or sufficient condition for the development or practice of moral codes (Atran, 2004; Boyer, 2001). Developmental psychology research shows that preschool children cross-culturally understand moral imperatives related to justice and inflicting harm on others. These moral understandings are present before children are cognitively capable of understanding and internalizing the religious concepts of their parents (Yau & Smetana, 2003). Therefore, it appears that moral codes exist prior to religious codes and that these moral codes are co-opted for religious purposes (Katz, 2000). The main difference between a moral code and a religious code is "that it adds an imagined agent (a god or ancestor) as a morally competent witness of one's own actions" (Boyer & Bergstrom, 2008, p. 120).

On cursory examination, the theistic moral argument is very weak indeed, and clearly does not account (i) for failures to adhere to or uphold the moral code (ii) the logical problem of 'evil' (although theists attempt to explain evil[2] as God's way of allowing His creation the free will to choose either evil or God (good) (Plantinga, 1974)); and (iii) the temporal and cultural specificity of morality (Krebs, 2008). That is, the theistic moral argument cannot account for the changes in moral normativity through history or across cultures. Issues for which the moral norm has changed over time are countless – corporal punishment, the death penalty, homosexuality, gay marriage, equality between the sexes, women in the priesthood, adultery, child exploitation and slavery, to name a few.

A more plausible explanation for morality is that it is a social construction that ensures the survival and function of social groups. Indeed, the earliest moral codes were those related to social organization and cohesion (e.g., norms about sharing, cooperating, doing no harm to others) (Nichols, 2002). While religious moralists argue that God is the supreme arbiter of moral law and conduct, rationalists state that moral law is enshrined in human law, which society promulgates and upholds. Sanctions are required to give legitimacy and force to the laws, suggesting that moral behaviour is not universal, nor necessarily intrinsically motivated. Moreover, the laws themselves are not universals – there are irreconcilable differences between Western law and Sharia law, for example. Like human law, divine law has its sanctions, not the least of which is the promise that transgressors and non-believers will burn in the fires of hell for all eternity!

Darwin (1874) proposed that the origins of so-called moral behaviour lay, like most human characteristics, in adaptive processes that served strategic social ends. As we will see in the coming discussion on totemism in Chapter 3, early humans constructed complex 'moral' codes in order to ensure the uniform conduct of tribal members that was geared to maximize the collective good. Over time, effective codes were selected and reproduced and out of these tribal laws, moral codes developed that are culturally relative in their expression but universal in their intent. Examples of universal codes include the rights of all people to liberty, equality and justice. Other examples include the duty to fulfil one's social obligations, to treat others as you yourself wish to be treated, to do no harm, and so on. These values ideally cohere under the rubric of the Golden Rule (Hauser, 2006), although there are now vast differences in the way that this set of rules is interpreted in different cultural and religious groups (Vasquez, Keltner, Edenbach & Banaszynski, 2001).

Psychology offers three possible explanations for the development of moral behaviour – the first derived from social learning theory (Kurtines, Gewirtz & Bandura, 1991), the second from cognitive-developmental theory (Kohlberg, 1984; Piaget, 1932) and the third from object relations theory (Klein, 1975; Winnicott, 1969). Social learning theory posits that children internalize their parents' and wider culture's values through a process of socialization that involves reward for the 'right' behaviour, sanction for the 'wrong' behaviour, and by example from respected elders, whom children model and imitate. Cognitive-developmental theory proposes that children begin with a primitive sense of morality that becomes increasingly complex and elaborated as the child develops and becomes capable of more complex mental operations. Some adults, by virtue of cognitive limitations or inadequate socialization, reason morally at levels consistent with that of young children, and appear incapable of perceiving or reversing irrational, all-or-none and egocentric thinking (Kenny, 2013; Kohlberg, 1984). When such thinking is embedded in and embellished by religious doctrine, or more properly dogma, fundamentalism flourishes. I will discuss this issue further in the final chapter.

The third explanation, derived from object relations (psychoanalytic) theory, proposes that we live in an "irreducibly moral universe" (Black, 2006, p. 6) but the motivation to repair the damage that we do to others, in either our internal worlds (i.e., our objects) or in external reality, remains an affective issue. On the path to emotional maturity, Winnicott (1953) proposed that children create, in fantasy, transitional objects on which they practise their emotional relating. For example, a teddy bear can be, at any given time, a younger sibling, a secret friend, a naughty child who must be punished or an aspect of the child himself who needs comfort. Winnicott argued that this form of play, based on illusion, provides the foundation of adult creativity and shared culture, of which religion forms a part. This notion was taken up by Ana-Maria Rizzuto (1979) in her book *The Birth of the Living God*, which applied the concept of the illusory transitional object to an understanding of how one's "God image" or "God representation" forms and changes over time. She proposed that God belongs to this category of objects. The child leaves home "with his pet God under his arm" (Rizutto, 1979, p. 8) which then interfaces with official

God images or representations promulgated by his culture. Just as the child's early image of his parents is never completely abandoned as he grows to adulthood, nor too will this pet image of God.

> [W]hen the human objects of real life acquire profound psychic meaning, God, like a forlorn teddy-bear, is left in a corner of the attic. ... A death, great pain, or intense joy may bring him back for an occasional hug or for further mistreatment or rejection, and then he is forgotten again.
>
> (Rizzuto, 1979, p. 179)

Complex factors come into play when we try to explain how people use moral codes, why they conform selectively to some and not others, why they use moral codes to justify immoral behaviour, and how self-serving biases can override adherence to a moral code (Krebs & Denton, 2006). Darwin (1874) proposed four stages in moral development that neatly subsume subsequent theories in conceptualization. The first was the formation of social groups; the second and third the development of higher cognitive functions and language, which potentiated the development of a conscience; and the fourth was the cementing of moral habits by repetition, thus ensuring obedience to the required social standard. Altruism makes a significant contribution to the survival of a species. This occurs through the three processes of sexual selection, kin selection and group selection, with each involving sacrifice, including of one's own body (as the transporter of genes) to preserve other carriers of its genes.

Many species have been shown to sacrifice their personal and biological interests for the sake of their kin (Alcock, 2005). Similarly, altruism at the level of the group would have the effect of preserving more group members than those in groups where selfishness and self-interest took precedence over the common good. However, selfishness is never far away – dominant animals exploit weaker or submissive animals, and weak and submissive animals may 'cheat' rather than compete according to the 'rules' with a stronger adversary because of the low probability of a successful outcome. Hence, decisions to act morally, altruistically or otherwise are based on complex decision-making strategies of the 'if-then' kind. Krebs (2008) concluded that

> the evolution of strategies that give rise to deferential, cooperative, and biologically altruistic behaviors [can be explained] in terms of the adaptive benefits of avoiding punishment, coordinating effort, exchanging goods and services, selecting fitness-enhancing mates, supporting kin and others on whom one's fitness is dependent, and upholding groups ... such strategies have evolved in many species. Our closest phylogenetic relatives, chimpanzees, are naturally disposed to behave in deferential, cooperative, sympathetic, altruistic, reconciliatory, rule-following, rule-enforcing, and group-upholding ways of the "if-then" variety.
>
> (p. 157)

Believers view the existence of altruism and morality as a sign that God exists (as a beneficent creator), having made man in His own image. They have greater difficulty explaining all those with no altruism or morality! Indeed, in this respect the very character of Jesus may be called into question. For Bertrand Russell (1957) any deity who believed in hell was seriously flawed because "any person who is really profoundly humane can[not] believe in everlasting punishment" (p. 7) or express such "vindictive fury" as Jesus did on more than one occasion against those who did not accept his teachings. "You brood of vipers, how can you who are evil say anything good? For the mouth speaks what the heart is full of" (Matthew 12:34); "Ye serpents, ye generation of vipers, how can ye escape the damnation of hell?" (Matthew 23:33). There are multiple examples of this aspect of Jesus's character. See, for example:

> Why do you not understand what I am saying? It is because you cannot hear My word. You are of your father the devil, and you want to do the desires of your father. He was a murderer from the beginning, and does not stand in the truth because there is no truth in him. Whenever he speaks a lie, he speaks from his own nature, for he is a liar and the father of lies. But because I speak the truth, you do not believe Me.
>
> (John 8:43–45)

and:

> The Son of man shall send forth his angels, and they shall gather out of his kingdom all things that offend, and them which do iniquity; and shall cast them into a furnace of fire: there shall be wailing and gnashing of teeth. Then shall the righteous shine forth as the sun in the kingdom of their Father.
>
> (Matthew 13:41–43)

Russell felt that the wisdom and humanity of Buddha and Socrates, who were not filled with narcissistic rage at those who thwarted them, were far more commendable and set a much better example for humanity than Jesus. In fact, there is evidence from his intemperate outbursts that Jesus operated from a grandiose and narcissistic state of mind. He treated others as his property, with no minds of their own. Thinking of this kind represents a primitive mode of relationship in which the individual does not recognize others to be separate beings with separate minds. In effect, Jesus was saying, "If you don't do as I say, think as I think, I will become enraged and disavow, disown and punish you. I will expel you from my psychic world (i.e., the Kingdom of God)." Now, reread the passages from the gospels of John and Matthew in this light and form your own opinion.

Atheists explain the existence of altruism and morality in terms of sociobiology and evolutionary psychology. What happens to reason in believers? It is there, we are told, but it is underpinned by revelation and faith which is beyond our understanding! Dawkins (2006) concluded that "Religious faith is a potent silencer of rational calculation" (p. 346) but does not offer an explanation as to why this might be so.

And so the arguments go! The interesting finale to these kinds of debates is that no minds are changed – there are no converts either way! I want to know why. This is one of the central aims of this book – to understand why "rational calculation is powerless in the face of religious faith". Bertrand Russell (1957) hinted at a possible answer:

> [T]here used to be … three intellectual arguments for the existence of God, all of which were disposed of by Immanuel Kant in the *Critique of Pure Reason*; but no sooner had he disposed of those arguments than he invented a new one, a moral argument, and that quite convinced him. He was like many people: in intellectual matters he was sceptical, but *in moral matters he believed implicitly in the maxims that he had imbibed at his mother's knee. That illustrates what the psychoanalysts so much emphasize – the immensely stronger hold upon us that our very early associations have than those of later times.* … *Most people believe in God because they have been taught from early infancy to do it, and that is the main reason.* … *The next most powerful reason is the wish for safety, a … feeling that there is a big brother who will look after you. That plays a very profound part in influencing people's desire for a belief in God.* [My italics]
>
> (pp. 5–6)

The anthropologists Boyer and Bergstrom (2008) make a similar point:

> In religious scholarship, commitment to religious ideas is often construed in terms of the relative weighing of belief vs. unbelief, given a set of accessible arguments. … However, this way of thinking about commitment may be a residue of defensive, post-Enlightenment religious institutions, in which "religion" is construed as an intellectual territory to be defended against other forms of knowledge more than a property of belief in general. Indeed, it would seem that for most people in most human groups, *norms and concepts are made compelling by processes that largely escape conscious scrutiny*, which may explain why the notion of "belief" is alien to most religious traditions.
>
> (p. 118)

Freud had a great deal to say about "very early associations" and matters that "escape conscious scrutiny", as will I in the coming chapters. For now, I wish to remark upon one of Freud's most profound insights. Contrary to the wisdom of the Bible and parenting practices through the ages – "When I was a child, I talked like a child, I thought like a child, I reasoned like a child. When I became a man, I put the ways of childhood behind me" (1 Corinthians 13:11) – Freud contended that, in fact, putting away the childish is a big mistake. One of the fundamental theses of the megalith of psychoanalysis is that mature (adult) functioning is in fact continuous with 'immature' (infantile/childish) functioning. If we cut ourselves off from our unconscious, we become emotionally impoverished and unable to account for ourselves. The cure in psychoanalysis and our attempts to navigate the enigmas of life depend on our reawakening of the ways of childhood that we have put behind us.

Science and religion

Spiritual, numinous, transcendent and neurological phenomena

> [P]sychology intentionally offers itself as a modern, non-traditional, even "unchurched" way of organizing and expressing the existential search for wholeness, numinous experiences, and individualization.
>
> (Parsons, 2010, p. 17)

Exceptional experiences that include, among others, extraordinary clarity of vision or understanding, feelings of benevolence, compassion, unity or merging with the universe, perceptual experiences, loss of control and the presence of supportive, non-physical entities or spirits have fascinated many students of human behaviour, not the least of whom was William James (1902). Before proceeding with a discussion of these experiences, we need some consensus regarding linguistic signposts that will help us navigate this territory, which lies outside our everyday world, so we will commence with some definitions.

The word 'spirit' derives from the Latin *spiritus*, meaning 'breath' and by extension denotes non-corporeal beings such as demons, deities, spirits and ghosts in contrast to material bodies or entities. The word 'numinous' derives from the Latin *numen* (pl. *numina*) which expresses the idea of the power of a divinity – that is, a supernatural power, deity or spirit and/or a sense of the transcendent, mystical or sublime. The German theologian Rudolf Otto explored the concept in *Das Heilige* (English translation *The Idea of the Holy*: 1917). He identified two components of the numinous experience. The first is the quality of fascination, attraction or compulsion and a feeling of communion with another. The second quality – *mysterium tremendum* – is its capacity to invoke fear and trembling, a state purportedly caused by man's egotism and hence self-imposed separation from God (Huxley, 2004). A related concept, transcendence, refers to a religious experience that overcomes the limits of one's physical body, during which one feels in a state of grace or otherworldliness. Such a state may be achieved through prayer or meditation, or indeed perturbations in the brain's electrical signals.

Some people who have used psychoactive drugs report similar otherworldly or 'out-of-body' experiences, or a feeling of oneness with the universe (Heydrich & Blanke, 2013). This sense of 'oneness' is frequently described in Eastern, non-theistic religions, such as Buddhism, Jainism, Confucianism and Taoism. Buddhists strive for enlightenment, the full attainment of which is nirvana – a state of being fully self-awakened. In Hinduism, transcendence occurs with the merging of the self/other, the personal/impersonal (Hicks, 2006). Those reporting near-death experiences also describe similar experiences (e.g., Alexander, 2012; Todd, 2012). For example, Todd (2012) described a near-death experience during surgical complications following triple bypass heart surgery.

> [T]his was an experience in which my finite ego-consciousness felt connected to a rapturously beautiful Light, a loving Presence and Source of Wisdom, which seemed to be infinite, cosmic, numinous, timeless, and eternal. ... The unconscious God archetype which I seemed to have encountered filled me with a sublime sense of oceanic unity and wholeness of all people and faith traditions as well as the *integration of science and religion*. [My italics]
>
> (Todd, 2012, p. 58)

Anyone who has experienced such a profound state as that described by Todd and others will not be easily dissuaded that such experiences may stem from some form of perceptual distortion and/or brain dysfunction while in a state of altered consciousness, for example when under the influence of hallucinogenic substances, a general anaesthetic or while suffering migraine, an epileptic seizure, stroke or other brain injury. Notwithstanding, there is growing evidence from cognitive science and brain imaging that shows self-consciousness is linked to the processing and integration of multi-sensory bodily channels (Heydrich & Blanke, 2013).

The underlying assumption of the neurosciences is that the way in which we think, feel and behave is determined by neurological processes – that is, by how our brains work. The link between brain damage or dysfunction in particular regions of the brain and the loss of function that was governed by that region has been documented for hundreds of years and is now highly specified. The relationship between damage and loss is easy to grasp logically. However, the relationship between damage and positive (as opposed to negative or loss) symptoms is more difficult to explain (Frith, 2004). Positive symptoms include various numinous phenomena, auditory and visual hallucinations, illusory bodily sensations and perceptions, telepathy and communication with the 'spirit world' that most of us do not experience. In a pre-scientific age, such phenomena were treated as realities. I have included a couple of detailed case studies from Freud – the first, Christoph Haizmann, a case of medieval demonio-mania, and the second, Daniel Schreber, who suffered a severe psychotic illness that was characterized by religious delusions – in Chapter 5 that provide an excellent analysis of the psychic meaning of seemingly bizarre symptoms.

In fact, such was the academic and personal interest in psychical phenomena in the late nineteenth century that a group of researchers interviewed 17,000 individuals and documented in detail their narratives of their psychic experiences (Sidgwick, Johnson, Myers, Podmore & Sidgwick, 1894). The report found that 10 per cent of the sample had experienced hallucinations. The report concluded that hallucinations originated in the brain, and not the sense organs as previously believed, although the sense organs are integrally involved in such experiences. We now know that the sense organs can be bypassed for some sensory experiences, which can be elicited through direct stimulation of the brain centre concerned. For example, direct electrical stimulation of the visual cortex produces visual hallucinations (Lee, Hong, Seo, Tae & Hong, 2000). Even the most incomprehensible cognitive and perceptual distortions seen in severe mental illnesses such as schizophrenia have been found to have a neural location. For example, delusions of control appear to be associated with overactivity in the parietal cortex (Blakemore & Frith, 2003). People with schizophrenia may also report mystical and religious experiences (Austin, 1998), which brain imaging has associated with hyper-activation of the left temporal lobe (Puri, Lekh, Nijran, Bagary & Richardson, 2001). We will now examine some of these positive symptoms more closely.

Autoscopic (AS) (from the Greek *autos* (self) and *skopeo* (looking at)) phenomena are illusory body perceptions that take three main forms. The first are out-of-body (OBE) experiences. While perceiving themselves to be awake, people report seeing their bodies from a vantage point outside their physical body. A second related phenomenon called autoscopy is characterized by the experience of seeing one's body duplicated in extrapersonal space. A third form is the héautoscopic experience, which is a variation of an autoscopic experience in which the individual hallucinates a *doppelgänger* (in German 'double walker') or double that he perceives to be himself. It was once commonly thought that we all had a *doppelgänger* that remained unseen and became visible just before our death. The song, "Der Doppelgänger", in Franz Schubert's song cycle *Schwanengesang* (Swan-song), set to a poem by Heinrich Heine, depicts such a scenario. A young man, disappointed in love, is standing under the night sky, wringing his hands in anguish. As he contemplates his emotional devastation, he sings: "The moon shows me my own form! O you *Doppelgänger*! You pale comrade! Why do you ape the pain of my love?" It was written in 1828, the year of Schubert's death. There are many such examples in nineteenth-century literature that depict the meeting of one's *doppelgänger* when death is imminent. The concept of the *doppelgänger* was used symbolically to address questions of 'otherness' and to explore alienation and projections[3] of the 'evil' (i.e., hateful, rageful, vengeful) characteristics in the self (Webber, 2011). Perhaps Freud's notion of projection as a defence mechanism, in which the individual splits the 'good' from the 'bad' and evacuates unwanted bad aspects of the self into others, while keeping the opposite attribute interiorized and safe (Fayek, 2007), had its roots in the German Gothic and Romantic literary traditions, of which Freud was a scholar.

A third variant is the autoscopic hallucination in which one hallucinates the self or part of the self, such as a hand or a face. The image is often just within or beyond one's grasp. These images often occur in the context of other visual hallucinations unrelated to the self. Notwithstanding huge general interest and many self-reports, such experiences are very rare and very few have been medically or scientifically documented. However, recent scientific papers have presented a series of case studies of such reports that have documented the phenomenological, neuropsychological and neuroimaging correlates of OBE and AS in neurological patients. These have identified shared central mechanisms, including pathological sensations of position and movement. For example, most patients report vestibular sensations, such as floating, flying, elevation and rotation. Such reports have

TABLE 2.2 Classification criteria for héautoscopy, out-of-body experience and autoscopic hallucinations, as well as lesion location suggested by previous case reports and small case series

	Autoscopic hallucination	Out-of-body experience	Héautoscopy
Self-location	Centred at physical body, stable	Centred at illusory body, stable	Centred at physical and/or illusory body, unstable
Self-identification	With physical body	With illusory body	With physical and/or illusory body
First-person perspective	Centred at physical body, stable	Centred at illusory body, stable	Centred at physical and/or illusory body, unstable
Second own body (autoscopic body)	2D image of own body, often of the face and upper trunk	3D image of whole own body	3D image of whole own body
Vividness/realism	Low	High	High
Lesion location	Bilateral, occipital, temporal	Right, temporal, parietal	Left, temporal, parietal

Source: Heydrich & Blanke (2013).

been found to be associated with the patient's body position prior to the experience, and in most patients are also associated with brain damage or dysfunction in the temporo-parietal junction (TPJ), suggesting the presence of paroxysmal cerebral disorders of body perception and cognition created by ambiguous input from the various information channels that inform our body consciousness (i.e., proprioceptive, tactile, vestibular and visual) while in a state of impaired awareness or consciousness (Blanke, Landis, Spinelli & Seeck, 2004).

In a case series of eight patients with epilepsy secondary to brain tumour or other lesion or brain structure atrophy who reported héautoscopic experiences, seven showed left temporal lobe and one showed right temporal lobe damage on MRI (magnetic resonance imaging), EEG (electroencephalography) and/or PET (positron emission tomography) examination. A classification system was proposed that links the particular type of autoscopic experience with a specific brain lesion location (Table 2.2).

One patient in the series, a 15-year-old girl with intractable epilepsy emanating from the left temporal lobe, reported that during a seizure she saw a white, transparent 'body' leaving her body and hovering above her hospital bed. At that moment she believed that her 'soul' was leaving her physical body; when her seizure abated, the girl reported that she felt her soul return to her body. At no time did this young woman 'believe' in the reality of these experiences; she remained aware of her actual bodily location in her hospital bed and retained her first-person perspective. However, some patients with temporal lobe epilepsy have shown personality alterations during the inter-ictal period (i.e., the time between seizures) that has been described as hyper-religiosity (Bear, Levin, Blumer, Chetham & Ryder, 1982).

More compelling evidence for the origin of OBEs comes from studies in which OBEs have been experimentally induced in healthy volunteers by creating an illusion related to the location of the body in space. Such demonstrations provide compelling evidence that OBE is determined by perceptual processes, in particular the visual perspective in conjunction with multi-sensory stimulation of the body, emphasizing the sense of touch (Ehrsson, 2007). Tactile stimulation of the experimentally induced illusory body produced emotional reactions that one would expect from stimulation of the actual physical body. Volunteers felt as if the 'virtual' body created by the use of video-display goggles was actually their own body. Further, when asked to locate themselves in the experimental space, most went to the location of their illusory body. These studies show that the brain is malleable; in other words, it can be tricked by incoming sensory information. One of the intriguing issues related to these body distortion experiences is that individuals must accept a set of propositions that override a fundamental 'truth' about our physical existence, that is, that "the perception of the self conforms to the borders of the physical body" (Miller, 2007, p. 1020).

Bodily self-consciousness is a non-conceptual, pre-reflective awareness that is essential to the development of a sense of self or (psychological) self-consciousness. Under experimental conditions that induced multi-sensory conflict, healthy individuals were induced to believe that their illusory body parts were in fact their actual body parts in the same way that has been observed in people with somatoparaphrenia, a condition due to right temporo-parietal damage, in which one's own hand or foot is attributed to another person (Lenggenhager, Tadi, Metzinger & Blanke, 2007). This overriding of a fundamental 'truth' that is required to retain a belief in OBE is exactly what occurs in religious belief, but more of this later.

Religion, religious experience and brain imaging

In the previous section, we discussed the association between bizarre bodily experiences and particular brain lesions located by various brain-imaging techniques in people who had known neurological deficits or severe psychiatric illness. Now we ask the question: Is it a step too far to make inferences about religious experience from the results of brain imaging? In this section, we will consider whether brain imaging techniques can cast new light on religious experience and perhaps even the origin of religion.

The prevailing neurological hypothesis, called the 'limbic marker hypothesis', states that religious experience is associated with abnormal brain states, most likely located in the limbic system, and that limbic system activity is necessary for 'religious' experience (Newberg & d'Aquili, 2001). As you can imagine, this is not a popular hypothesis among religious scholars or believers. It is difficult to consider that one's cherished religious beliefs and experiences might arise from primitive neural circuitry involving non-cortical brain structures and that religious experience and hence religion might have primitive evolutionary roots (Capps, 1995).

Recent research has, however, challenged this hypothesis, arguing that religious experience is not pre-cortical, but is, rather, a product of complex cognition. In one well-controlled study, Azari et al. (2001) assessed the differences between a group of committed Christians, who were members of an evangelical fundamentalist community, had reported having a conversion experience and who interpreted the Bible literally as the word of God, with a group of non-religious individuals matched for age, sex and level of education. After encouraging the two groups to self-induce a religious state by reciting religious texts, the researchers found that only the religious subjects reported achieving a religious state. The results from functional brain imaging during their religious state showed peak blood flow activation in the right dorsolateral prefrontal and dorsomedial frontal cortex, a pattern of activation not seen in the control (i.e., non-religious) subjects. Subsequent research showed that this pattern of activation was different from that observed with a non-religious, happy emotional state, which was associated with activation in the left amygdala, a limbic structure that was not activated during religious experience. This research challenges the limbic marker hypothesis; it appears that the prefrontal cortex, which is important for social-relational cognitive processes, social reasoning and decision-making, mentalizing, empathy and sympathy (Azari & Slors, 2007), is more centrally implicated in religious experience (Azari, Missimer & Seitz, 2005) than limbic structures. In a related study of Buddhist meditation using the same self-induction paradigm, Newberg et al. (2001) assessed the brain scans of experienced, practising Tibetan Buddhist meditators at the point at which they indicated that they were in an intense state of meditation. Changed blood flow was observed in the prefrontal cortex and the posterior parietal lobe, but there were no changes in the limbic structures, again suggesting that complex cognitive processes are involved in religious experience.

What do these associations between brain activation and religious experience actually tell us about the origin of religion? Some have argued that the quest for the origin of religion has been futile and should be abandoned (e.g., Masuzawa, 1988). Logically, we cannot use these data to explain origin because a religious experience had to be invoked to obtain the association. Further, the patterns of brain activation alone are unlikely to be sufficient, in the absence of other contingencies, for religious experience to emerge as a consequence of these neural activation patterns. Similarly, physiological arousal alone is insufficient to ascribe an emotional experience in the absence of other cues. Schacter and Singer (1962) showed that individuals with no immediate explanation for their arousal will label their feelings according to available environmental cues. When individuals were given an explanation for their physiological arousal (e.g., they had been given an injection of adrenaline), they did not seek an explanation in the external environment. This two-factor theory is not a complete explanation of emotion, first, because we sometimes experience emotion before we actually think about it and second, because there are actual physiological differences between emotions that may give the initial cue as to which emotion is being experienced. The same problem exists with neurological or non-cognitive (i.e., emotional) explanations for religion – non-cognitive states cannot cause religious experience until those experiences have been interpreted as religious, which is a cognitive process.

In the previous section, we noted that there were neurological explanations for other epistemologically indefensible experiences such as hallucinations and delusions that do not necessarily give rise to religious sensibilities. Further, beliefs similar to a belief in God, for example belief in the spirit world, did, in the nineteenth century, give rise to spiritualism, some forms of which borrowed several of their rituals and beliefs from religion, in particular that the spirit lives on after death. I conclude this section with the observation that while neurological phenomena have been differentially associated with religious experience, on their own they are not a sufficient condition to explain religion. Other cognitive and social factors must also be considered in order to develop the most complete picture possible of our domain of interest. Accordingly, we will now turn our attention to the role of cognition.

Religion and cognition

The application of theories of cognitive development to religion may cast new light on our understanding about how religious ideas develop and are maintained and how they motivate behaviour. The basic thesis of the cognitive approach to religion is that the development of religious ideas is not conceptually different from the development of everyday concepts and that 'ordinary' cognitive processes that are common to other forms of cognitive development can be applied in the same way to understand the development of religious beliefs and concepts (Barrett, 2000). These include concept formation, the presence of implicit ontological concepts, mental and metaphorical representation and intentional attribution. There is neurological support for this view, discussed above, that the areas of the brain activated during religious experience are associated with cognition, suggesting that beliefs and religious concepts are an inseparable part of religious experience, which presupposes an underlying religious tradition given that descriptions of the various forms of religious experience conform to particular religious orientations.

Let us take as an example Peter Todd's (2012) description of the numinous experience he reported while undergoing triple bypass heart surgery. I am particularly struck that his experience not only included a "sense of oceanic unity" with all people and all faith traditions, but that he also experienced "the integration of science and religion". Few descriptions of such experiences are as all-encompassing as Todd's or so dense with complex psychological concepts (e.g., "finite ego-consciousness"). The point I am making here is that Todd's numinous experience is densely cognitive and context-bound. For example, the word 'oceanic' used to describe the expression of a mystical feeling of limitlessness, unboundedness, timelessness and oneness with the universe would perhaps be familiar to students of psychoanalysis, but not generally. It was first used as a descriptor of numinous experience by Romain Rolland, Nobel prize-winning author, pacifist, religious mystic, Freud's friend and correspondent and critic of Freud's attack on religion. Rolland wrote to Freud in 1929 after the publication of *The Future of an Illusion* in 1927. Rolland described in this letter how this oceanic feeling is the basis of all "religious energy". Freud, who declared that he could not find such a feeling within himself, suggested that it may arise from the "feeling of ourself, of our ego which continues inward ... into an unconscious mental entity" (Freud, 1930, p. 65) that must seem fathomless and boundless, like infant helplessness, and which encapsulates a "wish for the restoration of limitless narcissism" (p. 72). My point here is that numinous experience contains cognitive content that simultaneously expresses one's heartfelt but often magical wishes. The sensory component (e.g., bright lights and long tunnels) is more uniform across those reporting such experiences, perhaps because human brains operate more or less similarly under the influence of the particular form of stimulation that is occurring. However, the cognitive interpretation of these sensations is more personal, based as they are in one's unique personal history and experience (Greenfield, 2000). Perhaps our perceptions of the character of God also arise from our deepest personal experience – that which resides in the Unconscious? Bomford (1990) observed that God and the Unconscious shared certain fundamental qualities. Table 2.3 presents these perceived parallels.

Lay belief and early research on religion cast religion as distinct from everyday life and 'ordinary' thinking, and focused on the 'extraordinary' elements commonly associated with religion, such as ecstatic or other forms of altered states of consciousness, conversion narratives, supernatural forces and events and beliefs beyond reason, that is, faith. The newer approach suggests that "religion is developed, communicated and regulated by natural human perception and cognition" (Barrett, 2000, p. 29) in much the same way as other human conceptual systems. Language, for example, is a complex human cognitive process that arises as a result of an innate predisposition to develop language (universal grammar) (Chomsky, 2000) and exposure to a particular enabling sociolinguistic environment that determines how the deep innate structure of language is expressed, that is, whether you will speak English, Cantonese or Arabic. The parallels between language development and the development of religious concepts are immediately apparent. Just as language is believed to be an evolved innate structure waiting to be potentiated, so too humans have a deep need to explain the meaning of their lives, and to search for a numinous experience that will satisfy an eternal longing that Freud argued derived from infant helplessness.

What is acquired in religion is a belief in the concept 'supernatural' and expectations about how supernatural phenomena influence people and the natural environment. The potentiated expression of those beliefs is socioculturally determined in the same way that factors responsible for the development of language operate. Whether we adopt the premises of the Jewish faith, Christianity, Islam or extreme cults will depend on our exposure to such expressions of religion and eventually, as we mature and encounter other experiences, our capacity to sustain a belief in the religious system to which we have been initially exposed.

TABLE 2.3 Shared characteristics of the Unconscious and God

The Unconscious	God
Timelessness	Eternity (Everlastingness)
Spacelessness	Infinity (Ubiquity)
Non-contradiction	Ineffability
Displacement/condensation	Partlessness or indivisibility
Equivalence of inner and outer reality	Pure Act (Omnipotence)

Source: after Bomford (1990).

For the purposes of this discussion, we will define religion as a "shared system of beliefs and actions concerning superhuman agency" (Barrett, 2000, p. 29). People hold such beliefs at different levels of complexity, in the same way that people understand the laws of physics or music theory at various levels of complexity. It depends on the general and specific cognitive capacities of individuals, the extent of their interest and exposure to the discipline under study, and the cognitive demands of the situation in which those concepts will be used. For example, singing nursery rhymes with children in preschool makes low cognitive demands compared with preparing a concerto for performance at the Julliard School of Music. With respect to theology and religion, religious concepts will be expounded differently in classes undertaken by trainee priests in a seminary or theological college from the pulpit of a working-class parish (Lawson & McCauley, 1990). In this regard, it is interesting to note that religious institutions themselves were, and continue to be, limited by their collective cognitive capacity and the social negotiations that occur around which beliefs are acceptable to their flocks (Boyer & Bergstrom, 2008).

At all levels of conceptual difficulty, people apply a number of implicit assumptions about the properties of both familiar and novel objects or experience, one of which is based on ontological category membership. For example, children as young as five years old can express the perceptual differences between an ordinary human being (their best friend) and God. They know that knowledge available to their friend, but not to God, was constrained by perceptual processes and that their friend's life cycle, but not God's, was constrained by biological processes (Giménez-Dasí, Guerrero & Harris, 2005). In another experiment, six-year-old children confronted with an animal that they had not encountered previously knew intuitively that it possessed the qualities of other animals – that it is a living thing that must eat to survive, that has the capacity to negotiate survival in its environment, that cannot pass through a solid barrier or be in two places at the same time. On the basis of these ontological assumptions, the child is able to generate hypotheses and explanations and to accurately categorize the new object (Keil, 1989). Because these ontological concepts are primordial, they may restrain religious concepts. When people from America and India were asked to reflect on their religious concepts and the nature of their God (gods), most reported that God did not have spatial, temporal or physical properties, and was omniscient and omnipresent. However, when these conceptions of god were embedded in narratives, the character of god took on much more human characteristics (Ward, 1994). While the god of abstract theological reflection violated most of the ontological assumptions related to other living organisms, the gods of the narratives were more 'human' in their character-istics and limitations (i.e., they were located in one place at a time; they needed to see and hear in order to know; they required food to live) (Barrett & Keil, 1996). Boyer (2001) concluded that people's actual religious concepts are not consistent with what they state they believe. For the most part, supernatural beings are con-ceptualized as people with ontologically counterintuitive properties in one or more domains – psychological, biological or physical. Boyer expressed his view as simple algorithms of the type:

(a) Omniscient God = person + special cognitive and physical powers;
(b) ghost = person + no physical body;
(c) zombie = person + no cognitive functioning;
(d) angel = person + special physical powers and exemplary moral rectitude.

There are timeless, mythical versions of these supernatural beings – Santa Claus and the Easter Bunny – and modern versions such as Frankenstein, the Wizard of Oz, Wicked Witch of the West, Peter Pan, Buffy the Vampire Slayer, Superman, Batman and Spiderman, the Incredible Hulk, Harry Potter, the X-Men and Wolverine, to name a few. Interestingly, on close inspection, the various categories of these super-natural beings such as God, gods, angels, devils, ghosts, ghouls, goblins, zombies, vampires and fairies are all more alike in their humanness and their endowment with human qualities than otherwise. Most of these creatures can see, hear, think, make plans, form attachments and have and express feelings. Importantly, they are perceived to be intentional, agentic beings because they are commonly believed to interact with humans in intentional ways. The extra-human qualities that they pos-sess are well within our imaginative grasp – for example, some can fly, some have superhuman strength, some have extrasensory perception, one can spin a spider's web out of his fingertips, another can bring forth deadly daggers out of the knuck-les of his hand.

Herein lies a paradox: on the one hand, people have innate ontological assumptions but also seem predisposed towards religious, or at least, numinous beliefs that violate these assumptions, leading to the conclusion that "religious beliefs [may] be the result of a rationally indefensible epistemic procedure, to which people are nevertheless prone given their psychological make-up" (Azari & Slors, 2007, p. 77). Both Freud (1913a, 1927, 1939) and Todd (2012) have argued the case, but from very different perspectives. Others have asserted that belief in the existence of supernatural beings is a cultural universal (e.g., Brown, 1991) and that such beliefs are not limited to primitive cultures or children. For example, in America, 94% of a large population sample reportedly believed in the existence of God, 70% believed in Satan and 78% believed that angels existed (Winseman, 2004). To reconcile these conflicting tendencies, people set a limit to which religious concepts may violate innate ontological assumptions and still be acceptable – the less the violation, the more acceptable the concept (Boyer, 1996). Hence, religious groups will cohere around religious concepts to which people are more receptive, which occurs when the supernatural beings are more human than otherwise. The internal longing for the 'religious' explains why such beliefs become so prevalent and widespread (Sperber, 1996) (if that is not too tautological an argument!).

The pervasiveness of beliefs in the supernatural is of immense interest from a cognitive science perspective, first because the object of study of supernatural entities cannot be observed, demonstrated by experimentation or proven by inference; rather, such beliefs are acquired through 'testimony', persuasion and other forms of cultural transmission, such as story-telling, modelling, imitation, inculcation, indoctrination and religious art and music. Barrett (2000) has proposed the hyperactive agent detection device (HADD) as a possible explanation. It works like this: People will react with an orientation response to novel stimuli; this interacts with our imaginations; and the idea builds and repeats. Here is an example: I am lying in my hut trying to sleep and I hear a noise. It is coming from the direction of the tree just outside. In my drowsy state, I think, "What's that? Did that tree just talk to me?" I wake my partner and say "I think there is a talking tree out there", to which he replies, "Where?" In this way the original fanciful idea becomes amplified and elaborated in a process known as 'group think' (see Chapter 7). Every tribal culture has a system of invisible supernatural agents in which they believe. Even highly civilized cultures are populated in their art and literature with witches, wizards, talking animals, animate objects, imps, goblins, fairies, gods and leprechauns, all of which compete for rehearsal space. These imaginings are the wild ancestors of today's organized religions (Dennett, 2006).

In addition, research has shown that minimally counterintuitive concepts are highly memorable, thus making transmission easier (Shtulman, 2008). However, a review of art and literature through the ages shows how conceptualizations of supernatural beings have changed throughout history and across cultures. For example, unlike Christianity, Islam and Judaism prohibit pictorial representations of God. Christianity distinguishes between idolatry, which is forbidden, and religious iconography, which is a mark of profound respect. One needs only to enter a Greek, Russian, Serbian or Ukrainian Orthodox church to observe the artistry and reverence that has been poured into its religious icons. Political, geographic and social issues have also influenced the way in which God has been depicted; for example, the nomadic herding communities of the ancient Near East envisage a male god, while in Hindu and other Eastern religions there are many female gods (Hicks, 2006). Today, God is overwhelmingly conceptualized as a white, Western male, although variations in this depiction have been made. For example, in the movie *Bruce Almighty*, God was black; in the movie *Dogma*, God was female, but these are not serious attempts to address religious scholarship. They do, however, uncover our assumptions about the nature of God that are so taken for granted that they remain implicit and unproblematized.

Naturally, there is also a developmental dimension to the acquisition and acceptance of ontologically counterintuitive beings. Contrary to the view that children cannot be Christian (or religious) in their own right (Dawkins, 2006), recent research has shown that even young children are naturally receptive to ontologically implausible beings like Santa Claus, the Easter Bunny and God, reasoning about these entities using the same cognitive skills that they use for reasoning in other domains. For example, by five years of age, children have developed a rudimentary concept of 'soul' ('the ghost in my body') (Richert & Harris, 2006) and notions of immortality and omniscience (Giménez-Dasí, Guerrero & Harris, 2005). Interestingly, Shtulman (2008) asked parent/child dyads to describe supernatural beings, including God. The most frequent attribution that both children and their parents attributed to God was the feat of creating life and the universe, that He is everywhere, guides people and is all-powerful. Children were more likely than their parents to say that God is a person or like a person and although He is everywhere, He lives in heaven; that is, they are more likely to anthropomorphize God (Gorsuch, 1988). There were very few differences between their descriptions of other supernatural beings like fairies and angels and their descriptions of God; children described angels and fairies as like a person who can fly, do magic, etc. Parents were more likely to attribute human characteristics to other fictional supernatural beings than to God, but still tended to attribute psychological, physical and biological characteristics to God. This tendency to anthropomorphize God was also related to their self-reported belief in God, with stronger belief related to lower anthropomorphization, possibly due to their greater exposure to theological and scriptural descriptions of God to which they had been exposed in the exercise of their faith. Intelligence and educational status do not confer immunity from the tendency to anthropomorphize God. Barrett and Keil (1996) showed that university students resorted to anthropomorphizing God in their attempts to comprehend non-natural entities.

Both Boyer (2001) and Shtulman (2008) have noted that perhaps a more accurate ontological characterization of supernatural beings is that of 'intentional agent' who possess a mind, rather than that of a 'person' who possesses both a mind and a body. Having a mind would retain the being's social and psychological characteristics, but free them from the constraint of requiring biological and physical properties (Dennett, 1987). An alternative hypothesis is that some adults might hold multiple concepts of God simultaneously. For example, God may be conceptualized as human to express His intentional qualities ('God's plan for me'), while a metaphor will be used to express His physical properties (e.g., God is Light). Others have argued that people develop metaphorical representations of God rather than an internally consistent cognitive concept (Lakoff & Johnson, 1980). Indeed, some people may hold shifting, diametrically opposed views either serially or simultaneously that God is both creator and destroyer, beneficent and vengeful, involved with mankind and a dispassionate observer of man's mistakes and its consequences.

Herein lies another paradox. In this chapter, we have discussed the idea that surrender and subjugation to deities was a universal characteristic of most religions.

However, people universally ascribe intentionality and agency to their gods, perhaps using Freud's mechanism of projection, in which (un)acceptable parts of the self are expelled into the external world. This is a very clever, if unconscious strategy that works like this: I want to be seen to be a humble supplicant among my church-going brethren, who has surrendered my will to a higher power and who seeks guidance. I project my desires, wishes and needs into the deity to whom I pray and he answers with guidance about how I should behave, which is, of course, in exactly the manner in which my needs will be met! What a marvellous win–win situation for all!

Notes

1 There are at least 10 different spellings of the name. I have selected the spelling used in the Arab world.
2 Evil has several meanings that need to be clarified. Originally understood as the absence or privation of goodness, the more frequent religious meaning is the presence of something destructive and painful. Nietzsche defined evil as intense resentment and hatred consequent upon feelings of impotence, while Stolorow defined evil as human destructiveness arising from and reactive to trauma.
3 Projection: a mental process whereby a personally unacceptable impulse or idea is attributed to the external world. As a result of this defensive process, one's own interests and desires are perceived as if they belong to others, or one's own mental experience may be mistaken for consensual reality (Moore & Fine, 1990).

3

THE COMMON ORIGINS IN HUMAN NATURE OF TABOOS, CONSCIENCE, NEUROSIS AND RELIGION

The origin and meaning of totems and religion

[W]here there is a prohibition there must be an underlying desire.

(Freud, 1913a, p. 70)

We will begin our discussion by examining the beliefs and behaviours of primitive tribes whose social structures were organized around elaborate taboos that arose in response to hidden (we now say unconscious) aspects of human nature that Freud uncovered during the development of psychoanalysis. In *Totem and Taboo*, Freud (1913a) argued that prehistoric man is still our contemporary, and that the psychology of primitive people, our 'modern' conscience, obsessional neurosis and religion are uncannily concordant in their origins and psychodynamics. Freud further made the astounding claim that taboos, conscience, neurosis and religion have common roots in human nature, and the particular aspects of human nature upon which each of these phenomena are built have remained constant across centuries and between different civilizations. The aim of this chapter is to interrogate Freud's claims.

Totemism

Totemism is one of the most ancient and most singular cultural phenomena in human history, and it is intimately linked with the origins of other human cultural phenomena such as religion, law, writing, exogamy, surnames, anthroponymy, to ponymy and the symbols and signs of social organizations.

(Xingliang, 2003, p. 1)

Totemism is a system comprising both social and religious practices that provided the basis for the social organization of a number of primitive cultures, including those in Australia, America and Africa. Because many totemic practices date back to prehistory, it is difficult to know for certain how such systems evolved.

> The most barbarous and the most fantastic rites and the strangest myths translate some human need, some aspect of life, either individual or social. The reasons with which the faithful justify them may be, and generally are, erroneous; but the true reasons do not cease to exist and it is the duty of science to discover them.
>
> (Durkheim, 1912, pp. 14–15)

Frazer (1910b), upon whose work Freud relied to form his own views about totemism, demonstrated that very diverse tribes all over the world shared similar totemic beliefs, and despite some intertribal differences, the common practices across tribes deserved a common description. The fundamental common practice was the development of a relationship between a group of kindred people with natural (or occasionally, artificial) objects. Lévi-Strauss (1963) also examined the structure and variety of totemic cultures and concluded that they were social structures that had a common purpose – to express the relationship between nature and society and to connect the material with the spiritual world.

Frazer (1910b) cautioned that attempts to understand the exact origins and relationships between people and their totems was not possible because of the primitive thinking of 'savages' who were not troubled, as we are, by contradictions and illogicality. Totemism, said Frazer (1910b), "was not a consistent philosophical system … but a crude superstition, the offspring of undeveloped minds, indefinite, illogical, inconsistent" (p. 4). Frazer theorized that totemism may have arisen as a result of the failure of primitive tribes, such as the Aranda (Arrernte) people of central Australia, to identify the role of the male in human reproduction. The Aranda do not believe that children are conceived by sexual intercourse. Rather, a woman believes herself with child only at the moment that she first feels it moving *in utero*. Her location near a tree, rock, billabong or animal at the moment of sensation indicates whence the spirit child has emanated and entered her body. Other explanations for the origins of totemism abound, and include, among others, self-preservation and kinship needs, which also served self-preservation (Xingliang, 2003).

If the totem were an animal, clansmen believed themselves to be members of the same species of animal, and imbued their totem animal with human qualities. They treated their totems in the same respectful manner in which they treated their family and friends. There have been a number of suggested derivations of the word 'totem' (Ember, 1988). The one generally accepted is from the Ojibwa (Ojibwe) language of the Native Americans via the words *nintotem* (also *nindoodem*) (my totem) and *ototeman* (his totem). The related French word, *aoutem*, has been used in a similar way by the Mi'kmaq tribe of Nova Scotia. In all its usages, the totem signalled 'kinship-related', belonging and filiation. Primitive people did not regard their totems as god-like or superior to themselves, which Frazer argued was a necessary condition for a religion; he was insistent that totemism, in its original form, was not a religion and that the most primitive tribes did not worship their totems. The concept of totemic kinship thus preceded the concepts of totemic ancestors and totemic deities, which may be considered a form of proto-religion.

However, behaviour towards the totem was rule-governed, including, for example, that the totem animal could not generally be killed or eaten, except at annual mystical feasts and only by some tribes, and that this act represented a form of incorporation of the totem that permitted a closer identification and allowed tribal members to acquire magical power over the totem. Such tribes (e.g., Australian Aborigines) used also to eat their dead relatives as a sign of affection and respect. These practices died out as clans became more focused on the social, as opposed to corporeal aspects of totemism and as they proceeded towards civilization and religion. Members of most totem clans were and continue to be exogamous – they were prohibited from having sexual intercourse or marrying within their clan. This represents a form of the universal taboo against incest (Frazer, 1910b). Totems were passed from one generation to the next. Members of a totem clan believe that they are direct descendants of their totems and have a common ancestor.

Durkheim (1912) argued that paring back the ever-increasing complexity of more recent religions, theological interpretations and religious practices and exploring the simpler, primitive religions would allow us to access the essential religious nature of man. Durkheim believed "La religion est le plus primitif des phénomènes sociaux" (religion is the most primitive of social phenomena) and that all religions were tied together "by fundamental representations or conceptions ... that have the same significance and fulfil the same functions" and which constitute "that which is permanent and human in religion" (p. 17). Durkheim attempted to access the essential and indispensable elements, that is, the necessary and sufficient conditions that cohere with the concept 'religion'. Durkheim rejected the usual definitions that contain notions of the mysterious, unknowable and supernatural that place religion in opposition to science and the natural order, because many early religions were directed towards the preservation of that order through the control of the physical forces of nature, hence the widespread practices of fertility rites, sun worship and rain worship.

Durkheim did not subscribe to the view that the presence of gods or other spiritual beings defined religion, because several religions (e.g., Buddhism, Jainism and Brahmanism) do not have such beings in their doctrines. The basis of religion, argued Durkheim, was the belief in two classes of 'things' – the sacred and the profane. This begs the question about how such a dichotomy was formed. Durkheim, and later Lévi-Strauss (1966), argued that what became sacred was decided by society, and that what stood in opposition to the maintenance of the social order became profane. Durkheim noted that in totemism, three classes of things – the totemic animal (or plant), the totemic emblem and the members of the totem clan – were considered sacred, and thus concluded that totemism was one of the most elementary forms of religion. Religious rites provided a system of injunctions about how clans should behave in the presence of the sacred. Thus, these religious (totemic) beliefs and (totemic) rites constituted the essence of a religion. Expressed succinctly, "society, of which the gods are only a symbolic expression, cannot do without individuals any more than these can do without society" (Durkheim, 1964, p. 347).

Some clan ties were nominalistic (i.e., clan members bore the same name) and were not based on blood relationships. The question arises as to why an incest taboo and the practice of exogamy became such dominant principles of ancient clans who were not blood relations. Freud offered two possible explanations: (i) because clan members believed that they were all descendants of the same (totem) ancestor, they treated each other as if they were blood relations or members of a single extended family; (ii) the second explanation relates to the question of "woman ownership" and is discussed in the section "From totems and taboos to religion".

The clan mark – a drawing of the totem animal – was used first, then the clan name, followed by the experience of a bond between man and the animal after which he was named. Durkheim argued that it was the symbolic representation in the form of totemic emblems and symbols of the totemic animal or plant that became sacred and imbued with magical powers. From there it was a small step to venerating a 'force' possessed by the totemic symbol (Guizzardi, 2007). Some extant tribes in Africa and the Australian Aborigines continue to believe in the literal kinship between humans and animals. For most other clans, with the dawning of the understanding that animals and humans cannot be kin, the more abstract concept of the totemic deity as symbolic guardian of the clan was born.

Totemism was also a cosmology based on a strict social organization and distribution of goods among the various clans. Sociological theory posits a socially based derivation of totemism, whereby each clan undertook to supply one particular food or service to the whole community (Frazer, 1910b). Those clans with non-animal totems, such as wind and rain, undertook to control these natural forces by conducting ceremonies to make rain and sunshine. This totemic cooperative, composed of groups of "magicians, each group charged with the management of a particular department of nature" aimed to "regulate the course of nature and accommodate it to the needs of man" (p. 18). The injunction against eating one's own totem, according to this theory, had a social derivation – to fulfil that clan's obligation to produce enough to meet the needs of those outside their clan. Hence, a primitive form of economic and social collectivism may have contributed to the development of totemism.

Subsequent scholarship has shown that totemic systems are much more complex than outlined here, and space allows only a couple of examples. Evans-Pritchard (1961), in his study of the totemic affiliations of Sudanese clans, discovered that in most clans from that region individuals belonging to the same clan had different totems, which weakens somewhat the theory of totemism as a kinship structure. Ancient China had a very complicated totemic structure, sub-classified into four categories – (a) horde totemism; (b) local clan totemism; (c) tribal totemism; and (d) national totemism – all of which were associated with ancestor worship. Each tribal unit worshipped the founding ancestor's spirit. A god was master of the founding ancestor; there was a different ancestor and a different god for each local clan (Wei, 1968). With the advent of feudalism in China and the subsequent amalgamation of tribal societies into feudal states, the character of totemism changed to both accommodate and serve these political and social changes. The rise of Confucianism and Taoism heralded the end of sacred totemism in China. The point here is that the varied forms of totemism discussed in this section served particular economic, social and political aims, and transmuted into other forms of 'religion' when the social structures in which it was practised changed.

Totemism and pre-logical thinking

[T]he ultimate basis of man's need for religion is infantile helplessness.
(Letter from Freud to Jung, 2 January 1910)

All primitive forms of totemism are predicated on pre-logical thinking – a feature noted by Lévy-Bruhl (1910) – which is a form of cognitive functioning universally observed in very young children (Piaget, 1927, 1936, 1947, 1954), most primitive societies (Arieti, 1976) and religion (Barrett, 2000; Barrett & Keil, 1996). It is characterized by the fusion of subjectivity and objectivity and fantasy and reality. There is also a failure to distinguish between the human and natural world and between humans and animals which lies at the heart of totemic animal kinship.

Some of the central characteristics of pre-logical thinking, also called pre-operational thinking and 'magical thinking', are animism, artificialism, substantialism and realism. Animism is the belief that everything in the world is alive, like me. Piaget defined animism as a child's mistaken belief that non-living things are alive or have attributes of animals or people (e.g., the sun was angry with the clouds, so he chased them away). In the Japanese religion Shinto, natural phenomena like waterfalls and trees are *kami* (i.e., supernatural beings, gods); they are alive and have a spiritual being. Piaget noted that many animistic expressions survive in adult language (e.g., "the sun is trying to break through the cloud"; "the steam is trying to escape") and such expressions, while metaphoric and heuristic in adult usage, no doubt enhance, at least for a time, animistic understandings and expressions in young children. Piaget, Tomlinson and Tomlinson (1929) identified three stages in the genesis of animism: (i) during the first stage, the child confuses self and objects (things) and believes that wishes and desires can exert a magical influence on reality; (ii) in the second stage, the child can differentiate self from objects, but still attributes subjective qualities to inanimate objects. The child still believes that s/he can operate on objects from a distance. The concepts of mental and physical activity are not yet separated. During this stage of cognitive development, both magical and animistic explanations are given for physical phenomena. For example, if the child perceives that the sun or moon 'follow' him as he walks, he may attribute causality to infantile omnipotence ("I am making the sun and moon move") or to animism ("the sun and moon are following me"). In the third stage, (iii) the child understands that thoughts and words are not located in things, but rather in 'my head'.

Although the child eventually gives up his magical notions, he retains his animistic interpretations of causality. Animistic thinking provides a window into the magical world of fantasy where everything is under one's own control and can be done and undone, atoned for and forgiven – unlike the stark reality of ungovernable and capricious forces in nature and ourselves that act at random on hapless humanity. The precepts of animism and religion are thus remarkably similar – they represent a flight into fantasy and wish-fulfilment, are superstitious, magical and reversible and imbue their believers with unfettered powers of control over nature.

Artificialism is the belief that deities or humans have made all the objects on earth in order to fulfil particular functionalist purposes that will satisfy human needs. For example, the sun is created to provide warmth and light to humans. Thus, the intentions of the sun are imputed from the intentions of its creators. In this form of thinking, there is no chance or probability. Artificialism was Piaget's term for the belief that natural phenomena are all ultimately products of human engineering – made from, for example, blocks, sand or clay. Children gradually develop an understanding of the differences between naturally causal and fabricated phenomena. Some are eventually able to understand that neither humans nor 'gods' can make natural phenomena, at which point they are able to correctly attribute causal-empirical explanations. A child in the early stages of artificialism, when asked about the origin of natural phenomena like rain, answers, "The rain is in the sky; God sends it down to us." Q: "Where does God get the water from?" A: "From his taps. He fills up buckets and throws the water down to us" (Piaget et al., 1929, p. 312). Another example: Q: "Where does wood come from?" A: "From the forest". Q: "How?" A: "God helps men to make the wood and then they plant it in the ground". The idea that humans can make natural phenomena like stars, clouds, sun and wood is common in pagan religious rituals.

A related characteristic of pre-logical thinking is substantialism, whereby qualities are endowed with substance. For example, snow is considered a sign of cold and cold a sign of snow, with each producing the other. Cold is thus identified as a substance derived from snow on the one hand and as a causative element of snow on the other. Evidence suggests that similar substantialist thinking is present in primitive societies. Stone Age man was aware of the connection between blood and life. He believed that a picture of an animal drawn in blood would transmute into the living animal depicted. Similarly, Australian Aborigines engage in a ritual of shedding blood on their sacred stones in order to induce the totem to reproduce itself. Some North American Indian tribes are prohibited from drinking the blood of animals because they believe that their blood contains their soul. Indeed, it could be argued that psychology is guilty of the same logical error, beginning with the duality of Descartes's Cartesian mind and Freud's concepts of id, ego and superego. It should be noted that Freud did not make this error and indeed warned others against it, but it is cognitively easier to reify such concepts than struggle with a "radically non-substantialist process-psychology" (Riffert, 2002, p. 1). Piaget was one of the great strugglers for this approach – the view that organisms are "open systems, with dynamic change processes and primary activity in contrast to a primitively conceived reactivity" (Piaget, 1967, p. 157).

Another characteristic of the pre-operational (i.e., pre-logical) thinking of young children is realism, which is the attribution of tangible, material qualities to dreams, words or wishes which actually have no concrete physical existence. That is, realism is the inability to differentiate psychic (subjective) from physical (objective) phenomena (Oesterdiekhoff, 2013). Young children believe that they think with their mouths and ears, because these organs are associated with talking and listening. They believe that words, which are equivalent to thinking, exist in the air around their mouths and ears (Piaget, 1954). A six-year-old boy responded to Piaget as follows: Q: "Is it possible to see thinking?" A: "Yes". Q: "How?" A: "In front" (points to a spot parallel to mouth). Q: "Can you touch thinking?" A: "Sometimes, the true things" (p. 50). Words thus have the characteristics of the things that they signify; the word dwells in and is a part of the object. "The name for the sun is the sun, because the sun is shining" (Oesterdiekhoff, 2009, p. 175). This is conceptual realism, the belief that universals have a real and independent existence. In the third stage, children come to understand that the word is an arbitrary signifier of the thing.

Similarly, in their study of children's dreams, Piaget et al. (1929) found that children in the pre-operational stage of cognitive development reported that their dreams were either images or voices originating from outside themselves. Older children recognize that the image is not 'real' but still ascribe an independent objective existence to their dream image; that is, it is not yet 'mental'. Very young children believe that the dream originates from the objects that occur in the dream and that others could also see their dream. Older children know that others cannot see their dream, but also assert that they too are unable to see their dream because their eyes are shut while they are dreaming and it is night; yet, they simultaneously state that it is with their eyes that they see the dream. These contradictory assertions show a combination of realism and subjectivism, that is, that the dream is starting to be understood as a subjective experience rather than a physical reality.

One theory (animism) states that the idea of the human soul arose from the experience of the 'self' in dreams; primitive man postulated a second self within that was not bound by the natural laws of their physical self. Upon death, the soul becomes spirit, detached from the physical body but with the power and capacity to involve itself in earthly affairs, for good or ill. To avoid ill, the living offered up prayers and sacrifices and performed rituals to appease the spirits. By extension, 'second selves' were subsequently attributed to all non-human entities, including plants, animals and nature (rivers, stars, sun, moon). Durkheim (1912) concluded that, according to this theory, "men find themselves the prisoners of this imaginary world of which they are, however, the authors and models" (p. 68). The opposing theory (naturism) argued that religion was based on nature and natural phenomena, which were transformed into spirits or gods who have the same characteristics and capacity for consciousness as humans, and which were described in animistic (anthropomorphic) terms (e.g., "the wind sighs with grief"). These characteristics were noted above to feature in the language of very young children. Once these spirits were named, the myths, fables and legends of the ancient religions were born. From here, the ancestor cult, a defensive development against the terror of death, allowed men's souls/spirits, upon separation from the physical body, to become immortal.

The cognitive characteristics operating in the pre-operational stage indicate an inability to distinguish living from non-living; humans from animals; and human society from the natural world. People from primitive cultures and even today's illiterate adults retain in their thought processes the pre-operational thinking of very young children that, without education, will not progress to concrete or abstract (formal operational) thinking. Advancing age does not, of itself, move cognitive processing to higher conceptual complexity. Although an illiterate adult has more knowledge than a seven-year-old child, this knowledge does not necessarily contribute to qualitative advances in cognitive processing. While some children, under certain conditions, will display the Piagetian stages identified in concrete operational thinking, without the intercession of culture and education, children and adolescents are unlikely to attain either concrete or formal operational (i.e., abstract/conceptual) thinking. Hence, the view that there are universal laws of cognitive development is not supported – rather, "it is not in the nature of humans to develop abstract-logical ways of thinking and related forms of civilized behaviour" (Oesterdiekhoff, 2009, p. 147).

Close examination of the cultures built on totemism can be seen to display all of these pre-operational characteristics. It is evident in tribal beliefs that the totem provided a safe haven for clan members' souls in times of danger. When a primitive man entrusted his soul to his totem, he became invulnerable, but only while the totem was also safe, hence the injunction against killing any member of the totem animal species. Another theory deriving from American Indians is that a totem is the guardian spirit of an ancestor (Frazer, 1910a,b). Wilhelm Wundt (1916), a physician, physiologist, philosopher and one of the foundational figures of modern psychology, proposed the theory that totemism is related to a belief in spirits and souls, and is animistic in nature. Totem animals and their 'soul animal' (e.g., birds, snakes, lizards, mice) provided a suitable resting place for the souls of the deceased.

Onians (1954) also observed all of these features of pre-operational thinking in the theories of mind in pre-Socratic ancient Greece. For example, the belief that objects were alive and created by god permeates the writing of the time. Homer identified thinking with speaking, thoughts with words and breath with mind. These same features are present in tribal and totemic societies and survive into early European philosophy. They are also characteristic features of the thinking of young children that we have just discussed. Scholars of the European Middle Ages showed the same characteristic thinking as young children, primitives and illiterates. For example, they ascribed 'holy' significance to every number, viewing each number as having its own individuality or personality. The number '3' was holy because Jesus was resurrected on the third day. The number '7' implies the addition of eternal and earthly life because it is the sum of '4', which represents the four earthly elements of earth, fire, water and air, and '3', which represents the three bodily organs required for the adoration of god (Oesterdiekhoff, 2009). Principles of pre-operational thinking are at work here – syncretism and parataxis underlie the transductions (Kenny, 2013) which produced unresolvable contradictions for these early scholars. Oesterdiekhoff (2009) concluded:

> [C]onceptual realism is a prerequisite to understand magic and animism across pre-modern cultures ... [it] explains the belief in sorcery, witches, magicians, shamanism, and all other beliefs in supernatural powers. ... Conceptual realism is a part of the direct connection between cosmos and person, which is the basis for magic and superstition ... [and] the belief in paranormal phenomena.
>
> (p. 173)

There are also compelling correspondences between children's artificialism and myths, legends, religions and other spiritual practices. For example, fire ceremonies were conducted to sustain the energy of the sun. These have been recorded in ancient Europe, the Mediterranean and China in March, June and December of each year (Frazer, 1910a,b). Sun cults promoted good crops, but humans were needed to give energy to the sun and to nature through magical rituals, seasonal rites and human sacrifice. Thus, the fundamental artificialistic belief that nature depends on human activity is borne out – humans and nature were interdependent and shared the same fate; both are born, they die and are reborn. Perhaps it was in the cycles of nature and its constant seasonal death and rebirth that the idea of reincarnation took hold in some primitive cultures. Similarly, the ritual killing and eating of a totemic animal served similar functions – the gods were incorporated into humans, reinvigorating them, thus symbolizing the eternal circle of life. The role of humans in sustaining the survival and rebirth of nature in order to sustain their own lives is the common thread that links the artificialistic cultural practices of most primitive cultures (Durkheim, 1912).

Freud believed that there was a developmental progression over the course of history – from animistic and magical, to religious, and then to scientific explanations – in the way in which we view and explain our universe. Each explanation becomes progressively less omnipotent and egocentric, ending in the scientific view that we are mortal, finite, small in a vast universe, and helpless against the forces of nature. There are several developmental theories of moral and religious development in the individual which parallel those historical stages identified by Freud, to which the interested reader is referred (e.g., Kohlberg, 1984; Meissner, 1984).

Taboos: *Totem and Taboo* (1913)

Wundt (1906) regarded taboos as the "oldest unwritten code of laws" (p. 308, in Freud, 1913a, p. 18). The word 'taboo' is Polynesian in origin, although it also appeared in other cultures in the South Pacific, for example, Tongan *tabu*; Maori *tapu*. It was introduced into the English language by Captain James Cook after his visit to Tonga in 1771 (Encyclopaedia Britannica, 2010). The concept was also present in the ancient world – in Latin *sacer*; in Hebrew *kadesh*; in Greek *agos*. However, Joyce (2001) cautions that the various words and concepts depicting taboos are not entirely interchangeable. The definition of 'taboo' in Western cultures is 'morally forbidden', while the concept of *tapu* refers to the quality of contaminating and contagious uncleanliness that resides in objects that are *tapu* and which may be relieved through washing or other cleansing rituals. A similar element is present in the ancient Greek and Roman usages. Freud (1913a) recognized these two converging meanings of the concept, describing one as sacred or consecrated and the other as "dangerous, forbidden, unclean" (p. 18).

Joyce (2001) argued, from a philosophical and logical perspective, that these concepts are defective; that an assertion of the form "[action x] is tapu" is never true. "[R]eflection on the kind of metaphysical uncleanliness that an application of the term presupposes leads to recognition that nothing is tapu" (p. 2). However, this assertion does not explain why the concept is held to be true and indeed is embodied in whole races of otherwise intelligent and logical people. For an explanation, we turn to Freud. Freud (1913a) commenced his analysis of taboos with Wundt's (1906) conclusion that taboos "have their origin in the source of the most primitive and at the same time most lasting of human instincts ... fear of 'demonic' powers" (p. 307, in Freud, 1913a, p. 18). Wundt continues:

> Taboo is originally nothing other than the objectified fear of the "demonic" power which is believed to lie hidden in a tabooed object. The taboo prohibits anything that may provoke that power and commands that, if it has been injured, whether wittingly or unwittingly, the demon's vengeance must be averted.
>
> (p. 308, in Freud, 1913a, p. 24)

Wundt believed that "the unspoken command underlying all the prohibitions of taboo, with their numberless variations ... is originally one and one only: 'Beware of the wrath of demons!'" (p. 24).

Wundt observed that both the sacred and the demonic share a common characteristic – the dread of contact and the prohibition against touching, characteristics that are observed in people with obsessional neuroses, which today we call Obsessive-Compulsive Personality Disorder (OCPD). Wundt argued that this common element suggests that the sacred and the taboo have common roots that at some point in their evolution diverged in other ways into the opposites of veneration (sacred) and horror (taboos). Purification and sacrifice rituals were developed to appease the demons who had been wronged by violation of the pertaining taboo, just as today's patients with OCPD engage in endless hand-washing. Violation of a taboo portended disaster. Any person who violated a taboo became himself taboo, with whom contact is forbidden, because such a person was thought to be able to arouse forbidden desire in others, and place their fellow clansmen at risk of imitation.

Taboos, obsessional neurosis and magical thinking

Freud was not satisfied with Wundt's explanation about the origin of taboos, arguing that fear of demons as the root cause for the development of taboos would only be plausible if demons actually existed; even fear cannot be a root cause, because it begs the question, "Fear of what?". Freud (1913b) noted the strong resemblance of primitive taboo practices and those of people suffering from obsessional neuroses. Neither primitive man nor obsessional patients can adequately account for their obsessions, compulsions/taboos, and both are intrinsically motivated to perform them, not out of a fear of externally imposed punishment, but out of primal fear that an annihilating disaster would befall them for failure to do so. Freud concluded, through the analysis of his obsessional patients, that at some point in their development, they experienced a strong desire to touch.[1] This desire was met with an external prohibition against touching. The prohibition proves stronger than the instinct (desire), and although it succeeds in preventing the touching, it does not succeed in abolishing the instinct, which is repressed into the unconscious. The patient subsequently develops an intense ambivalence towards the simultaneously desired and prohibited object, which cannot be resolved through reason. The 'magical' power of the taboo, according to Freud, is its capacity to arouse temptation, which must be resisted through obsessional acts and compulsions and with the use of other defensive measures. If all these strategies fail, the person may atone for their 'sin' by renunciation and the performance of ceremonial acts. Freud (1909) noted that many of his obsessional patients were superstitious and believed their premonitions and prophetic dreams. Freud (1907, 1913a,b) also observed the similarities between obsessive rituals and religious practices; both display 'magical' thinking, rely on charms, relics and icons, make illogical associations between events and accept that external forces will protect believers from adversity.

The worlds of intensely religious and obsessional individuals resemble the world of the pre-operational child, who occupies a magical world in which the law of causality does not apply. Pre-operational children believe that their thoughts control objects, that thinking causes actions and outcomes. Wishing is omnipotent; dreams represent reality. Freud and others (Einstein & Menzies, 2004a, b, 2008) have argued that these features are the underlying commonalities between religious and obsessional rituals that have survived childhood's stage of magical thinking. "This explains why obsessional neurotics find themselves guilty of the crimes that they commit in imagination, and are compelled to atone for their sins and restore their innocence with the symbolic rituals of purifying and undoing" (Yu, 2013, p. 60). Is this not also what the religious penitent does?

Over time, taboos came to serve useful social functions. Some became embedded in the social structure of the kinship group, tribe or clan and took on the status of a ritual, custom, tradition or moral precept and, in some cases, even law. Some were imposed by clan leaders – kings, priests and chiefs – as a way of protecting their property and privileges. Rulers, both secular and religious, were endowed with immense powers, including control over the sun, wind and rain, and with importance to their people, over whom they exercised sovereign control. Hence, the ruler must be both guarded from danger and guarded against to make sure he uses his powers judiciously. Failure to do so would precipitate the ruler's fall from idealized reverence and veneration to hatred, contempt and dismissal from his exalted position, in some cases followed by execution. Indeed, this pattern of events is in evidence today in the Middle East. The inherent ambivalence and unconscious hostility that tribes harboured against their rulers were expressed indirectly through ceremonial acts and the imposition of a complex set of taboo practices imposed upon the ruler as a form of control and "as punishment for their exaltation" (Freud, 1913a, p. 51). Japan is key example of the stifling rituals under which the ruling emperors were and still are required to live their lives.

Taboos and conscience

[R]elaxation of all the moral ties between the collective individuals of mankind should have had repercussions on the morality of individuals; for our conscience is not the inflexible judge that ethical teachers declare it, but in its origin is "social anxiety" and nothing else. When the community no longer raises objections, there is an end, too, to the suppression of evil passions, and men perpetrate deeds of cruelty, fraud, treachery and barbarity so incompatible with their level of civilization that one would have thought them impossible.

(Freud, 1915, p. 280)

Many taboos related to one's enemies and to the dead. For example, rites of appeasement have been observed in several South Pacific, African and American Indian cultures whereby the victors seek to appease the souls of those they have slain through expressions of remorse and respect for the enemy, sacrifice rituals and other acts of expiation in order to fend off the avenging ghosts of the slain. Freud believed that these acts were motivated by guilt at having violated the primary prohibition against killing. Other cultures, including the Australian Aborigines, Polynesians and tribes from India, Africa, South America, Japan, the Philippines and Indonesia, have a strong prohibition against speaking the name of the deceased, as it is considered tantamount to having contact with him and to invoking the return of the deceased's ghost. A number of anthropologists have observed the widespread fear of the dead among, for example, Australian Aborigines, Maoris and Inuit, and concluded that it was based on the belief that an individual becomes, upon death, a demon who has malevolent intent towards their living relatives from which they must protect themselves. If the deceased met their death through violent means such as murder, they became evil spirits who went in vengeful pursuit of the wrongdoers. Freud argued that the concept of demons and other forms of evil spirits had their origin in human corpses, which originated in the emotional ambivalence "between conscious grief and the unconscious satisfaction at death" (Freud, 1913a, p. 103), but also in the fear of death, and human imagination about the deeds of which corpses were capable. To find out, spirits that could provide vital information on the disposition of the demons were conjured.

Freud noted that the obsessive self-reproaches that occur in some bereaved individuals have much in common with these more primitive, magical processes characteristic of ancient tribes. The conscious content of these reproaches relate to feelings of responsibility for causing the death of their loved one through carelessness or neglect. However, Freud believed that the reproaches related to ambivalent feelings towards the deceased, on the one hand, conscious feelings of love and on the other, an unconscious wish to be rid of the deceased person: that "[b]ehind the tender love there is a concealed hostility in the unconscious" (Freud, 1913a, p. 60). This unconscious hostility is projected (or displaced) into the dead, thereby transforming the souls of the dead into 'demons' who return to torture their bereaved relatives. The defensive mechanism of projection allows survivors to deny their own hostile feelings because they now reside in the object of their hostility, against whom they must protect themselves with taboos and rituals. Taboos against contact with the dead and appeasement rituals require the adherent to submit to punishing renunciations and restrictions that have the character of penances.

Hence, both taboos and neurotic symptoms arise from feelings of ambivalence that serve multiple functions, including expressions of grief, concealment of hostility and self-defence against the perceived malevolence of the souls of the departed. Thus, the origin of demons can be explained as "projections of [unconscious] hostile feelings harboured by survivors against the dead" (Freud, 1913a, p. 62), who now become animate in part (through their 'soul'), since they have the capacity to act on the living. In this process, the living exchange internal discomfort for the external oppression of taboos, rituals and ceremonials that attempt to assuage their fear of retribution from the demons. Taboos were therefore conceptualized as an attempt to deal with ambivalent feelings towards the deceased. As civilization progressed, ambivalence towards the dead decreased and the practices of taboos accordingly became less prevalent or were transmuted into other forms, such as piety and penances.

However, Freud noted that both taboos and conscience, which he defined as "the internal perception of the rejection of a particular wish operating within us" (Freud, 1913a, p. 68), developed in response to emotional ambivalence and the awareness of the guilt we experience for enacting a forbidden wish. Further, analysis of the prohibition taboos in primitive societies indicates that the strongest temptations were to kill their priests and kings, to commit incest and to maltreat the dead. Since many of these taboos create emotional ambivalence through the experiencing of simultaneous but conflicting impulses of love and hate, desire and repulsion, we can now see how taboo, neurosis and conscience are associated, both in their origin and in their 'rituals'. The ambivalent attitude of the living towards the dead has also given rise to "opposed psychical structures: on the one hand fear of demons and ghosts and on the other hand, veneration of ancestors" (Freud, 1913a, p. 64).

We have not yet discovered from Freud's analysis how the dominant culture 'chooses' which side of these ambivalent feelings will become socially acceptable. Margaret Mead (1930) correctly argued that differences in cultural practices among different tribes has resulted in differential privileging of one side of these ambivalent feelings as conscious, while its obverse remained unconscious. For example, in Western culture, "the memory of the beloved dead must be kept green at all costs" (Mead, 1930, p. 298). In contrast, for the tribes of aboriginal Siberia, for example, all traces of the dead are removed as soon as possible, accompanied by rituals to bewilder and baffle the deceased's spirit so that it cannot find its way back to the village. Further, the same cultural practice may carry different signification. Before burial in both Western and aboriginal Siberian cultures, someone is in attendance on the deceased, but for different reasons. For a Westerner, it is a mark of respect, reflection and remembrance; for the aboriginal Siberians, it is a safety precaution that prevents the dead from reviving and doing harm. Mead argued that neuroses developed in those whose feelings were in cultural opposition to the majority. "The conscious personality, carefully shaped by a vigorous cultural tradition, would thrust such dangerous, anti-social, wicked attitudes away from it" (Mead, 1930, p. 301). In Western culture the feeling of excessive relief, in the Siberian, the feeling of excessive sorrow at a death would produce conflict. This is not to deny Freud's contention that ambivalence about death occurs in all humans, regardless of culture, but to add that "a civilization may seize upon one or the other of these (ambivalent) attitudes, elaborate it, ramify it, institutionalize it, until the reverse attitude, outlawed by society, is made an outlaw in each individual personality which is shaped by that society" (Mead, 1930, p. 301). Mead applauds those cultures who exercise a belief in multiple souls, which, she argued, allows for the free expression of both sides of the ambivalent feelings towards death. The Bagobo of the Philippines maintain that everyone has a right-hand (benevolent) soul and a left-hand (malevolent) soul. The good soul goes to the city of the dead, which is described as heaven-like (e.g., a place where the "rice … is of immaculate whiteness", (Mead, 1930, p. 304)), while the bad soul continues to roam the earth in perpetuity doing harm. Such a system allows the conscious expression of both sides of the ambivalent feelings towards the dead, thereby obviating internal conflict and the consequent development of neuroses.

From totems and taboos to religion

Freud argued that his purpose in writing *Totem and Taboo* was not to draw a straight causal line from totem to religion, but that this direct route presented itself to him in the course of his investigations into the origins and function of taboos and the evolution of religion.

> In *Totem and Taboo* it was not my purpose to explain the origin of religions but only of totemism. Can you … explain the fact that the first shape in which the protecting deity revealed itself to men should have been that of an animal, that there was a prohibition against killing and eating this animal and that nevertheless the solemn custom was to kill and eat it communally once a year? This is precisely what happens in totemism. … [I]t is hardly to the purpose to argue about whether totemism ought to be called a religion. It has intimate connections with the later god-religions. The totem animals become the sacred animals of the gods; and the earliest, but most fundamental moral restrictions – the prohibitions against murder and incest – originate in totemism. Whether or not you accept the conclusions of *Totem and Taboo*, I hope you will admit that a number of very remarkable, disconnected facts are brought together in it into a consistent whole.
>
> (Freud, 1927, p. 22)

What might the timeline from totem to religion look like? Frazer (1910b) envisaged a rude awakening of the kind described here:

> The imperious attitude of the magician towards nature is merely a result of his gross ignorance both of it and of himself; he knows neither the immeasurable power of nature nor his own relative weakness. When at last he gets an inkling of the truth, his attitude necessarily changes … he ceases to be a magician and becomes a priest. Magic has given place to religion.
>
> (p. 29)

Frazer is here ascribing the transition from totemism to religion to the cognitive development of individuals. Although undoubtedly one component of this shift, changes in the social organisation of clans over time were also influential. Initially, the rules governing ritual practices in relation to the totem were paramount and any direct link between individual members of the clan with the totem was less important than adherence to the rules. The totem thus provided a starting point for the collectivization of individuals into a society in which individual members became bound by the collective ideals. We discussed earlier how the symbol of the totem assumed greater significance and potency than the actual totem, and came to be imbued with a force or 'moral energy' that was diffused through ritual practices into members of the clan. To be influential in controlling behaviour, this force must penetrate into individual consciences; that is, the collective moral energy must also be taken in by each clan member and individualized, such that failure to adhere to ritualistic rules instilled fear of retribution in the recalcitrant. This is a process akin to the development of a superego and ego ideal in Freudian metatheory, which will be discussed later. It was this fear that became the foundation of the moral life of the clan (Guizzardi, 2007). Because of this capacity of the totem to integrate groups of individuals and bind them with common beliefs and rituals, religion was viewed as essential to the creation and maintenance of society (Pickering 1984). Durkheim defined religion thus:

> A religion is a unified system of beliefs and practices relative to sacred things, that is to say, things set apart and forbidden – beliefs and practices which unite into one single moral community called a Church, all those who adhere to them.
>
> (Durkheim, 1912, p. 62)

Durkheim and more contemporary scholars (e.g., Friedland, 2005; Shilling, 2005) argued that the 'god' of the clan, that is, the clan's totemic principle, is the clan itself. Religion represents the collectively shared sentiment of the clan, which is embodied in the sacralized totemic object. Thus, the social group, or the tribe or the church worships itself. This is one mechanism that perhaps assured the survival of such processes, beliefs and practices, enshrined as they were in the group as a whole. Freud (1921) noted in *Group Psychology and the Analysis of the Ego* that individuals behave differently in groups than when alone, an observation that later developed into the disciplines of social psychology and sociology. Mackay (1841) pre-empted Freud by 80 years in his commentaries on irrational mass behaviour and the economic behaviour of investors. "Men … think in herds; they go mad in herds, while they only recover their senses slowly, one by one" (Mackay, 1841, p. 2). Freud concurred: The individual becomes more credulous, open to influence and obedient when part of the 'herd'. 'Herd' behaviour is characteristic of groups of which the Christian Church takes full advantage, promulgating a message of sharing equally in the love of Christ (as the idealized Father God) as a brotherhood of believers who have been bound together by a collective inherited guilt regarding the original sin of the murder of the primal father.[2] This original sin is kept alive in successive generations of individuals who re-experience the same ambivalent feelings that resulted in the 'original sin' in relation to their own fathers.

Frazer noted that the most primitive totemic cultures were democratic and magical, compared with the monarchical and religious character of more developed cultures (e.g., Polynesia, Melanesia, America), which in the extreme manifested as the brutal absolute rule and murderous rituals of the Ashantee and Ugandans. Frazer also points out that there are a significant number of totemic cultures that did not proceed to the creation of totemic deities (e.g., the Bantu tribes of Africa, the 'negro' tribes of Guinea). In contrast, the majority of totemic cultures abided by the principle of collective responsibility which supported the development of moral codes of conduct.

In *Moses and Monotheism*, Freud (1939) returned to a consideration of totems, concluding:

> I think we are completely justified in regarding totemism, with its worship of a father-substitute, with its ambivalence as shown by the totem meal, with its

institution of memorial festivals and of prohibitions whose infringement was punished by death … as the first form in which religion was manifested in human history and in confirming the fact of its having been linked from the first with social regulations and moral obligations.

(Freud, 1939, p. 83)

Freud (1939) accepted Darwin's thesis that the early social structure of primitive societies mirrored the social organization of apes, placing a powerful male at the head of small groups of individuals clustered into hordes.[3] This male exercised enormous power over his dominion, which he protected by the most violent means, including murder, if his authority were threatened. All females, including his wives, daughters and sisters, were chattels and his sons and younger males in general were a potential and ever-present threat. If any dared arouse the parental ire, they were killed, castrated or cast out. The spurned sons would collect and start their own community, perhaps stealing wives from other communities, and if the opportunity presented itself, would defeat their father, kill him and devour him. Fathers became objects of fear and hate, but also of honour and awe. The social structure based on the father-horde was eventually replaced by the brother-clans, who, realising that they could have no peace unless the issue of "woman owner-ship" was resolved, instituted the practice of exogamy. The patricidal act, at some point, developed into the yearly ritual totem meal, at which the clan could do together what no individual could do alone – slaughter, kill and eat the totemic animal (i.e., father-substitute), which was first mourned to expiate their guilt and then celebrated in lavish festivals, cementing a sacred bond between the sons and their father.

Freud (1913a) argued that primitive man's attitudes to his ruler are mirrored in the modern child's infantile attitude towards his father. Indeed, he goes further in arguing that primitive society's disposition towards its rulers may have con-tributed to the "myths of Christendom" (p. 51). For example, he draws a parallel between the cannibalistic devouring of hated/feared fathers and totemic animals with the Last Supper and the Christian ritual of Holy Communion, in which "the believer incorporates the blood and flesh of his god in symbolic form" (Freud, 1939, p. 84), thereby re-enacting the ancient totemic meal. Freud also argued that the notion of original sin in Christian religions may have derived from the mur-der of primal father(s) who were later deified in patriarchal, monotheistic reli-gions. These primal murders were ritualistically replayed by Jesus, the Son of God, who submitted willingly to death by crucifixion to absolve all sons of the guilt of their original sin of murdering their fathers. There is a remarkable concord-ance between this doctrine and attachment theory (Bowlby, 1969), whereby the infant, who initially feels blissfully bonded to doting parents, becomes enraged by parental empathic misattunements, feels guilt about the rage because he loves his parents, and grief about his rage because he has symbolically murdered his parents. Freud further noted that the original religion of the Jews – Judaism – was a religion of the father, while the later Christian religions exalted the son, who triumphed over his father in the same way that the primal sons conquered the fathers of the primeval hordes. The guilt and remorse for the murder of Moses was perhaps the stimulus for the wishful fantasy of the messiah, a role that was admirably filled by Jesus.

Freud and Durkheim on religion

[I]n the absence of consideration of psychic mechanisms, sociological formulations about the individual [are] less than satisfactory.

(Golding, 1982, p. 548)

Freud and Durkheim developed independent theories on the socialization of the individual and the role of religion in society. They have much in common although they begin from a different perspective – Durkheim from the sociology of groups and Freud from the psychology of the individual. Both begin with the premise that to live collectively requires rules that need to be enforced, thus requiring the exertion of authority of one or a few over many. These rules are reinforced by having some form of external, symbolic expression around which (religious and social) rituals are organized. Durkheim argued that whether a society became monotheistic or pantheistic was secondary to the notion that sacred practices surrounding the deity(ies) derived from group experiences and group loyalty (Durkheim, 1912). Durkheim (1892) argued that the sociology of work and the division of labour may give rise to *anomie*, an outcome of particular social forces and dissatisfactions that lead to disobedience and rebellion. Anomic members of society become fringe dwellers – criminals, drop-outs or suicides – because they have no power to change society or to fit in with society in its current form.

Durkheim recognized that society can honour some of its members and denigrate others, but fell short of recognizing that both experiences can occur within the same individual, a situation that creates ambivalence, a theme central to Freud's work, but overlooked by Durkheim. Freud argued that man is aggressive, inquisitive and exploratory but also accepting of authority. This latter quality of compliance, he argued, was genetically selected to allow collectivization and the development of higher intelligence and culture. However, there are inherent tensions in such arrangements – between aggression and passivity, assertion and obedience, individuality and sociality, love and hate – that Freud argued were the foundations of both the infant's experience with his parents and between members of the social collective.

Envy arises between unequals and jealousy arises between equals, just as they do in the nuclear or extended family structure as inevitable expressions of man's fundamental instinctual nature. These same characteristics, according to Freud, define society. The two forms of idealized society are based on a vertical or horizontal social structure, the first with its rulers and hierarchies of authority, the latter with absolute equality between members and 'true' democracy that is often yearned for but rarely achieved by the anomics of mainstream society who form breakaway groups and cults. If *anomie* becomes pervasive, it may be a springboard for rebellion and revolution, processes that are currently occurring in several countries in the Middle East.

Freud tended to overlook particular characteristics of society such as its scale and the speed of change processes that can both influence and explain the ways in which it functions. For example, larger societies are more diversified, necessarily have more hierarchies and leaders, multiple authorities and systems of authority, greater risk of conflict between leaders, greater risk of injustice and discrimination, both real and perceived, and increased multi-group memberships leading to role confusion or diffusion (Scharf, 1970). Thus, larger societies that naturally tend to cultural and religious plurality, and are at greater risk of conflict and disintegration, require stronger systems of authority and necessarily allow less individuation among their members, although subgroups are tolerated, subject to the highest authority. In some situations, religion itself becomes the justification for conflict and revolution – for example, the nine Crusades (holy wars) of the Middle Ages, commencing in 1095, in which the Christian nations of Europe waged war against the Muslims to rescue Palestine, in particular the holy city of Jerusalem, which had been overrun by the Turks in 1065. Subsequently, the Crusades extended their reach – to rescue Spain from the Moors and Eastern Europe and the Mediterranean from the Slavs and Pagans (Tyerman, 2006). I will discuss the unholy religious wars of our own era in the final chapter.

Scharf (1970) offers a Durkheimian analysis of why Judaism – the religion of the Jews – has survived 4,000 years and resisted all internal and external challenges to its disintegration. Some of the factors that have contributed to its longevity include the supremacy of religious law (as opposed to secular laws) in Jewish society, the role of Judaism in cementing tradition and the absence of transformations or ruptures in ideology, rituals, ceremonies and rules over the course of its existence. Historical events also intervened to ensure that the Jewish 'tribe' remained small. Once established and consolidated in Palestine, the population expanded as a result of determined efforts at conversion and the establishment of small communities of Jewish settlers across the Middle East.

Perhaps inevitably, the settlers in Palestine became subject to schisms and the growth of sectarianism, a process which also occurred during the Christian expansion. The Jewish community was divided into aristocrat and commoners, rich and poor, educated and uneducated. Four main groups emerged – Sadducees, Pharisees, Zealots and Essenes – who nonetheless retained common religious scriptures and traditions. The main external pressure came from the hostility of the gentiles, whose numbers were rapidly increasing, prompting a permanent schism between Jews and gentiles that persists today. The next major challenge to Judaism was Islam, which, after Muhammad's initial failure to convert the Jews in Medina, pursued a policy of tolerance of both the Jews and the Christians. In subsequent centuries, permutations of religious beliefs and practices crept in, as they had in Christianity, from the influence of Greek (Aristotelian ideas), Spanish (kabbalism) and Italian (religious humanism) religious cultures.

The largest threat to Judaism came from the Shabbetaian movement. Tired of the impersonal oligarchic authority of the rabbis, a charismatic leader, Shabbetai Tzevi, steeped in the Jewish mystical writings of the Kabbala, appeared in the seventeenth century, declared himself the messiah and promised renewal and redemption to the adoring masses of converts in much the same way that occurs in Christian messianic movements in which the authority of the Church is replaced by a divinely inspired prophet or leader. Shabbetaianism, as the movement became known, was short-lived as a result of the conversion of Shabbetai to Islam to avoid torture following his arrest by the sultan in Turkey, whereupon he was appointed the sultan's doorman! A splinter group remained and continued to operate outside the bounds of Jewish orthodoxy. Shabbetai was declared a false messiah who threatened rabbinical authority in Europe and the Middle East; he fell out of favour with the sultan, was banished and died in Albania. Interestingly, however, mystical kabbalism was incorporated into Jewish orthodoxy.

For Durkheim, "the experience of social living is the raw material of all religions" (Scharf, 1970, p. 162). Such movements, argued Durkheim, reflect social change, disillusionment with current social arrangements, particularly for the poor and disenfranchised, or the need to provide a better template for an ideal society; for Freud, messianism is motivated by the infantile yearning for utopia, disappointment that it cannot be found and the subsequent turning to a messianic leader to help them create it.

Let us pause here to consider the role of social structure in the manner in which Christianity was promulgated in the Dark Ages and Patristic era. Christianity did not have its foundations in the philosophical thought of ancient Greece and Rome. Many of its earliest acolytes originated in unschooled tribes from Egypt, Greece, Asia Minor, Syria and Spain. Christianity was promulgated through the formation of 'study groups' or *didaskaleion* (i.e., from the ancient Greek διδασκαλειον, meaning school). Each group had an appointed leader who became the authority on questions of doctrine. Most did not have access to biblical texts; inevitably, leaders exercised interpretative licence that resulted in a diversification of teachings that later posed a problem for the Church's desire for unification of doctrine. It was this desire for absolute power over doctrine and religious observance that sowed the seeds for the development of the concept of heresy and the brutal suppression of beliefs and practices that too strongly resembled Jewish or pagan practices (Robinson, 2003). This did not end religious schisms, however; social forces are always in play between the struggle for totalitarian control, in this case, by a dictatorial Church, on the one hand, and the exercise of dissent and rebellion of its followers, on the other.

If we combine the theses of Durkheim and Freud, we achieve a stronger explanation for these radical religious schisms. The splinter leader is a rebel (i.e., anomic) against the prevailing social order and seeks to establish his own community of followers. Eventually, group values reappear as do the social problems of the mainstream religion or society that they sought to escape. Religious idealism turns to disillusion and the movement disintegrates. Freud argued that all social structures are fragile by virtue of man's ambivalence towards his leaders; put together with Durkheim's theory of the division of labour, the individual's relationship with society and incipient *anomie*, it appears that all social structures are placed under pressures from within and without, from which they may not recover. What, then, we may ask, are the factors leading to the survival of Judaism? Scharf (1970) concluded that the longevity and continuity of Judaism were due to "a monotheistic belief sanctioning religious laws whose provisions clearly marked off the community, kept it small and limited its internal diversity" (p. 159).

Notes

1 Current aetiology of OCPD is understood as an effort to relieve anxiety by preventing objectively unlikely dangers. Obsessions and/or compulsive behaviours prevent the breakthrough of unconscious anger, aggression, resentment, shame and fears about loss of control. Magical ideas originating in childhood often underlie the manifest anxiety of OCPD patients (PDM Task Force, 2006).
2 Freud's use of the term 'primal' or 'primitive' denotes a basic element of the unconscious and does not necessarily only refer to the historically early stages of human development in primitive cultures.
3 Darwin (1874) defined a horde as an organized group ruled over by a despotic, violent, jealous, primal father, who appropriated all the women and denied them access to his sons and other young male members of the horde. This view is generally accepted by anthropologists (Atkinson & Birch, 1970) and psychoanalysts (Schoenfeld, 1962).

4

FREUD, RELIGION, CULTURE AND PHILOSOPHY

Exposition: *The Future of an Illusion* (1927)

> [R]eligion becomes, in Freud's terms, the universal obsessional neurosis of mankind, participation in the rituals and magical thinking of which spares the believing individual from a personal neurosis.
>
> (Kovel, 1990, p. 70)

Freud's three other works on religion – *The Future of an Illusion* (1927), *Civilization and its Discontents* (1930) and *Moses and Monotheism* (1939) – argue that religion is a cultural product that serves important social and political purposes, a view strongly supported by Karl Marx (1843), who argued that:

> Man's self-esteem, freedom, must be awakened once more in the heart of ... men. Only this feeling, which disappeared from ... the blue mists of heaven with Christianity, can once more make from a society a fellowship of men working for their highest purposes, a democratic State.
>
> (p. 561)

In these works, Freud tackled the vexed question of why religious beliefs are embraced by millions and concludes that religion, just like other political and cultural products, serves a vital function that maintains the social fabric of civilization – the renunciation or suppression of instinctual urges, without which social structures would crumble into anarchy and annihilation.

Freud experienced the form of appropriation to which Marx alluded of his own work for religious purposes. Freud stated in a letter to Oskar Pfister, pastor of Zurich, that he wished to protect analysts from physicians and priests. "I want to trust it [psychoanalysis] to a profession that doesn't yet exist, a profession of secular ministers of souls [in German *Seelsorger*], who don't have to be physicians and must not be priests" (Kovel, 1990 , p. 82). It is not difficult to understand why Freud felt so protective of his method against corrupting misinterpretations and self-interested applications. You will understand why from the following example: Pfister's (1923) book, *Some Applications of Psychoanalysis*. It attracted the following comment from its reviewer in the *Psychoanalytic Review*:

> So Pfister classes all other religions as hysterical or neurotic and recom-mends elimination of their manifestations and the "introduction of the Protestant religion, which is free from neurosis." The Japanese and the Chinese are to be instructed by the missionary that their religion is merely indicative of father fixation, the Brahmin and the Buddhist learn that their Nirvana is a catatonic paradise.
>
> (Anon., 1924, p. 223)

Freud structured *The Future of an Illusion* as if it were addressed to a hypothetical adversary who argues against his assertions. The adversary, akin to a Greek chorus, also questions the character of a person (i.e., Freud) who has the audacity to present such a seditious account of religion, which risks dislodging the bedrock on which our civilization rests. Not surprisingly, Freud often used this defensive literary man-oeuvre to pre-empt criticism of his work, as he felt the need to be constantly on the alert to critical attacks upon his ideas.

> If our work leads us to a conclusion which reduces religion to a neurosis of humanity and explains its enormous power in the same way as a neurotic compulsion in our individual patients, we may be sure of drawing the resent-ment of our ruling powers down upon us.
>
> (Freud, 1939, p. 55)

Although mindful of the negative reception that he would receive from some quarters for his seditious ideas, Freud was somewhat defiant of those who would denigrate him, boldly announcing the thesis of this work by its title – that religion is an illusion propagated to satisfy the believer's wishful fantasies and to control their behaviour. With the rise of the Nazis in the 1930s, Freud's work, along with the work of other brilliant minds including Albert Einstein, H.G. Wells, Thomas Mann and Marcel Proust, was burnt in public bonfires for the "their soul-disintegrating exaggeration of the instinct-ual life" (Lemma & Patrick, 2010, p. 3). Freud and Darwin were also charged with "subverting the high values of fair-skinned races" (Lemma & Patrick, 2010, p. 3).

Freud begins his thesis by arguing that civilization is the outcome of a process whereby man, through skill and knowledge acquisition, raised himself above the animal kingdom in order to "control the forces of nature and extract its wealth for the satisfaction of human needs" (Freud, 1927, p. 6). However, collective living, as a foundational requirement of civilization, is not a natural state. Paradoxically, every individual is also an enemy of civilization – man realizes simultaneously that he cannot exist in isolation but resents the heavy burden demanded of him by civilization that nevertheless makes communal living possible. Hence, civilized society needs protection against its own members and achieves this through a complex system of rules, laws and prohibitions. Civilization must also monitor its products – science and technology – which can equally enhance the quality of life and hasten its destruction. Civilization is thus imposed on a reluctant majority by a minority who have attained power by various means over the masses – in its most benign form, through a direct or representative democracy and in its most extreme form, through a totalitarian dictatorship that rules with brute force and swift and lethal retribution for any form of disobedience.

Hence, civilization is necessarily built upon coercion and a "renunciation of instinct" (Freud, 1927, p. 7). Instincts are frustrated by the imposition of prohibitions against the expression of man's natural (i.e., destructive, antisocial and anticultural strivings) instincts, thereby creating a state of deprivation. In order for a civilized society to survive, ways need to be found to both lessen and compensate for the individual's instinctual burden. Freud argued that this could be achieved by the modelling of the desired behaviour by its leaders, who have presumably mastered their own instinctual desires. Successive generations would find the task more manageable if children were reared with kindness and taught to value reason. In this way, the task of renouncing sexual and aggressive impulses, or at least finding acceptable ways to express them through sublimated activities or structures (e.g., sport, artistic pursuits, marriage), would feel less onerous. However, regardless of these developments, a degree of restlessness and discontent persists within groups or minorities who feel themselves disadvantaged that can fester into revolts or revolution. Some groups reject the cultural prohibitions imposed upon them and express hostility aimed at overturning them, normally as a means of redressing imbalances or actual or perceived injustices in the current organizational structures. There are, sadly, many contemporary examples (e.g., the Israel–Palestine conflict, Syria, Egypt) of this struggle to redress actual or perceived imbalances.

Fortunately, for the majority, the external constraints on the unfettered expression of instincts are eventually internalized, and man thereby acquires the capacity to control his own behaviour through the operation of the superego, which Freud described as "the most precious cultural asset" (Freud, 1927, p. 10), second only to religious ideas that he argued were the "most important item in the psychical inventory of a civilization" (Freud, 1927, p. 14), although Freud believed that instincts, like the forces of nature, can never really be fully restrained. Further, being subjected to the majesty, cruelty and inexorability of nature confronts us with our own finitude, insignificance and helplessness. Civilization is thus charged with the task of consoling us and assuaging our terror. For Freud, this process begins with the "humanization of nature" (Freud, 1927, p. 16). He explained it thus:

> [I]f the elements have passions that rage as they do in our own souls, if death
> … is … the violent act of an evil Will, if everywhere in nature there are
> Beings around us of a kind that we know in our own society, then we can
> … feel at home in the uncanny and can deal by psychical means with our …

anxiety. ... We can apply the same methods against these violent supermen outside that we employ in our own society; we can try to adjure them, to appease them, to bribe them, and, by so influencing them, we may rob them of a part of their power. ... [T]his situation is nothing new. It has an infantile prototype ... once before one has found oneself in a similar state of helplessness: as a small child, in relation to one's parents.

(Freud, 1927, pp. 16–17)

The humanized (i.e., personified) forces of nature became "gods" whose tasks were to (i) exorcize the terrors of nature; (ii) reconcile men to the cruelty of Fate, particularly death; and (iii) compensate man for the sufferings and privations which a collective civilized life imposes upon him. Man soon realized that the gods could not relieve the "the perplexity and helplessness of the human race" (Freud, 1927, p. 18), leading to the conclusion that the gods themselves were subject to the same vicissitudes as man and that a power above the gods – Fate/a unitary Deity – was operating. In order to render our helplessness and fear of finitude more tolerable, we decided that our transitory physical life in this visible world served a higher purpose in eternity – that of perfecting man's nature. To accomplish this, the eternal part of man, his 'soul', becomes detached from his temporary, earthly body through death, which need not now be perceived as extinction, "a return to organic lifelessness" (Freud, 1927, p. 19), but as a gateway to an exalted existence, in which good is rewarded and evil punished.

The transition from multiple gods to a unitary Deity in Western Christian religion replicated the early infantile attachment to one's father, who is both loved and feared, whom one attempts to please and appease, and from whom one expects a just reward, to be his beloved child and, by extension, his "Chosen People" (Freud, 1927, p. 19). Freud observed that the ambivalence of the relationship between father and child is mirrored in every religion. The helplessness of childhood is never resolved; it transmutes into feelings of helplessness as an adult in the face of one's own instinctual drives, the recognition of one's finitude and the unwinnable struggle against the forces of nature, which are, according to Freud, the underlying motivations for the development of religion. Once intertwined in the fabric of civilization, tacit injunctions are invoked that religious beliefs must not be questioned; they must be defended against the collective insecurity that these religious doctrines would not survive such scrutiny. Notwithstanding, Freud identified two strategies that have been invoked to shore up what are, at their heart, logically insupportable positions. The first, propagated by the Church, was to proclaim that religious doctrines are not subject to reason. One must have a revelatory inner experience of their truth. The second involves the adoption of an 'as if' stance. Even if one believes these "fairy tales of religion" (Freud, 1927, p. 29) to be false, one must behave as if they were true in the interests of supporting the structure of human society, to prevent it from descending into chaos through the unfettered expression and satisfaction of every "asocial, egoistic instinct" (Freud, 1927, p. 34) of man, freed of his obligation to adhere to the precepts of civilization.

This leads us to a consideration of Freud's question: "In spite of their incontrovertible lack of authentication, why have [religious ideas] exercised the strongest possible influence on mankind?" (Freud, 1927, p. 29) To answer this question, Freud returns to his opening argument that religious ideas have their origins in wish-fulfilment. The "benevolent rule of a divine Providence" (Freud, 1927, p. 30) relieves our fears and feelings of helplessness and promises eternal prolongation of our earthly existence in the realms of heavenly bliss for those who have faithfully obeyed His commandments. Further, religion's gatekeepers – ministers and priests – were shrewd enough to understand that "God's kindness must lay a restraining hand on His justice" (Freud, 1927, p. 37). Given the wretchedness of their existence, even when enfolded in the comforting arms of religious illusions, humans will falter and sin. In order to maintain the flock in the fold, there evolved the complex system of sacrifices and penance for sins that permitted some leeway for the expression of base instincts but also maintained the submission of the masses to the authority of the Church, which deliberately withheld the provision of opportunities for their intellectual enlightenment, such as teaching them to read and to think their own thoughts. The religious enterprise was based on the placement of faith above knowledge and rationality. The easiest way to instil faith was to instil fear and withhold knowledge.

Like all illusions, religious ideas are motivated from the deepest recesses of the human psyche that have no regard for reality. These illusory ideas cannot be proven or refuted and can teach us nothing outside of the contents of our own emotional life. Freud was critical of all the permutations of the Deity found in various religions and in the versions created at the hands of philosophers, who make of God "nothing more than an insubstantial shadow and no longer the mighty personality of religious doctrines" (Freud, 1927, p. 32). He universally condemned these efforts as intellectually dishonest because they represented a form of circular logic that merely created a doctrine that satisfied their original needs and wishes. We will examine this proposition in more detail presently. Insistent inculcation of the "absurdities of religious doctrines" (Freud, 1927, p. 48) into the minds of young children led, according to Freud, to "intellectual atrophy" (Freud, 1927, p. 47), thus making belief in these doctrines unassailable.

Freud argued that there were satisfactory, non-religious reasons for imposing injunctions against killing and stealing and that God could be comfortably removed from the development and implementation of societal regulations. Further, there will always be a minority, with or without religion, whose impulses will override reason and regulation, and who will necessarily become subject to the judiciary as well as or instead of the Deity. Freud hastened to point out that religious doctrines are not the only offenders with respect to errors of flawed and circular logic; the criticism could equally be applied to political doctrines that have, for centuries, subjugated women, and other minority groups, but more of this later. The antipathy to science within some religious circles had similar origins – it was perceived to be a threat to the means of controlling the masses, and must be discredited for the very reason that it has exposed the "fatal resemblance between the religious ideas that we revere and the mental products of primitive peoples and times" (Freud, 1927, p. 38).

Freud, who worshipped at the shrines of the twin gods *Logos* (Reason) and *Necessity*, alludes ironically to the possible consequences of his seditious ideas: "[U]tterances such as mine brought with them a sure curtailment of one's earthly existence and an effective speeding-up of the opportunity for gaining a personal experience of the afterlife" (Freud, 1927, p. 36). In his final analysis, Freud viewed religious precepts and edifices as nothing more than "neurotic relics" (Freud, 1927, p. 44); he drew an analogy between religion and obsessional neurosis, arguing that believers' acceptance of a universal neurosis "spares them the task of constructing a personal one" (Freud, 1927, p. 44). After all, religion is a warmer and more comforting blanket than reason, which demands that we "admit to ourselves the full extent of [our] helplessness and insignificance in the machinery of the universe" (Freud, 1927, p. 49). Rather than adhere to "the mythical structures of religion" (Freud, 1939, p. 45) Freud urges us to "concentrate all [our] liberated energies into [our] life on earth" (Freud, 1927, p. 50).

Civilization and its Discontents (1930)

> It is impossible to escape the impression that people commonly use false standards of measurement – that they seek power, success and wealth for themselves and admire them in others, and that they underestimate what is of true value in life.
>
> (Freud, 1930, p. 64)

In *Civilization and its Discontents*, Freud (1930) further develops the thesis that religion arises to tame the forces of nature without and the instinctual urges within, and to provide solace for relinquishing our human nature in order to live collectively in civilized society. Freud distinguishes the different purposes of this work compared with those of *Future of an Illusion*. He states that his main concern in the earlier work was to elucidate

> what the common man understands by his religion – with the system of doctrines and promises which on the one hand explains to him the riddles of this world with enviable completeness, and, on the other, assures him that a careful Providence (who takes the form of an "enormously exalted father") will watch over his life and will compensate him in a future existence for any frustrations he suffers here.
>
> (Freud, 1930, p. 74)

In *Civilization and its Discontents*, Freud was unable to restrain his disdain for religion, which he found

> so patently infantile, so foreign to reality … it is painful to think that the great majority of mortals will never be able to rise above this view of life. It is still

> more humiliating to discover how large a number of people living to-day, who cannot but see that this religion is not tenable, nevertheless try to defend it piece by piece in a series of pitiful rear guard actions.
>
> (Freud, 1930, p. 74)

In this work, Freud was concerned with further elucidating "the irremediable antagonism between the demands of instinct and the restrictions of civilization" (Strachey, 1930, p. 59), "the deepest sources of the religious feeling" (Freud, 1930, p. 74) and to account for the role of guilt and the superego in the development of civilization (p. 61). Freud identified three basic instincts, as follows:

1. sexual instinct (libido);
2. aggressive (destructive) instinct – hate, cruelty and sadism (origins in the early object relations with love-hate bipolarity);
3. self-preservative instincts.

He then identified three sources of suffering arising from these three instincts:

1. our bodies, which are "doomed to decay and dissolution";
2. the external world, "which may rage against us with overwhelming and merciless forces of destruction";
3. our relationships, against which we may protect ourselves through "voluntary isolation" thereby achieving a "happiness of quietness" or by becoming a better member of our human community (Freud, 1930, p. 77).

According to Freud (1930), in order to avert suffering, we engage in a number of strategies, as follows:

1. the use of palliative measures or "substitutive satisfactions" such as "powerful deflections" that make light of our misery, as Voltaire enjoins us in *Candide* (p. 75);
2. intoxication, which physically induces pleasurable states;
3. renouncing instinctual pressures through Eastern practices such as yoga;
4. satisfaction of wild instinctual impulses;
5. displacement of libido through the defence of sublimation into artistic or cultural pursuits and the enjoyment of beauty;
6. indulging in the life of the imagination, which is "exempted from the demands of reality testing" (p. 80). In the extreme, imagination turns to illusion through a further separation of oneself from the external world;
7. regarding reality as the enemy and the "source of all suffering" such that one must break contact with reality and retreat into reclusion, neurotic illness, delusion or madness;
8. "delusional remoulding of reality" (p. 81) which can occur on a grand scale and become a mass-delusion, as happens in the various religions of the world,

and in totalitarian states such Hitler's Nazi Germany, Stalin's Russia or Mao's China. Religion restricts choice and adaptation, since it imposes equally on everyone its own path to the acquisition of happiness and protection from suffering. Its technique consists in depressing the value of life and distorting the real world in a delusional manner – which presupposes an intimidation of the intelligence (p. 84);

9. adopting a way of life that makes love the centre of everything, which looks for all satisfaction in loving and being loved, including sexual love (p. 82).

Fromm (1964) provided the following account of the relationship between the individual and civilization from a humanistic theoretical perspective:

> [S]ociety forms the social character not only by stimulating certain strivings and drives, but also by repressing those tendencies which are at odds with the social patterns. ... This repression operates not only with regard to certain socially tabooed strivings, but particularly with regard to one basic fact: in all societies in which there is conflict between the human interests of all individuals and the social interest of the existing society (and its elite), the society will see to it that the majority of the people do not become aware of this discrepancy. The greater the discrepancy between the specific interests of the survival of a given social order and the human interest of all its members, the more must a society be conducive to repression. Only when social interest and the human interest of the individual are identical will the need for repression disappear.
>
> But why, we must ask ourselves, is man so ready to repress what he feels and thinks and experiences? Freud thinks that the reason lies in the fear of the father and of his castration threat. I believe the fear is deeper and of a social character: *man is afraid of nothing more than of being ostracized, isolated, alone.* ... If a society lays down the law that certain experiences and thoughts must not be felt or thought consciously, the average individual will follow this order because of the threat of ostracism which it implies if he does not. ... [W]hat is unconscious and what is conscious depends (aside from the individual, family-conditioned elements and the influence of humanistic conscience) on the structure of society and on the patterns of feelings and thoughts it produces.
>
> (p. 76)

Freud's and Fromm's accounts are remarkably similar in their understanding regarding the need for repression in civilization, but they differ with respect to the content of repression. For Freud (1930), civilization is built upon the "renunciation of instinct" (p. 97) that creates "cultural frustration" which breaks through in hostilities. Fromm asserts that fear of ostracization motivates repression, but he does not specify the content of the repressed material, only that it is the "human interest of the individual" that is at odds with the "social interest". The fear of being cast out of one's society for failure to comply with its dictates is implied, if not directly stated in *Civilization and its Discontents*. It is interesting to note, however, that Fromm believed the father's castration threat is the significant element in Freud's theorizing about the tensions between collective and individual good, when the issue of castration does not receive a single mention in *Civilization and its Discontents*. In this work, Freud is more concerned with the protective role of the father in infancy, and who, over time, becomes "enormously exalted" in the minds of believers who trust that he will compensate them in a future existence for all the cultural frustrations they must endure in this life.

Moses and Monotheism (1939): Freud's final religious and philosophical contemplations

It was this one man, Moses, who created the Jews.

(Freud, 1939, p. 106)

Moses and Monotheism, Freud's last study of religion, has a strong historical and philosophical turn. Freud expressed uncertainty "in the face of [his] own work" (Freud, 1939, p. 58), which was not due to any lack of conviction about the veracity of its argumentation but whether he had been sufficiently persuasive to convince others. The central concern in this work was to understand the concept of historical truth in the context of the religious believer's conviction that God exists despite the absence of verifiability of the proposition and, indeed, in the presence of realities incompatible with a belief in God (Blass, 2003). Freud, as an uncompromising seeker after truth, also examined the proposition that religious ideas might be accepted because they are, in fact, true.

Freud observed that he was struggling to make sense of the origins of a Jewish monotheistic religion at a time when the world was allying itself with barbarism, by which he meant the rise of fascism in Italy, Nazism in Germany and the brutalities imposed upon the Russian people by Soviet Russia under Stalin. He was particularly critical of Germany, which had "relapsed into ... prehistoric barbarism ... without being attached to any progressive ideas", a reference to the fact that Russia had at least "withdraw[n] ... the opium of religion" and granted greater "sexual liberty" to its people even though these advances occurred in the context of "cruel coercion" and a loss of freedom of thought (Freud, 1939, p. 54).

Freud also noted the irony of the fact that only the Catholic Church stood between Nazism and cultural preservation and advance, and that he needed to be cautious about incurring its wrath in his current writings on the development of monotheism, but admitted that this was a difficult enterprise in view of the fact that "our work leads us to a conclusion which reduces religion to a neurosis of humanity and explains its enormous power in the same way as a neurotic compulsion in our individual patients" (Freud, 1939, p. 55). Freud complained that, just as the Jews wandered in the wilderness with no home, psychoanalysis, while enjoying a universal diaspora, never found a proper home in the city of its birth. He, too, lost that lifelong home of his childhood when the Catholic Church in Austria proved to be "a broken reed" (Freud, 1939, p. 59).

Despite the tumultuous political upheavals and personal[1] crises confronting Freud during the preparation of this work, he claimed that his sole purpose in writing *Moses and Monotheism* was the "introduc[tion of] the figure of an Egyptian Moses into the nexus of Jewish history" (Freud, 1939, p. 52). While this was a very bold and contentious thesis, the work achieves much more than this. Although Freud did not waiver from his atheistic convictions – e.g., "We must not expect the *mythical structures of religion* to pay too much attention to logical coherence" (my italics) (Freud, 1939, p. 45) – he once again concluded, as he had in *Totem and Taboo* 25 years earlier, that religion had a social and psychological value so important that its survival was assured. See, for example, this passage:

> [T]otemism, with its worship of a father-substitute, with its ambivalence as shown by the totem meal, with its institution of memorial festivals and of prohibitions whose infringement was punished by death – we are justified …
> in regarding *totemism as the first form in which religion was manifested in human history* and in confirming the fact of its *having been linked from the first with social regulations and moral obligations*. [My italics]
>
> (Freud, 1939, p. 83)

A similar argument has been mounted by Robert Bellah (2011), a sociologist of religion, in his book *Religion in Human Evolution*, which includes, as does Freud, the supposition that a unitary God is not a necessary condition of human religion. I have elsewhere noted that Freud had a special affinity with Moses. Indeed, Max Graf, the father of "Little Hans", told Kurt Eissler that Freud had a 'Moses complex', by which he meant that Freud had a similar desire to withstand and indeed rise above the scepticism and hostility to his work in order to lead his chosen people into the promised land of his psychoanalytic worldview (Kenny, 2013). This represented, like Judaism, "an *advance in intellectuality* … in which ideas, memories and inferences became decisive in contrast to the *lower psychical activity* which had direct perceptions by the sense-organs as its content, [and which] was unquestionably one of the most *important stages on the path to hominization*" (my italics) (Freud, 1939, p. 113).

Moses is known to be a historical figure and not a figure of myth or legend, who did in fact lead "his chosen people" out of Egypt. Freud mounted a number of arguments favouring the hypothesis that Moses was Egyptian. (For example, the name 'Moses', meaning 'child', was Egyptian, not Hebrew, and was commonly used as a suffix to the names of Egyptian kings (e.g., Ra-mose(s), denoting that the king was a child of the god, Ra); there is evidence that Moses introduced circumcision, which was commonly practised in Egypt, as a religious custom to the Jews.) There are other hypotheses about his origins (e.g., that he was a Midianite to whom God revealed Himself) or there were, in fact, two Moses, one Egyptian and one Midianite. If it be the case that Moses were Egyptian, what would induce him, Freud asks, to forsake his own culture and standing in (purportedly royal) Egyptian society to "put himself at the head of a crowd of immigrant foreigners at a back-ward level of civilization and to leave his country with them" (Freud, 1939, p. 18), become their political leader and law-giver and force them into the service of a new religion which was vastly different from that of Egypt?

The Jewish religion bequeathed to the Jews by Moses was strictly mono-theistic, in stark contrast to Egyptian polytheism. The Egyptians' host of gods comprised personifications of natural forces and animals, and a god of the dead, Osiris, whose images in clay, stone and metal adorned the city. All gods required the performance of ceremonial acts and the giving of "charms and amulets" (Freud, 1939, p. 19) to please and appease them. Egyptians denied death and went to enormous lengths to prepare their passage into the next world. By con-trast, the Jewish faith worshipped one God, forbade the carving of graven images and denied the possibility of an afterlife or immortality. How did such a reli-gion develop? Freud argued that the young Pharaoh, Amenophis IV (who later changed his name to Akhenaten in honour of the sun god, Aten), introduced a monotheistic religion into Egypt at around 1375 BCE. During his father's reign, the idea that the sun god (Aten) could become an ethical, universal god had gained traction amongst its priests, the sun cult of On. The religion of Aten may be the first example of a monotheistic religion in recorded human history. As Egypt's influence spread in the coming millennia, it was politically propitious to offer a universalistic and monotheistic religion to Egypt's dominions – just as Pharaoh became the sole ruler of the ancient world, so too the sole Egyptian god became the exclusive deity of his empire. It was a harsher version of this Aten religion that Moses passed on to the Jews, with the important difference that the Mosaic religion no longer worshipped the sun (or sun god). With the collapse of Egyptian dominance after the death of Amenophis IV and in the ensuing inter-regnum and anarchy, Moses led the Jews out of Egypt to the land of Canaan, having relinquished any ambition he may have harboured to rule over them in Egypt. Freud frequently cautions that there are few verifiable historic facts in the Mosaic saga: "No historian can regard the Biblical account of Moses and the Exodus as anything other than a pious piece of imaginative fiction, which has recast a remote tradition for the benefit of its own tendentious purposes" (Freud, 1939, p. 33). However, he noted from various sources that Moses was a powerful and imposing leader, but irascible, impatient, quick to anger and indig-nation. Historians of Freud's day (e.g., Ernst Sellin) found evidence to suggest that Moses was murdered by his chosen people. So ashamed of their actions were the Jews that a myth arose that he would one day rise from the dead and again lead his people into a "kingdom of lasting bliss" (Freud, 1939, p. 35). These events may have been the origin of the messianic myth of the second coming.

Following their exit from Egypt, the Jews joined other tribes in the region between Egypt and Canaan and adopted a new religion and deity – Yahweh, a vol-cano god – that was common to the amalgamated tribes. Yahweh had a demonic nature and was variously described as "jealous, severe and ruthless" (Freud, 1939, p. 33), characteristics also attributable to Moses that had perhaps contributed to incurring the wrath of his people, resulting in his assassination. This new tribal religion extended the restrictions against creating images of Yahweh to prohibition on speaking His name. The word 'Adonai' (Lord) was used to refer to Yahweh. In the 800 years between the Exodus from Egypt and the writing of the biblical scriptures of the Old Testament, the Yahweh religion reverted to the original religion propounded by Moses, with a moral, all-embracing single deity, who disdained sacrifice and ceremonials and demanded only that his followers live in truth and justice and serve Him.

Freud argued that a monotheistic god served the purpose of Egyptian imperialism, while, for the Greeks, by contrast, the disintegration of their polytheistic religion resulted in developments along humanistic lines, including the birth of the discipline of philosophy. However, in making the argument that contemporaneous social and political factors influenced the form that deities took in different regions, Freud was also concerned with the evolution from polytheistic to monotheistic religions, which, he argued, were centred on the cult of the 'great man', of which Moses was a cardinal example. Eventually, Moses became indistinguishable in the minds of "the poor Jewish bondsmen" (Freud, 1939, p. 110) whom he had chosen and rescued from Moses' God, as a result, no doubt, of the injection into 'God' of the personality traits of the 'great man'. Thus, "the figure of the great man [grew] to divine proportions (p. 110) "and [a]nyone who believed in this God had … a share in his greatness" (p. 112). Freud, somewhat wearily and nostalgically, concluded that

> [w]e can only regret that certain experiences in life and observations in the world make it impossible for us to accept the premise of the existence of such a Supreme Being. As though the world had not riddles enough, we are set the new problem of understanding how these other people have been able to acquire their belief in the Divine Being and whence that belief obtained its immense power, which overwhelms reason and science
>
> (Freud, 1939, p. 123)

before making an attempt to explain the phenomenon via the mechanism of the 'return of the repressed'. Freud believed that children always identify with their fathers in early childhood and that these identifications become unconscious. Even if there is a period later in life when this identification is consciously repudiated, the individual appears always to return to the initial form of identification. Freud used this idea of the 'return of the repressed' as an analogy for the effect of traditions, often long since forgotten or abandoned, in the minds of a clan or tribe. Freud emphasized that he was not referring to a Jungian 'collective unconscious', although he stated that the content of the unconscious was the "collective, universal property of mankind", that man shares an instinctively acquired "innate symbolism" and that "the psychical precipitates of the primaeval period became inherited property which, in each fresh generation, called not for acquisition but only for awakening" (Freud, 1939, p. 131).

In this way primitive man progressed from a belief in totemism to a belief in a supreme and singular deity. Freud noted that as hordes became clans, clans tribes and tribes nations, so too did the structure of the society of deities accompanying these social transitions become organized in the same way – into families and hierarchies. Eventually, the "supremacy of the father of the primal horde" (Freud, 1939, p. 133) was reasserted in the development of monotheistic religions, which tolerate only one god as supreme lord and master. The rapturous devotion displayed to the great father resembles that of the helpless infant seeking succour and refuge from its human father. However, the infant's relation to his father is not without ambivalence, as we have discussed, and hostility and rebellion will break through if the great father fails to satisfy. There was no place in Mosaic religion for any open expression of murderous rage towards God. The feelings were expressed as a reaction formation – abject guilt about the hostility and the need to atone for having sinned for the symbolic murder of the great father. This strategy served two very powerful purposes – expiating the guilt of the worshippers and exculpating God for His failures to fulfil their wishes and longings. And so began for the Jews the development of ever-increasing moral injunctions and instinctual renunciations that bear an uncanny resemblance to the reaction formations of both obsessional neurotics and Orthodox Jews.

Notes

1   Freud was in advanced old age, was suffering from mouth cancer and no doubt contemplating the end of his life.

5

FREUD, THE DEMONIC, MADNESS AND THE FANCIFUL

Historical context embeddedness of demonic phenomena and madness

> Psychological phenomena cannot be understood apart from the intersubjective contexts in which they take form. Intrapsychic determinism thus gives way to an unremitting intersubjective contextualism.
>
> (Stolorow & Atwood, 1996, p. 182)

Gadamer (1975), in *Truth and Method*, argues that our worldview is circumscribed by the language we use to describe our experiences. We are all embedded in a historically conditioned set of prejudices enshrined in culture and language, which constitute pre-formed understandings that organize our subjective experience. Put simply, if everyone around us, including authoritative and powerful members of influential organizations like the Church, is ascribing demonic possession as the cause of bad or bizarre behaviour, this explanation becomes 'taken for granted' – it must be right because the Church has so decreed it. The search for other possible explanations ceases because we have the answer from a trusted and reliable source.

Freud believed the process of cultural and linguistic embeddedness was responsible for the presentation of neurotic illnesses. He argued that these illnesses assumed characteristics, in the form of symptoms, which were historically and culturally comprehensible. For example, devils and demons have had a long literary as well as religious history. As we discovered in Chapter 3, the practices of many primitive cultures centred on the mastery of evil spirits. Demons existed in the writings of the ancient world, and are depicted in Latin theological treatises. Similarly, during the Middle Ages, the neurotic's forbidden wishes and impulses were projected into the external world and given corporeal form as demons.

Primitive man has no choice; he has no other way of thinking. It is natural to him, something innate … to project his existence outwards into the world and to regard every event … he observes as the manifestation of beings who at bottom are like himself.

(Freud, 1927, p. 21)

I will here focus on medieval demonic conceptions because a dramatic shift occurred in the conceptualization of devils and demons during the Middle Ages that exemplifies the historical context embeddedness of expressions of psychological conflict that are conflated with religious scholarship and influenced by the prevailing social and political culture of the time. Ruys (2012) describes the transformation of the conceptualization of demons from "impersonal manifestations of a divinely ordained world with labile frontiers between the natural and the supernatural … [to] passionate beings … portrayed as envious, angry, and vengeful, with a particular animus towards morally upstanding humans" (p. 184); that is, demons acquired human emotions. This shift was predicated upon the emergence of the concept of *interior homo* (inner man), and an understanding of (internal) emotional states from which the notion of evil as temptation (i.e., a struggle between id and superego)[1] or demonic possession (i.e., disowned or dissociated self-states) arose. This conception of the demon-within, that is, the presence of unwanted emotional states (e.g., envy, greed, rage, sexual and aggressive impulses) that feel alien to the self (i.e., that conflict with a punitive superego) started to appear in the first-person life narratives of medieval monks. These proto-autobiographical texts provide a glimpse into the tortured souls of the religious struggling against their own human nature in a 'persecuting society' that was driven by a paranoid Church dedicated to eradicating perceived threats to its dominion from paganism and heresy (Moore, 2006). This paranoia was motivated by the Church's efforts to control the beliefs and behaviours of the people; it also motivated the brutality and madness of the Crusades and the Catholic Inquisitions, which represented a manic determination to impose orthodoxy by force. Sadly, the universities of the day played a key role in the persecution of difference and disobedience, in particular, by developing a prescriptive scholastic theology.

The first cardinal example of the medieval proto-autobiography is *Liber de temptatione cuiusdam monachi* (The book of the temptation of a certain monk), written in 1070 by Otloh of St Emmeram. It is a painful account of a celibate's struggle to suppress his sexuality, to overcome his fear and doubt about the existence of God, and the provision of advice about how to avoid succumbing to temptation. In Freudian terms, Otloh projects (i.e., externalizes) his temptations (demonic 'wiles and stratagems') into the Devil and draws on his good objects ('divine grace') to support him in his struggle. However, his doubts signal that his internalized good objects are not fully sustaining. After all, his struggle to contain his God-given sexual impulses is unnatural and masochistic; the fight against one's own nature is monumental and exhausting. Eventually, he took comfort in the sense of community and the shared suffering of the faithful who take up the yoke of belief ("Noli ergo mirari, quia mihi placet omnes probari", Otloh of St Emmeram (1070, p. 270). Nonetheless, the Devil is a constant and menacing presence for the very reason that the 'menace' – forbidden sexual and aggressive impulses – emanates from within and therefore cannot be excised. God and the Devil in Otloh's text represent the struggle between id impulses and the punitive superego. However, the struggle is characterized as a struggle of the will/intellect and remains emotionally dissociated, despite the enormous emotional pain that is evident in the account. God's "compassionate paternal feeling" (p. 264) is an internalized good object that is cathected with pain. It is noteworthy that the account contains no statements about the Devil's intent, motivation or emotional investment. Demonic temptation was taken as a given, as an inevitable trial of a fallen creation (Ruys, 2012).

In subsequent accounts, for example, Guibert of Nogent's (1115) autobiographical *Monodiae*, the hostile motivations of the Devil in tempting the faithful are more explicit. The statement that demons are "more violently embittered" (p. 118) against believers points to the psychoanalytic concept of envy and the dynamic of envious 'spoiling' (Klein 1975). "It must be believed how grievously that sudden movement of will towards good gnaws at diabolical hearts" (Guibert, 1115, p. 120). Similarly, the scholastic philosopher William of Auvergne (*c.* 1230) noted "the magnitude and vehemence of the wraths and hatreds and envies with which they [demons] burn against humans" (p. 1021bA).

The miracle tales of the thirteenth century – exemplars include Peter the Venerable (1988) (*De miraculis libri duo*) and Caesarius of Heisterbach (*Dialogus miraculorum*, 1219) – were the natural heirs to these highly personal narratives of the twelfth century. In these tales, demons are individualized and are reported to have specific emotional reactions ("turbulent demonic passions") in response to the success or failure of their temptations. They explicitly envy men because not only do they have a relationship with the Creator, but share earthly friendships among themselves, a concept foreign to demons (Caesarius of Heisterbach, 1219, p. 324). In addition, a new creature appears – the demoniac – a person possessed by demons, who becomes a conduit of demonic messages, which clearly indicates the shift to interiority of demonic temptation.

William of Auvergne, Bishop of Paris from 1228 to 1249, was a scholar of magic and demonology (de Mayo, 2007). These were important subjects because, from the inception of the early Christian Church, it was decreed that magic operated through demonic power. All pagan religious rites were denounced and pagan deities were understood to be demons cleverly disguised to lead unsuspecting believers off the path of righteousness (William of Auvergne, *c.* 1230). William claimed that there were three categories of 'wondrous' events – divine miracles, demonic illusion and acts of nature (i.e., natural magic). He stridently demanded the extermination of idolaters by fire (i.e., burning at the stake) and sword. William's evident underlying extreme misogyny – he claimed that women were idolaters and temptresses with supernatural powers who were in league with the Devil – laid the theological foundation for the later witch trials, which I will discuss in the final chapter.

Although Arabic scholars had proposed that not all spirits were demonic, and that, in fact, some were neutral or benevolent, William rejected these notions and reaffirmed that demonic spirits were fallen Christian angels, hence corrupt and evil at their core. He distinguished between demonic spirits and demons, proclaiming that demons could operate only according to natural law and only God had the power to overturn their actions through miracles (Mayo, 2007). William's was a savage and persecutory perspective that promulgated the belief that there was a demonic conspiracy on earth whose goal was to lure humans into false worship. He denounced dissenting opinions as demonic lies and labelled those who propagated them dupes of the demons. These views persisted in ecclesiastical doctrine for several centuries.

Yet another contribution of William of Auvergne to the shameful history of the Catholic Church was his official condemnation of the Talmud in 1248, by which time the Church was using its scholars and power to insist on religious conformity. This date marks the beginning of Christian antagonism to the beliefs and practices of Judaism (Mayo, 2007). Prior to this date, the Church had upheld the rights of Jews to practise their faith, although there is evidence of anti-Semitism in the late twelfth and early thirteenth centuries.

William's entire doctrinal output may be understood as a manifestation of projective identification, a defence mechanism proposed by Melanie Klein (1975), which is capable of serving multiple functions, including the expulsion of a (hated) part of the self into the other. Both good and bad parts of the self can be projected into the object. In the case of William of Auvergne, it is probably true that he was exceedingly tempted by women, who aroused him sexually. As a priest, they were forbidden objects and his sexual feelings were taboo, so he expelled them into women whom he now perceived as demonic temptresses because they were the containers of his sexual impulses. The process of projective identification can be conceptualized as a process of coercive colonization of the internal world of the other with parts of one's own world. In time, the colonized person takes on the wishes and values of the person colonizing them, and they come to feel the projections as ego syntonic, as if they had arisen from within. This may have contributed (along with torture!) to some of the outrageous confessions that accused women made during the Inquisitorial trials.

In subsequent eras, it has been understood that 'demons' are symbolic products of the patient's internal emotional life that are seeking expression, relief and perhaps forgiveness and exoneration. Hence, even though the underlying dynamics of mental illnesses may be similar, the epiphenomena of their presentation may bear little resemblance to one another. As Freud (1923a) quipped, "the fact that we so seldom in analysis find the devil probably indicates that in those we analyse the role of this medieval, mythological figure has long since been outplayed. ... For various reasons the increase in scepticism has affected first and foremost the person of the devil" (p. 87).

In Freud's twentieth-century Vienna, neuroses were expressed in hysterical symptoms which took on "a hypochondriacal aspect and appear[ed] disguised as organic illnesses" (Freud, 1923b, p. 72). In the Middle Ages, neuroses were accompanied by 'demonological trappings' expressed in terms of demonic possession, ecstasy, convulsions and visions, such forms having been preserved for us in the art work of the time. See, for example, Duccio's *Descent to Hell* (1308), Crivelli's *Saint Michael* (1476) and Lochner's *The Last Judgement* (1435). It is interesting that while sacred figures like Jesus and the Virgin Mary assumed a uniform and highly recognizable form in art spanning hundreds of years, there is no standard depiction of Satan, which is limited only by the imagination (and early emotional experiences) of his artists. Satan would sometimes take human form, while at other times would assume animal-like or phantastical forms – Christoph Haizmann's nine characterizations of Satan are an apt example of the varied portrayals, ranging from the human form to more monstrous forms with accoutrements such as pitchforks or forked, weapon-like tails.

However, there are also continuities in history, which are instructive. For example, Freud observed that God and Satan have always been represented as male; hence, he drew the conclusion that the father is the "individual prototype of both God and the Devil" (Freud, 1923a, p. 86). Although at times it is the case that the Devil is depicted as female, as in some of Haizmann's depictions, Freud noted that "*the* Devil, who is a great individuality, the Lord of Hell and the Adversary of God, should be represented otherwise than as a male, and, indeed, as a super-male, with horns, tail and a big penis-snake – this, I believe, is never found" (Freud, 1923a, p. 86).

Can we then argue that depictions of *the* Devil shed light on the nature of the relationship with the earthly father? Freud offered an Oedipal explanation for Haizmann, prompted by Haizmann's bestowing of breasts on some of his depictions of the Devil in his nine portrayals. There is, however, another explanation: Haizmann had recently lost his father, was experiencing grief over the loss and a heightened longing for his father. Perhaps he perceived his father as a devil in order to find an acceptable home for his unconscious anger (rage) at having been abandoned. We cannot labour this point too much because of the paucity of factual information about Haizmann's early life and his relationship with his parents. The aim of the exercise is to lay the groundwork for understanding how religious, demonic and other mystical experiences and beliefs colour our human subjectivity. Freud remained puzzled all his life about the origins and adherence to particular belief systems that to him made no sense.

> I believe that a large part of the mythological view of the world, which extends a long way into the most modern religions, *is nothing but psychology projected into the external world.*
>
> (Freud, 1901, p. 258)

Just as the depictions of Satan and other demonic phenomena and expression change over the course of history, so too do psychiatric symptoms, which, like art, are historically transformed and culturally bound (Otsuka, Sakai & Dening, 2004), making it difficult to ascertain whether descriptions from the past represent today's recognizable psychiatric illnesses. It is noteworthy, for example, that people living in medieval times more frequently reported visual hallucinations, while people diagnosed with schizophrenia today are much more likely to report auditory hallucinations (Kroll & Bachrach, 1982). To further complicate matters, group processes that operate in religious groups and cults result in behavioural contagion that may manifest as speaking in tongues, frantic dancing, falling into trances and reporting similar psychic phenomena, such as the content of hallucinations, across its members (Schwab, 1977). Some behaviours and experiences that are valued in religious contexts as mystical experiences occurring in God's specially chosen few are, in medical contexts, considered bizarre and indicators of mental illness. Such people, far from being viewed as favoured by God and specially chosen, are marginalized in closed wards of psychiatric hospitals or wander the streets homeless, unnoticed or shunned.

Hence, as society, culture, religion and scientific understanding change and develop, so too does our identification and understanding of mental illness and demonic phenomena. Although Haizmann's presentation – convulsions, visual hallucinations, belief that he had sold himself to the Devil – may seem bizarre and deviant to us today, such presentations were not unusual in the Middle Ages. Another famous account – that of Father Theophilus, who also believed himself to be in contract with the Devil – was well known in the medieval world. His story was translated into many languages and recounted in many churches across Europe (Guiley, 1989). During Haizmann's lifetime, there were competing opinions about the proper place of demons in religious scholarship. The Reformation of the sixteenth century (1517–1648) and the new Protestant theology were critical of the belief in the existence of demons and the use of exorcisms and confessions to expel the Devil. In response, the Catholic Church, in the Counter-Reformation, reasserted its acceptance of such beliefs and practices, and was responsible for executions at witch trials in Germany in the late seventeenth century (Mildefort, 1972).

Freud's great contribution to the understanding of madness was his recognition that symptoms have meaning; they represent "intentional, meaningful, and symbolic communication" as "signifiers of previously dissociated intersubjective knowledge … [or] buried and unformulated experience" (Gentile, 2010, p. 88). Failure to search for the meaning of symptoms represents a failure to grasp the patient's personal experience and his/her struggle for emotional survival. Contemporary psychoanalysis understands divine and demonic self-images as a metaphorical communication of different states of being – the former grandiose and megalomaniac and the later devalued and debased (Eigen, 1985). Symptoms provide the portal through which the therapist may enter into the patient's inner world that has been beset with unmet needs, empathic failures, environmental impingements and disruptive affective self-states. When the early deficits have been severe, they result in a loss of personal agency and feelings that one's body and mind are not one's own, but are being controlled from the outside, as occurs in delusions of reference and persecution in psychosis.

Our sanity and our worldview are based on the quality of the social matrix of relationships into which we are born and out of which our human subjectivity is formed. Madness is an attempt to reclaim and reintegrate a shattered self; the accompanying delusions tell the story of the descent into the abyss while also containing the hopes for redemption. In the same way, our belief in God and the Devil and their ascribed characteristics may tell us much about our early object relationships and the quality of the caregiving environment. We will take up these themes again in Chapter 8 when we try to understand fundamentalism.

A demonological illness: the case of Christoph Haizmann

Thou believest that there is one God; thou doest well: the devils also believe, and tremble.

(James 2:19)

Freud was intrigued with witchcraft, the concept of 'possession' and demonological phenomena, no doubt ignited during his period of study with Jean-Martin Charcot at Salpêtrière in 1885–6. James Strachey, in his editorial annotations of Freud's English translation of Charcot, noted a detailed account of a sixteenth-century case of demonic possession, which is followed by a discussion of "the hysterical nature of medieval 'demonio-manias'" (Strachey, in Freud, 1923a, p. 70).

Freud also studied a manuscript from the seventeenth century, discovered by Dr Payer-Thurn, director of what would now be called The National Library of Austria, which gives an account of a 'demonological neurosis' of Faustian proportions in which the seventeenth-century Bavarian painter Christoph Haizmann was delivered from evil by the Virgin Mary. The original material comprises a report written in Latin by a monk, together with diary notes from Haizmann written in German. Freud learnt of this manuscript because Payer-Thurn discovered that the subject of this miraculous deliverance had suffered from "frightful convulsions" (Freud, 1923a, p. 73) and visions, including being tortured in burning flames and being flogged, whereupon Payer-Thurn decided to consult Freud for an opinion on this aspect of his case study.

Haizmann suffered these convulsions while in a church in Pottenbrunn and was sent with a letter of recommendation from the village priest to nearby Mariazell – a place of pilgrimage in Austria – to seek assistance. Here he was examined by the Prefect "with a view to discovering what it was that was oppressing him and whether perhaps he had entered into illicit traffic with the Evil Spirit" (Freud, 1923a, p. 73). Haizmann apparently readily concurred with this interpretation of his affliction, explaining that he had indeed made a pact with the Devil during a period of despondency following the death of his father and the loss of his artistic motivations and capacity to work. The pact stated: "I, Christoph Haizmann, subscribe myself to this Lord (i.e., the Devil) as his bounden son till the ninth year. Year 1669" (Freud, 1923a, pp. 80–1). Freud interpreted this pact to mean that the Devil would replace the painter's lost father for nine years, after which Haizmann would be possessed 'body and soul' by the Devil, lead a sinful life and deny God.

Haizmann had written out his undertaking in blood and accompanied it with nine paintings, each representing one of the Devil's nine temptations. He then began a period of prayer and penance. On 5 September 1677, the Devil appeared to him as a winged dragon in the chapel while he was undergoing an exorcism and returned the pact. Shortly afterwards, Haizmann left Mariazell 'cured'. Alas, the cure was short-lived and his seizures returned in October of the same year. He confided to his diary that he suffered 'absences', temporary paralysis of his limbs and saw visions of Jesus Christ and Mary. Notwithstanding the sacredness of these visions, Haizmann believed that they were the Devil's work and returned to Mariazell in order to retrieve an additional bond he had made with the Devil that predated the bond written in blood. Freud argued that the 'invention' of this second bond was required to provide justification for Haizmann's second visit to Mariazell, and to avoid the imputation that the priests' intercessions on his behalf in September had failed, thereby running the risk that he might not be welcome there a second time.

Freud expressed the view that the consultation with the Prefect implanted in Haizmann, by suggestion, at a vulnerable time in his life, during which Freud believed Haizmann was suffering from melancholic depression, the idea that he had made a pact with the Devil. The pact, which Freud characterized as a "neurotic phantasy" (Freud, 1923a, p. 84), was motivated by the painter's desire to retrieve the lost love object (i.e., his father) – the Devil became a father-substitute – in the hope that he might regain not only the lost object but also his artistic motivation and creativity and his capacity to earn a living. It is interesting that the first of Haizmann's nine paintings depicts the Devil as a benign figure – an old man with a beard and walking-stick. The subsequent paintings became more sinister, mythological and terrifying, and the Devil is variously depicted with claws, horns or wings, as naked and misshapen, with breasts, a penis resolving into a snake and, finally, as the flying demon dragon in the chapel during his exorcism.

The question arises as to why the Devil can become the substitute for a loved father. Freud explains it thus:

> God is a father-substitute ... an exalted father ... a copy of a father as he is seen and experienced in childhood – by individuals in their own childhood and by mankind in its prehistory as the father of the primitive and primal horde. Later on in life the individual sees his father as something different and lesser. But the ideational image belonging to his childhood is preserved and becomes merged with the inherited memory-traces of the primal father to form the individual's idea of God.
>
> (Freud, 1923a, p. 85)

Freud stressed that children have an ambivalent relationship with their fathers: on the one hand, loving, submissive and longing, on the other, fearful yet defiant. This ambivalence is replicated in man's relationship with God, and in the subsequent religions that have been built upon this ambivalence towards the Deity.

Haizmann subsequently entered the Order of the Brothers Hospitallers, but continued to "be tempted by the Evil Spirit" (Freud, 1923a, p. 78) until his death in 1700. In this act, Haizmann simultaneously resolved both his spiritual struggle (i.e., his 'demonological' illness) and practical problems related to having to work and make a living. Further, he recovered from the loss of his father, first by seeking the Devil as a substitute father, and then by falling into the embrace of the 'fathers' of the Church.

In psychosis, neither the body nor mind is felt to be truly one's own and one is reduced to the role of being the bearer of meanings and demands imposed from the outside by malevolent others, as appears to be the case with Haizmann's assertion that the Devil was guiding his thoughts. Sadly, when the symbolic meaning of this assertion is lost, 'symptoms' are construed as delusions and overvalued ideation. Combined with his visual hallucinations, Haizmann's presentation would today be consistent with a diagnosis of schizophrenia. However, this is a mere label for his observable behaviour and provides no explanation as to its origin, dynamics or meaning.

Freud's explanation for the 'demonological illnesses' of Christoph Haizmann remains plausible. He concluded:

> The demonological theory of those dark times has won in the end against all the somatic views ... of "exact" science. The states of possession correspond to our neuroses, for the explanation of which we once more have recourse to psychical powers. In our eyes, *the demons are bad and reprehensible wishes, derivatives of instinctual impulses that have been repudiated and repressed.* We merely eliminate the projection of these mental entities into the external world which the Middle Ages carried out; instead, we regard them as having arisen in the patient's internal life, where they have their abode. [My italics]
>
> (Freud, 1923a, p. 72)

Psychoanalytic explanations for demonological and other 'religious' phenomena in psychotic illnesses

> For God hath not given us the spirit of fear; but of power, and of love, and of a sound mind.
>
> (2 Timothy 1:7)

Josef Breuer (1893) attempted to explain the presence of the demonic in the thinking of patients by hypothesising that part of the patient's mind enters a hypnoid state that gains ascendancy during lapses in waking states, such as during hysterical attacks, 'twilight states' and states of exhaustion or delirium. While the patient is in such states, alien thoughts, hallucinations and motor acts occur independently of conscious volition. Thus, Breuer argued:

> [T]he split-off mind is the devil with which the unsophisticated observation of early superstitious times believed that these patients were possessed. It is true that a spirit alien to the patient's waking consciousness holds sway in him; but the spirit is not in fact an alien one, but a part of his own.
>
> (Breuer, 1893, p. 250)

Although Freud abandoned hypnosis and theories based on hypnosis, he retained Breuer's notion of the divided mind, which was not a waking state and a hypnotic state, but a residue of primitive experiences that are no longer accessible to consciousness. Using this framework, Freud (1923a) understood demons to be "bad and reprehensible wishes, derivatives of instinctual impulses that have been repudiated and repressed" (p. 72). Thus, demonic states of possession can be understood to be manifestations of a psychodynamic process (i.e., neurosis) involving conflict that requires the repudiation and expulsion of a devalued part of the self. One of Freud's first patients was Emmy von N., whom Freud (1893) described as a highly suggestible 'hysteric', and thus a good candidate for hypnosis. She was also "morally oversensitive", self-deprecating and highly critical of any small fault in herself. Despite Freud's attempts to reassure her and to release her from her "tormenting recollections" (p. 65), by assuring her

> that there is a whole multitude of indifferent, small things lying between what is good and what is evil – things about which no one need reproach himself. She did not take in my lesson … any more than would *an ascetic mediaeval monk, who sees the finger of God or a temptation of the Devil in every trivial event of his life and who is incapable of picturing the world even for a brief moment or in its smallest corner as being without reference to himself.* [My italics]
>
> (Freud, 1893, p. 66)

Freud (1900) described a 13-year-old boy who began to have "devil-dreams" in which the Devil came to him in the night, "smelling of pitch and brimstone", burning his skin with flames, and shouting "Now we've got you!" (p. 586). In a state of great terror, the boy cried out for mercy. The frequency and intensity of these nightmares took its toll on his health and he was sent to the country to recover. Two years later, he was able to acknowledge that the source of his nightmares was his pubertal sexual awakening and his desire to masturbate. It is likely that he had either been threatened with punishment or was actually punished for masturbating. The conflict between expressing and suppressing his sexual urges created anxiety that was symbolically expressed in his dreams. The devil that appeared to him was a condensed, but terrifying version of the injunctions that he had introjected (i.e., taken in) from his religious education.

Freud (1911a) subsequently recorded a number of case studies in which demonological/religious phenomena played a central role. None is better known than that of Dr Daniel Paul Schreber, who wrote his own case history at the age of 63, *Memoirs of My Nervous Illness*, and published it in 1903 "for the advancement of science and the common good". He was a man of superior intellect who held highly respected judicial positions and was happily married, although involuntarily childless. He began his long career as a patient in 1884 when he experienced debilitating hypochondria for more than a year, during which time he spent six months in a clinic, unable to work. In 1893, he was appointed Senatspräsident of Dresden. Soon afterwards he began to suffer from sleeplessness, whereupon he returned to the clinic, but his condition deteriorated and he formed the belief that his physician was in conspiracy with God against him. He complained of a softening of the brain, fears that he was afflicted by the plague that was causing his body to decompose and that he would soon be dead. He also reported hyperaesthesia (sensitivity to light and noise) and delusions of persecution. He was so tortured by his illness that he attempted to drown himself in his bath and asked for cyanide so that he could end his life. His delusions then took on a mystical and religious character – Schreber believed himself to be the "plaything of the devil". By 1899, Schreber had recovered sufficiently to live independently and sought discharge from the asylum. His paranoid delusions remained in an encapsulated form that did not appear to exert a negative impact on the rest of his personality or his ability to function. However, he believed that he had a mission to redeem the world. This could only be achieved if he were transformed into a woman by a divine miracle, when by direct impregnation by God, he would conceive a new race. This delusion may represent an unconscious wish related to his desire to father his own child(ren).

Freud noted that Schreber's proposed emasculation was at first "a sexual delusion of persecution" in which God committed "soul murder" upon him. This transformed into a "religious delusion of grandeur" in which God became his ally. However, even as an ally, God is a deeply ambivalent and mistrusted figure in Schreber's system, who plotted against him, took him for an "idiot" and showed no understanding of "living men", who was so "blinded by His ignorance of human nature" that He attempted to prevent Schreber from urinating and defecating (Freud, 1911a, pp. 26–7) and visited other "tormenting ordeals" upon him. Schreber concluded that God was "ridiculous and childish", causing him to "scoff at Him aloud" (Freud, 1911a, p. 27). What is noteworthy in this case history is the "mixture of reverence and rebelliousness" in Schreber's attitude towards God, and the devilish and sadistic characteristics ascribed to Him. Notwithstanding, the account is filled with Schreber's longing for reconciliation with God and an end to his suffering.

To summarize, Schreber described a monstrous conspiracy being perpetrated against him by his physician and God, whose aim was to murder his soul and transform him into a woman, in short, to strip him of his identity as a man (to emasculate him) and to rob him of a right to his own existence. What can we understand from the religious delusions and hallucinations from which Schreber suffered? From an analysis of his upbringing, we know that Schreber was subject to extremely harsh paternal discipline and moral education, such that he had to engage with his father/ God in a struggle for his existence, his selfhood. Daniel was the son of the physician and pedagogue Daniel Gottlieb Schreber. The elder Schreber believed that children were demonic and morally bankrupt; accordingly, he proposed the harshest and most brutal forms of discipline to correct these defects in their nature. This included beatings, starvation and physical restraints that severely curtailed physical movement. Some of his contraptions were designed to prevent the child from masturbating (Schatzman, 1973). This is the form of parenting to which he subjected his own son. Schreber the elder professed love for his children while perpetrating hateful, abusive control of them. They were constrained both physically and emotionally through their father's demand for absolute obedience and submission. When viewed against this background, Daniel's delusions make sense; they were symbolic representations of his father's atrocities. Daniel was indeed the plaything of the Devil/father, who had committed soul murder upon him. "Schreber … was fashioned into a contraption that materialize[d] his father's fantasy of the perfect child" (Atwood, 2010, p. 349).

This case study demonstrates the way in which our 'gods' and 'demons' take on the characteristics of our primary caregivers, even when the individual is not able to identify or articulate the root of their madness in their early intersubjective experiences. Schreber's God was sadistic and exacting, relentlessly tormenting the hapless boy/man with His outrageous demands. Young Schreber seethed with unexpressed hatred and contempt for his father, which subsequently featured during his period of madness in his depictions of a ridiculous and childish God who was the object of his scorn and derisive laughter. Freud concluded that God and Satan are both "cop[ies] of a father as he is seen and experienced in childhood" (Freud, 1923a, p. 86). Support for this view comes from studies of cognitive development in young children. Piaget et al. (1929) noted that pre-logical children's conceptions of God necessarily contain the characteristics of human adults. Here is an example: Q: "Who is God? A: He is a man. Q: What does God do? A: He is in his house working" (p. 312).

Jung (1921) offered an alternative formulation through the construct of the psychological '(mother or father) complex', which he defined as "an unconscious constellation of cognitions, memories, images, impulsions, opinions, beliefs, associations and other content emanating from a core or nucleus of repressed or dissociated emotion, drive or instinct" (Diamond, 2011). Through the action of various defence mechanisms, the content of 'complexes' becomes dissociated from the 'conscious' personality and from a dark hiding-place in the mind influences consciousness, thought, emotions and behaviour. Jung believed that complexes were the depositories of archetypes that lie dormant in the unconscious until activated by particular experiences, such as early and prolonged abuse, as in the case of Haizmann and Schreber. Thus messiah or God archetypes, which appear to be innate and universal (according to Jung, 1921), become messianic or God (or satanic) complexes when the normal defences of everyday life breakdown, resulting in the misidentification of self with the archetypal image, which in patients with schizophrenia we call delusions or persecutory paranoia. There are many modern-day examples of this process, for example in cults, in which members respond with defensive violence against demonized outsiders or critics. David Koresh of the Branch Davidians cult, whose life and the lives of 74 other cult members ended in a gun battle with federal agents, comes immediately to mind. Cult leaders like Jim Jones of the People's Temple, who believed himself to be both Jesus and Buddha, and Marshall Applewhite of the Heaven's Gate cult, who declared himself the messiah, both inspired their followers to mass suicide. It is also worth noting that individuals rendered vulnerable by virtue of early unsatisfactory relationships with caregivers who have been thwarted in attaining more prosocial narcissistic strivings unleash these 'complexes' in a vengeful rage against a society that has slighted them. I am thinking here of Adolf Hitler, a frustrated artist, and Charles Manson and David Koresh, who both had thwarted aspirations for rock-star fame.

The psychodynamics of myth, legend and fairy tale

> [T]he connections between our typical dreams and fairy tales and ... other kinds of creative writing are neither few nor accidental ... the sharp eye of a creative writer has an analytic realization of the process of transformation of which he is habitually no more than the tool.
>
> (Freud, 1900, p. 246)

Freud (1915–17) believed that the story of the primal horde, with its envious father, rivalrous sons, their competition for the sexual favours of the horde's women and the eventual defeat of the father by his sons, is retold in many forms in the world's myths and fairy tales. Many of "the monsters of mythology are father-figures and the hero who slays them is their own son in disguise" (Schoenfeld, 1962, p. 217), a theme illustrated graphically in the Oedipus myth. Freud concluded that the symbols in fairy tales, legends, myths, religions and dreams share common origins. In fact, Freud believed that myths and fairy tales could be interpreted in the same way as dreams – as unconscious wishes or impulses that have not yet been fully realized. The role of the nightmare in the creation of mythical beings had certainly been canvassed by others. For example, Clodd (1891) linked the products of nightmares with religion.

> [T]he intensified form of dreaming called "nightmare", when hideous spectres sit upon the breast, stopping breath and paralysing motion, and to which is largely due the creation of the vast army of nocturnal demons that fill the folklore of the world, and that, under infinite variety of repellent form, have had place in the hierarchy of religions. Some mythologists even trace the belief in spirits in general to the experiences of the nightmare.
>
> (p. 85)

Interestingly, William of Auvergne (in *De Universo*) was also interested in night terrors and made a study of the "spirits of the night", many of which he associated with death and women. He claimed that cannibalistic female spirits killed infants while they were sleeping (a condition we today call Sudden Infant Death Syndrome) and ate the flesh and blood of children. William, ever the harsh disciplinarian, considered the loss of a child due punishment for his/her parents' lack of faith; he accused parents of loving their children more than God. One of the male spirits of the night, Ephialtes (whose name derived from the Greek Titan of Sleep), was a demon who sat on the chest, causing suffocation, paralysis or death. It was recognized by others, even at the time (e.g., John of Salisbury), that these "demonic attacks" were really symptoms of medical conditions. Today, we might suspect this cluster of symptoms to be indicative of a panic attack or a myocardial infarction (heart attack).

Otto Rank (1914) who made a particular study of the close connection between unconscious motivations and the fantastical content of myths, noted the cross-cultural similarities of mythical content. Each form – whether myth, dream or religious texts – derives from the same psychological universals. Consider, for example, the religiosity saturated in this excerpt from Hans Christian Andersen's *The Little Mermaid*. It occurs near the end of the story, after the mermaid, having lost her beloved prince, flings herself into the ocean, turns to foam, and becomes a daughter of the air:

> A mermaid has not an immortal soul, nor can she obtain one unless she wins the love of a human being. On the power of another hangs her eternal destiny. But the daughters of the air, although they do not possess an immortal soul, can, by their good deeds, procure one for themselves. ... After three hundred years, thus shall we float into the kingdom of heaven.
>
> (Andersen, 1836)

Similarly, the stories from *The Thousand and One Nights* are replete with references to Islamic religion. In Hindu cultures, the magical story of the devoted love of Rama and Sita from the *Ramayana* provides a template of a good marriage to which all Hindus should aspire. On her wedding day, a Hindu bride is called Sita and as part of the wedding ceremony she re-enacts scenes from the *Ramayana*.

All of these different literary forms of story-telling contain within them symbolic truths and the seeds of our own natures with their discontent, fears, magical thinking, destructive wishes and insatiable longings. They may be understood as manifestations of our primitive unconscious and childhood fantasies. Myths (and religion) allow us to anticipate and hopefully to master, even if fearfully, the brute fact of the finitude of our existence. For example, myths codify our fear of death and somehow make it more manageable by negating it in various ways through, for example, our belief in an afterlife (i.e., we don't really die), our capacity to commune with the dead (i.e., we are not really separated permanently from those we love) and, ultimately, our hope that loved ones will be reunited in a heavenly eternity. Here is the last paragraph of Hans Christian Andersen's *The Little Match Girl*, which illustrates all of these denials of death:

> [A]t the cold hour of dawn, sat the poor girl … leaning against the wall – frozen to death on the last evening of the old year. Stiff and stark sat the child there with her matches. … No one had the slightest suspicion of what beautiful things she had seen; no one even dreamed of the splendour in which, with her grandmother, she had entered on the joys of a new year.
>
> (Andersen, 1858)

Newberg and d'Aquili (2001), like Freud, proposed that myths developed as a result of the human need to grasp, analyse and understand the phenomenology of our experience. They termed this drive to understand the 'cognitive imperative'. Melanie Klein (1975) called it the epistemophilic instinct, which signifies that humans need to assign causes to events, even those that are inexplicable; we would rather postulate a cause, however fanciful, than leave the event unexplained. Our imaginations and our unconscious fill in the knowledge gaps – our mythical world contains aliens, the undead, the spirit world, magic and fantastical mythical creatures, all representing parts of our own human nature (see Table 5.1). We also apprehend reality in terms of 'binary operators'; for example, we can understand 'good' only if we also understand 'bad'. Our language and our stories reflect this binary operation: light/dark; tall/short; dead/alive; God/Satan; life/death; heaven/hell; true/false, and so on. Myths also operate in this way. There is little nuance; characters are either good or bad, situations are either right or wrong; good nearly always triumphs for the righteous and the bad are punished cruelly for their wrongdoing. Yet these explanations for the emergence of myths and indeed religion, if we class religious belief as a subset of mythological beliefs, are incomplete because we can see in myths and religion the pre-logical thinking of the very young child – they are also replete with animisms, artificialisms and realisms. We have already discussed the work of Piaget et al. (1929), who showed that in normal development, children believe that their dreams originate in images or voices coming from outside themselves. Likewise, the Welsh psychoanalyst Ernest Jones (1910) hypothesized that nightmares were the source of false ideas that are expressed in the creation of terrifying creatures like vampires, werewolves, witches and devils that have become incarnated in myth and legend. They also had a sociological function for primitive people that supported the tribe or collective, as reviewed earlier in our discussion on totemism.

Bruno Bettelheim (1976) analysed a number of fairy tales from a psychoanalytic perspective in *The Uses of Enchantment: The Meaning and Importance of Fairy Tales*. Because fairy tales deal with universal existential issues that are presented in a form that encourages psychic development, he found them useful in his work with severely disturbed children. Bettelheim argued that our dominant Western culture wants to focus only on the 'good', wishing to shun notions that our human nature is responsible for much of the 'evil' we see about us. Fairy tales thus fill a gap in our

TABLE 5.1 Mythical creatures and psychological function

Function	Examples of form
Projections of 'good'	God, angels, fairies, princes and princesses, 'white knights'
Projections of 'evil'	Satan, demons, devils, monsters, gargoyles, witches, sorcerers, Sirens
Idealized man (man made God)	Achilles, Amphiaraus, Heracles
Projections of ambivalence	Vampires, werewolves, Dr Jekyll and Mr Hyde
Projections of primordial father figures	Giants, God, Satan, monsters
Projections of the idealized mother	Fairy godmothers, the Virgin Mary, Diana of Rome, Cybele of Greece, Ishtar of Babylonia, Leto (Titan of motherhood), Gaia (Mother Earth), Persephone (Queen of the Underworld and goddess of spring), Hera (Queen of Heaven)
Projections of innocence	Hansel and Gretel, Snow White and the Seven Dwarfs
Projections of sadomasochistic sacrifice	Jesus Christ, Oscar Wilde's nightingale in *The Nightingale and the Rose*, Hans Christian Andersen's Eliza in the *Wild Swans*
Awakening sexuality	Little Red Riding Hood, Sleeping Beauty, Snow White
Rebirth and eternal life	Little Match Girl, Little Mermaid

Note: Many psychoanalysts since Freud have observed Freud's under-estimation of the role of the mother during infancy and consequentially the role of an idealized, exalted mother in the God-concept. Schoenfeld (1962) contends that the Judeo–Christian God demonstrates both male and female characteristics constructed from the image of both parents during childhood. Some creation myths, for example, Greek (Uranus and Gaia), Japanese (Izanagi and Izanami) and Australian Aborigines (Sun Mother and Father of All Spirits), have joint maternal and paternal deities.

emotional experience, providing as they do tales of the dark side of human nature that is home to our aggression, selfishness, rage and envy. The essential message of both psychoanalysis and fairy tales is that life is unavoidably difficult and challenging; both aim to assist us to "accept the problematic nature of life without being defeated by it" (p. 8) and to "civilize the chaotic pressures of the unconscious" (p. 23). The stories of both religion (i.e., parables) and fairy tales present existential dilemmas in symbolic form, at a safe distance that allows children to assimilate the message without experiencing overwhelming threat. The characters are starkly drawn, and are usually good or evil, without too much confusing nuance; the situations are simple and a common theme underscores the entire plot.

   Space does not permit an individual analysis of the characters or narratives of legend, myth and fairy tale so I will instead focus on codifying the symbolic meanings of some key exemplars from our wishful thinking and William of Auvergne's "vast army of nocturnal demons" – the types of distinct characters that symbolize our shared conscious and unconscious psychic content that populates these stories, the forms they take physically and psychologically and the unconscious conflicts that the stories try to resolve. We can cluster these imaginative creations according to their form and function as shown in Table 5.1. We will now examine three 'characters' in more detail.

Satan

> [E]ven Satan disguises himself as an angel of light.
>
> (2 Corinthians 11:14)

The arch-archetype, Satan (the Devil, Lucifer), enemy of man and God, is one of the most colourful, perverse and pervasive figures in religion. Variously characterized as our ancient foe, as Necessary Evil, as the origin of human suffering, the arch-heretic, as *hassatan* (the adversary), the opposer, the trickster and deceiver and tester of the faithful, Satan appears in some form in all of the major religions. Originally favoured by God as the brightest star in heaven's firmament, Satan was charged by God to tempt humans and to report on all those who had failed to observe heavenly decrees. However, the relationship between God and Satan soured from the moment of creation when envy, triggered by sibling rivalry with God's new creation, reared its ugly head.

> And so the devil, seeing that human beings were able to ascend by the humility of obedience to that from which he had fallen through pride, envied them. He who through pride had previously become the devil, which is the one who has fallen below, by the jealousy of envy was made Satan, that is, the adversary.
>
> (Peter Lombard, 2008, 92; bk. 2, d. 21, ch. 1)

Satan's murderous rage against his rivals was enacted in the serpent's temptation of Eve to eat the forbidden fruit from the tree of knowledge in the Garden of Eden. The temptation of Job, detailed in the Book of Job in the Old Testament, is another example. However, at this point in theological thinking, the Devil and his soldiers (demons) were simply following orders from their General (God) (recall the Nazi war crimes trials at Nuremberg after World War II!). They could tempt only those whom God had specified; the Devil had no personal axe to grind with Job. Similarly, Jesus's temptation in the Garden of Gethsemane was an impersonal act of a devil (God's soldier) following orders. After three temptations, which were unsuccessful from Satan's perspective, he simply left and "angels came and attended him" (i.e., Jesus) (Matthew 4:11, NIV). In other words, Satan was not affected personally by Jesus's refusal to give in to temptation. He simply did God's bidding and clocked off after he had completed his assignment.

In the story of Satan, we have a very human dilemma. Satan is originally portrayed as the one most favoured by God but subservient to Him and bound to obey His command. At some point, Satan rebels against God's authority, becomes God's enemy and is cast out of heaven. Because Satan had enjoyed an exalted position among the angels, his pride is severely bruised; that is, he experiences a narcissistic injury that demands revenge. He seeks to destroy God, and to harm God's creation by turning it against its creator. Narcissistic injuries of this kind unleash rage, envy, hatred and destructiveness. Yet, underneath this display of terrifying emotion are unacknowledged feelings of pain and loss. It is disturbing that God responds in kind, not like a loving parent who is willing to forgive a wayward son, but with savage rage and vengeance – His own narcissistic injury demands it – casting Satan into Revelation's "lake of fire" (hell), where he is condemned to suffer eternal torment. A similar, but less brutal account of the fall of Satan is given in the Qur'ān. In this version, Satan was cast out of heaven but was spared further punishment until the Day of Judgement.

Colman (1988) observed that

> Satan's situation corresponds exactly to those paranoid states of mind where the most violent attacks can be launched on others in the belief that they are justified – and indeed required – by the need to defend against others' violent intentions towards the self. It is chilling to recognize that in our own time this same Satanic spirit animates the global nuclear politics between East and West.

> (p. 77)

Ultimately, "Satan represents the extreme binary thinking that demonizes ... scapegoats and marginalizes persons, cultures, and ideas that are foreign to us and our interests" (Mobley, 2013, p. 239).

Vampires

Vampires are particularly intriguing because of the historical role of the Catholic Church in manipulating and promulgating the vampire myth, declaring vampires to be agents of the Devil, and then assuming the role of protector of true believers from this ever-present and sinister threat (Ivey, 2010). The Church's purpose was to expand its empire and its converts into the Balkans, where the myth is thought to have originated in the modern era (although mentions of vampire-like creatures were also present in the ancient world) (Silver & Ursini, 1993). Sacred items such as crucifixes, rosaries and holy water were used to repel vampires and protect the innocent. Vampires could not walk on consecrated ground (e.g., churches or church land) (Barber, 1988). Thus, the church represented itself as the only remedy against the evil perpetrated by vampires. Such was the mass hysteria generated by the Church in early eighteenth-century Europe about their pervasiveness and evil, it led to public executions of people accused of being vampires (Cohen, 1989).

The modern conception of the vampire has been immortalized in Bram Stoker's (1897) *Dracula* and its filmic representations (see, for example, the "Dracula" episode of Christopher Frayling's (1996) BBC TV series *Nightmare: The Birth of Horror*; Stephanie Meyers's *Twilight* series; and Joss Whedon's complex characterization of the vampire Spike in *Buffy the Vampire Slayer*). A vampire is a deceased person who nonetheless continues to be sentient, and through sucking the blood of the living, protects his body from decomposition, perhaps a metaphor for the infant's desperate need of the mother's life-giving milk. The act draws the living to the dead and the dead to the living, who become reanimated only with their living sacrifice. The modern vampire is the quintessential mythical creature – mysterious, sinister yet alluring, inhabiting the night, undead, yet intensely human, a complex mixture of hatred and love, pain and pleasure, longing and sexuality, with an insatiable need for human (life) blood. The word 'vampire' may have been derived from the Turkish *uber* meaning 'witch'; alternatively from the Greek *pinó* (πίνω) 'to drink' or the Hungarian *vampir* (Wilson, 1985). The vampire legend is found in most cultures and regions of the world, including Russia, Germany, Albania, Poland, China, Peru and India (Summers, 2005).

If we enter the emotional domain in search of understanding of the vampire metaphor it is evident that the vampire myth is an attempt to come to terms with our own death and the decomposition and decay of our bodies after death. Some cultures have elaborate burial rituals in order to prevent the deceased from becoming a vampire. For example, Tibetans cremate their dead in order to prevent the spirit of the deceased from re-entering their own dead body, which would transmute the deceased into a vampire (Dawa-Samdup, 2000). In ancient Greece, complex burial rituals (see, for example, accounts in *Antigone* and the *Iliad*) forestalled the return of the dead, including cutting off the limbs of the deceased (Lawson, 1910).

Freud, in *Mourning and Melancholia*, distinguished between complicated and uncomplicated grief. In uncomplicated grief, the loved one mourns his/her loss and eventually reconnects with the living. When grief is complicated by mixed emotions about the deceased person – love, hate, rage, guilt, regret, lack of resolution – the loved one projects these emotions into the deceased, believing that the deceased is also yearning for reunion and resolution. The projected longing is embodied in the vampire, who is hungry for love and will devour the loved one by sucking his/her blood (i.e., sucking the life out of him/her). The bereaved become stuck in grief, unable to let go or move on, longing for the return of the dead from the grave in order to create a better parting. Thus, the vampire myth of the eternally undead is like melancholia: I can never let you go; I can bring you back from the dead and repossess you. The ritual of eating and drinking the body and blood of Christ in Christian ritual bears an uncanny resemblance to the vampire myth and Freud's melancholia. The bread is the flesh of the dead Christ and the wine his blood. By eating his flesh and drinking his blood, God (Christ) is come alive again in me, reversing the melancholia, fear and guilt about the murdered Christ.

Jesus and Buddha

Jesus and Buddha occupy a slightly different position from the characters discussed above, which are figments (symbols) of our collective imagination. Jesus and Buddha were historical realities. They both existed and were, by all accounts, strong, charismatic characters who commanded attention and respect. Both were morphed, in the manner of fairy-tale characters, into superheroes and deities. (Muhammad, the last of the prophets of Islam, also underwent a similar transformation. We will discuss Muhammad in more detail in Chapter 8.) Jesus was aware that people constructed and reconstructed him in particular ways that suited their purposes and needs, such that he was prompted to ask his disciples, "Whom do men say that I am?" (Matthew 16:13). For Pontius Pilate, Jesus was "King of the Jews" and as such a threat to the Roman Empire. Jesus saw himself in a similar light, as a radical reformer situated within the Judaist tradition of his day. He behaved like a revolutionary, gathering followers to him, giving sermons to the masses (e.g., the Sermon on the Mount), attending the synagogue, overturning the tables of the money-changers (a symbolic act of defiance against those who would turn a house of prayer into a "den of thieves"), preaching an unpopular brand of religion in which the current order would be destroyed and replaced by the "Kingdom of God" on earth, thereby seditiously undermining the Roman Empire, for which he was finally crucified. This Jesus of history has subsequently been transformed into Jesus Christ, the Son of God, the divine saviour of the world by those who needed him to be so. This is a clear example of what Freud (1921) called the "lie of the heroic myth [which] culminates in the deification of the hero" (p. 137).

Buddha was similarly a man of his times, whose thoughts and works were politically motivated. For example, he maintained that all four castes of the Indian caste system were equal, declaring the unimaginably radical belief that all people are capable of attaining enlightenment. Buddha declared that a man should be known by his deeds and not by his caste; his was an early and radical attempt to abolish discrimination. He argued that no one by birth is born an outcast, but makes himself so through his deeds alone. In the *Madhura Sutta, Majjhima* II 87, Buddha stated that after death, all shall be reborn in accordance with their karmas and not in accordance with their caste (*jāti*).

> A man who is a murderer or a thief or a fornicator, or a liar, or a slanderer, or of violent speech or tattles or covets or is malevolent or holds wrong views, he will, after death at body's dissolution pass to the state of misery and woe, whether he be a brāhmana [priests], a kṣatriya [warriors or rulers], a vaiśya [merchants, tradesman, minor officials] or a śudra [unskilled workers].

Notwithstanding these radical views, Krishan (1986) argued that Buddha did not intend to transform or improve social conditions for the lower classes. Indeed, his sermons are addressed only to the 'respectable castes'. Note in the quotation above, Buddha did not include the pariahs or harijans (outcastes, 'untouchables', 'Children of God'). Even the *Mahāyāna* doctrine of the bodhisattva (from the Sanskrit: *Bodhi*, meaning enlightenment and *sattva* meaning being) contains no denunciation of the caste system or concern for the śudras or the Untouchables; its focus is on the relief of individual suffering and not with challenging the social structures that caused such suffering *en masse*. It was the need of Buddha's followers to make him a greater reformer than he actually was, in the same way that followers of Jesus needed to elevate him to the status of a deity, the Son of God.

The formative personal contexts of religious and philosophical thought

> [W]hen it is distress that philosophizes, as is the case with all sick thinkers — and perhaps sick thinkers are more numerous in the history of philosophy — what will become of the thought itself when it is subjected to the pressure of sickness?
>
> (Nietzsche, 1882, p. 34)

The principal thesis underpinning Freud's view of religion is that it is a form of wish-fulfilment that provides a window into the emotional life of the individual, which is always historically and culturally embedded. This thesis goes some way towards explaining why there are so many religions and so many permutations of the nature of God. A number of commentaries on the nexus between religion, philosophy and one's personal history have interrogated Freud's contention. Jung (1929) acknowledged that "every psychology – my own included – has the character of a subjective confession. ... Even when I deal with empirical data, I am necessarily speaking about myself" (p. 336). A more recent analysis of this issue concluded that "metaphysics [and by extension, religion] represents an illusory flight from the tragedy of human finitude" (Stolorow & Atwood, 2013, p. 405). Atwood et al. (2011) argued that any attempt to claim that intellectual products can be divorced from their creators and the life experiences from which they arose is a form of Cartesian madness that assumes that the life of the mind is autonomous and not in need of a personal context to be envisaged and understood. In this paper, the authors identified how the "formative personal contexts" (p. 263) of four philosophers – Søren Kierkegaard, Friedrich Nietzsche, Ludwig Wittgenstein and Martin Heidegger – shaped their philosophical theories, which in turn reflected the personal contexts in which they were developed. We will examine each briefly.

Søren Kierkegaard

> For we do not wrestle against flesh and blood, but against the rulers, against the authorities, against the cosmic powers over this present darkness, against the spiritual forces of evil in the heavenly places.
>
> (Ephesians 6:12)

Søren Kierkegaard had an extraordinarily unfortunate life. The youngest of seven children, he witnessed the successive deaths of five of his six siblings. His mother died when he was 21; his father died four years later. His own health was fragile – he lived a short 42 years. His father was a man tortured by (Christian) guilt, who instilled his ascetic Christian sensibilities into his young son through intense religious instruction. These experiences led to Kierkegaard's perception that he was destined to suffer, just as his father suffered – tortured with the belief that his children would die before him because of his sins against God. This perception created a profound philosophical dilemma. If God makes the innocent suffer, He is not benign and benevolent, thus leading to doubt and defiance of the Deity. If God be good, the sufferer is guilty of sin, without necessarily knowing how he has sinned, a position that can lead to despair. If the sufferer be Christian, then God expects him to suffer – "Ye must forsake all, take up thy cross and follow Me" (Matthew 16:24). Auden (1952) argued that Kierkegaard's philosophical polemic moved in two directions because it arose in two personal contexts – "outwardly, against the bourgeois Protestantism of the Denmark of his time, and inwardly against his suffering" (p. vi). Kierkegaard introduced the concept of 'angst' (dread, anxiety) to describe the fundamental grounds of (his) human existence.

As a young man, Kierkegaard described an experience that he called "the great earthquake", which has been interpreted in different ways by different Kierkegaard scholars. Some claimed it was Søren's discovery that his demanding and austerely Christian father had committed serious transgressions (e.g., cursing God for his hardships, impregnating his wife before marriage) that both father and son believed had brought down the curse of a wrathful God on the entire family. Søren had idealized his father and could not integrate the realization that his father was flawed. This discovery plunged the young man into despair and a period of alienation from his father, with whom he eventually reconciled in the year of his father's death. An alternative explanation offered by Atwood, Stolorow & Orange (2011) refers to a much more serious earthquake in the young Kierkegaard – a feeling of unbearable grief associated with multiple losses, constituting almost his entire family, that produced "a rift in his soul" that was even greater than a "shattering disappointment in a parent" (G.E. Atwood, personal communication, 20 May 2013). The rift is between the past and the present/future, with part of the self remaining in a mystical union with the deceased loved ones and the other part moving on without his family. I came across a very poignant example of the notion of a mystical union with the deceased in a newspaper report of a young father who had recently lost his 19-month-old daughter, Jem, to a brain tumour. Her father, Matt, stated, "When she died, I wondered, 'What does this mean? Where is she? Is she somewhere? Could she be there by herself? She is only 19 months old. Shouldn't I be there as well?'" He reported that for some time after her death, he thought that he himself would also die, and that he did not really mind because it might mean that he could be with his beloved daughter (Cadzow, 2013, p. 24).

In *The Sickness unto Death* (1849), Kierkegaard argued that man had lost sight of God because of his own despair, a thesis that mirrored his experience with his father, and the despair accompanying his profound grief. In *Either/Or*,

Kierkegaard (1843) deals with the struggle epitomized in his father and in all Christians, including himself, who sacrificed his love for his fiancée, Regine Olsen, for God, to choose between the temporal search for earthly happiness, which evaded Kierkegaard and which he eventually defensively eschewed, or to retain faith in the unchanging values of the eternal, which requires sacrifice and suffering, about which Kierkegaard knew much. Kierkegaard craved the stability and predictability of the eternal as an anchor in a life that was shattered by a great earthquake.

Friedrich Nietzsche

> The minds of others I know well;
> But who am I, I cannot tell
> (Nietzsche, 1882, p. 49).

Friedrich Nietzsche was a soul tortured to the point of madness. Nietzsche lost his father in early childhood and subsequently became a parentified child, assuming his father's mantle, comforting his mother in her grief and eventually becoming consumed by (over-)identification with his dead father. Thus, he, like Kierkegaard, was faced with a profound dilemma – living for his dead father or living his own life. This personal dilemma could be argued to have given birth to his thesis that everyone is destined to live lives that have already been lived – he explicitly stated in his autobiography that he had relived his father's life (Nietzsche, 1908). Nietzsche's work is permeated with nihilistic thinking about a chaotic world that is endlessly relived by succeeding generations. Surely this philosophy is a reflection of his own life's course? Nietzsche was a prolific writer until his "tragic collapse into madness" in 1889 (Black, 2006, p. 2). In *Beyond Good and Evil* (1886), Nietzsche foreshadowed Freud and the phenomenologists: "It has gradually become clear to me that every great philosophy has hitherto been [a] confession on the part of its author and a kind of involuntary and unconscious memoir" (p. 37). Thus, Nietzsche (1882) concluded that since all our thoughts are contextually embedded and perspectival, there can be no reality separate from human experience, and that, therefore, "God is dead". This statement was not made in the spirit of atheistic triumphalism. It is a statement often quoted without its context, which paints quite a different emotional picture:

> After Buddha was dead, his shadow was still shown for centuries in a cave – a tremendous, gruesome shadow. God is dead; but given the way of men, there may still be caves for thousands of years in which his shadow will be shown. And we still have to vanquish his shadow.
>
> ...
>
> When will all these shadows of God cease to darken our minds? When will we complete our de-deification of nature? When may we begin to

"naturalize" humanity in terms of a pure, newly discovered, newly redeemed nature?

(Nietzsche, 1882, pp. 108 and 110)

Nietzsche's conclusion that God was dead meant, to him, that everything was permitted – that the consequence of repudiation of God's existence was a deification of man. According to Black (2006), this led to his essentially "manic fantasy of an *Übermensch*, a superman, who would be heroically joyful and defiant despite the essential futility of life in a godless, post-Darwinian universe" (p. 2). These thoughts translate into Modernity's aspiration for personal autonomy and purpose in the face of the "original absence underlying all of reality, a fertile void in which all things are possible" (Hart, 2009, p. 21). Underneath the panicked grasping after meaning, though, is the nihilistic fear that there is nothing other than man's striving and torment. There is no Maker, no First Cause, no transcendental truth about our existence waiting to be discovered by those who ardently search for it. Nietzsche felt the profound implications of his declaration and worried whether he himself and all humanity who came after him could cope in a godless world. Hart (2009) takes a more optimistic view, arguing that to be a nihilist is to embrace the freedom to make of ourselves what we will, unencumbered by subjugation to creeds, dogma, fantasy or any moral or cultural absolutism.

Ludwig Wittgenstein

What can be said at all can be said clearly, and what we cannot talk about we must pass over in silence.

(Wittgenstein, 1921, p. 3)

The most distinguishing and shocking feature of Ludwig Wittgenstein's life is that all three of his brothers ended their lives by suicide and that he, himself, was chronically suicidal. Atwood et al. (2011), in trying to understand the irredeemable pathology of such a family, concluded that it lay in their father's profound narcissism that denied his sons any form of independent existence. They were merely items on their father's inventory of possessions. All four sons, like their father, became engineers. Any spontaneous agency, autonomy or authenticity was crushed to the point where the older sons were literally annihilated psychologically by their father until they "finally declined the destinies that had been designed for them ... rejecting a life of compliance by rejecting life itself" (Atwood et al., 2011, p. 275). Wittgenstein's saving grace may have been that he found alternate role models in Gottlob Frege and Bertrand Russell, who mentored him, not only in mathematical logic, but in the acceptability of having a mind of his own. Wittgenstein finally and courageously ended his relationship with his father. Ludwig nonetheless remained chronically suicidal and retained a precarious hold on his sense of his own personal existence. His philosophical writing reflected his personal struggle to account for his own "onto-logical vulnerability" (Atwood et al., 2011, p. 283) and to find his place in the world by "[disentangling] his identity from ... his father's self-centred universe" (p. 275). Note, for example, Wittgenstein's assertion that "There is no such thing as the sub-ject" and "The subject does not belong to the world" (Wittgenstein, 1921, p. 69).

Martin Heidegger

> For manifestly you have long been aware of what you mean when you use the expression "being". We, however, who used to think we understood it, have now become perplexed.
>
> (Plato, in Heidegger, 1927, p. 1)

Martin Heidegger was preoccupied with the ontological question of the meaning of existence, of 'Being' (*Dasein* – literally, 'being-there'), which he explored in *Being and Time* (1927). He subsequently constructed a number of hyphenated concepts – such as Being-in-the-world (*In-der-Welt-sein*) – to denote the indissoluble unity of a being-in-context; that is, "[a] bare subject without a world never 'is'" (Heidegger, in Atwood et al., p. 297). Heidegger's project was to dismantle the Cartesian dualism that separated mind from world, subject from object. Like Wittgenstein, Heidegger had a tenuous sense of his own identity. The annihilating force in his life was the Catholic Church, on whom he was dependent financially for 13 years for his edu-cation, but from whom he felt increasingly alienated and distant. He finally extri-cated himself from his training to become a priest by claiming a heart condition. In so doing, he disappointed his mother, another profound annihilating force, who died deeply distressed at his rejection of the Church. Heidegger left a copy of his masterpiece, *Being and Time*, on her deathbed as a futile last attempt to find accept-ance from her for the path that he had chosen.

Heidegger argued that death is embedded in our existence – we are all 'beings-towards-death'. We must embrace the grounds of our humanness, which includes our finitude, in order to live authentically. To do this creates anxiety and a state of 'uncanniness', which represents a giving up of our everyday certainties in a pre-dictable world and the denial of death to fully embrace our finiteness, selfhood and aloneness. Atwood et al. argued that Heidegger experienced three major crises of personal annihilation and world collapse that motivated his philosophical approach. First, his mother died in a state of bitterness and angry rejection of her son for having abandoned the Church, his lover left him at around the time of his mother's death and these personal devastations were followed by the uncomprehending reception of *Being and Time* among the academic community. Heidegger sought solace in the Nazi party for which he was derided after the war and banned from all university positions in Germany. He subsequently experienced a breakdown and withdrew into a life of solitary philosophical contemplation. Atwood et al. concluded: "Both in Heidegger's philosophy and in his personal experiential world, authenticity and homelessness, ownmost selfhood and radical non-relationality were inextricably intertwined" (2011, p. 283).

Richard Dawkins

> [W]hen two opposite points of view are expressed with equal force, the truth does not necessarily lie midway between them. It is possible for one side to be simply wrong.
>
> (Dawkins & Coyne, 2005, p. 19)

It may be instructive to comment here on the life experiences of Richard Dawkins, who has been one of the most strident critics of religion in recent times. Dawkins has recently (2013) published his autobiography – *An Appetite for Wonder: The Making of a Scientist*. In this book, we learn that he was sent to boarding school at the tender age of seven. He recounted that early every morning, Matron would make her rounds and as she did so, Dawkins imagined that she "would somehow be magically transformed into [his] mother. … I prayed incessantly for this." Later in the book he said that he "did this wishful kind of praying so often, I must have been deeply influenced by preachers telling me if you wanted something strongly enough you can make it happen." Richard experienced not one but three traumatic breaks from his mother (and family) – the second at age eight when he was sent to prep school and again at 13 when he went to public school. He developed a stammer at this time that perhaps reflects the unrelieved stress he experienced from these repeated attachment ruptures. Jane Wheatley (2013a), in an interview with Dawkins about the book, asked him whether life was more upsetting than he lets on. He responded, "I chose not to make this a misery memoir or talk about feelings too much." He did concede that he was beaten by his headmaster. However, he minimized this experience, stating "I wasn't beaten a great deal … they all did it and it's wrong to judge the past by the standards of today" (Wheatley, 2013a, p. 31). He also had an experience of what he described as "minor sexual abuse" from one of his masters at school. He stated that this experience was not as bad as the "horror of telling a child about hell" (Wheatley, 2013a, p. 31). Dawkins's family is populated by many men of the cloth, who perhaps warned the young Dawkins in graphic terms about the consequences of sin, hence his preference for sexual abuse over anxiety about hell. Richard was a fervent believer in his early life but rebelled in his adolescence and never returned to the faith of his forefathers. So … here we have a child who suffered repeated traumatic separations from his parents, his mother in particular, who prayed earnestly and "incessantly" to a silent God, whose prayers were not answered and who was abandoned to the frightening world of boarding school with its masters who beat and sexually abused the boys in their care. Here was a child who was very angry with mother (and perhaps also father), but who never "made a fuss" according to his mother, perhaps because he had already abandoned the hope of being nurtured by a responsive object. As an adolescent Dawkins became very angry with God, rejecting and abandoning his heavenly Father just as he had been abandoned by his earthly parents. Richard is now making the fuss (about the failings of God and, by extension, his parents) that perhaps properly belonged to his childhood.

Notes

1   Descriptors in parentheses describe the phenomenon in psychoanalytic terms.

6

CRITIQUES OF FREUD'S THEORY ON RELIGION

Religion as a social construction and a wish-fulfilling illusion

> Primitive man has no choice; he has no other way of thinking. It is natural to him ... to project his existence outwards into the world and to regard every event ... he observes as the manifestation of beings who ... are like himself. It is his only method of comprehension. And it is by no means self-evident; on the contrary it is a remarkable coincidence, if by thus indulging his natural disposition he succeeds in satisfying one of his greatest needs.
>
> (Freud, 1927, p. 21)

Freud presented arguments from a number of perspectives – historical, anthropological, genetic, epiphenomenological,[1] philosophical, and psychological – in support of his objections to religion, the most oft-cited being that religion is a form of wishful thinking derived from infantile neurosis, at the heart of which are our feelings of helplessness and our longing for a loving and powerful father. He concluded that: "Religious doctrines have to be discarded ... [because] nothing can withstand reason and experience, and the contradiction which religion offers to both is all too palpable. Even purified religious ideas cannot escape this fate" (Freud, 1927, p. 54). Freud maintained that religion is a social construction that was an inevitable but "delusionary" by-product of the collectivization and civilization of humans that served multiple purposes for rulers and followers alike. People, Freud argued (1930), "attempt to procure a certainty of happiness and protection against suffering through a delusional remoulding of reality" which becomes, in effect, a "mass delusion" (p. 81). The fact that religion, this "delusional remoulding of reality", takes so many diverse forms is evidence of social construction – that is, "civilization creates these religious ideas" (Freud, 1930, p. 21); the appearance and expression of these religious ideas arise from and are contextually embedded in the social milieu in which they take form.

Social and cultural phenomena are powerful determinants of beliefs and behaviours, even in biology. For example, menopause is viewed differently in different cultures and these differences in the social construction of menopause affect the way in which menopause is experienced by women. In cultures in which older women are valued, such as Thailand, Guatemala, Mexico, Japan and Papua New Guinea, women rarely report menopausal symptoms (Lock, 1995). This is in stark contrast to women in Western society, where ageism is rife and where menopause is medicalized, that is, constructed as a disease needing treatment, and dreaded by women approaching this stage of their biological life cycle (Wilson, 1966). Unsurprisingly, Western women report multiple symptoms not experienced (or at least not reported) in cultures that value older women. Freud (1926) expressed rather strong opinions regarding the menopause. Below is an example.

> People have not been spoilt by successes in the therapy of the neuroses; the nerve-specialist has at least "taken a lot of trouble with them". Indeed, there is not much that can be done; nature must help, or time. With women there is first menstruation, then marriage, and later on the menopause. Finally, death is a real help.
>
> (Freud, 1926, p. 232)

Freud was critical of an anthropomorphic God, specifically as characterized in the Judeo-Christian religions – he did not consider other representations of God and was critical of those who did:

> Where questions of religion are concerned, people are guilty of every possible sort of dishonesty and intellectual misdemeanour. Philosophers stretch the meaning of words until they retain scarcely anything of their original sense. They give the name of "God" to some vague abstraction which they have created for themselves; having done so they can pose before all the world as deists, as believers in God, and they can even boast that they have recognized a higher, purer concept of God, notwithstanding that their God is now nothing more than an insubstantial shadow and no longer the *mighty personality of religious doctrines*. [My italics]
>
> (Freud, 1927, p. 32)

"However, [all these meanings of God] have arisen from the same need as have all the other achievements of civilization: from the necessity of defending oneself against the crushingly superior force of nature" (Freud, 1913a, p. 21). The unifying concept, which Freud described as the "root of every form of religion" (Freud, 1913a, p. 148) is the longing for the father and protection against unassailable forces. Contrary to common opinion, Freud did not claim that his theory about belief in

God disproved God's existence. He conceded that even if he succeeded in demonstrating that belief in God fulfilled humankind's most primitive yearning, God
might, nevertheless, exist.

It is worth noting that Freud's anti-religious sentiments found fertile soil in the
chaotic political scene that unfolded in the early twentieth century, in which the
perpetrators of ethnocentrism, anti-Semitism, jingoistic nationalism and genocide
were all claiming the religious and moral high ground. Significantly, of the two
taboos that were central to Freud's understanding of totemism, one belongs to
intrapsychic processes and the other to social motives:

> The two taboos of totemism with which human morality has its beginning
> are not on a par psychologically. The first of them, the law protecting the
> totem animal, is founded wholly on emotional motives: the father had actu-
> ally been eliminated, and in no real sense could the deed be undone. But
> the second rule, the prohibition of incest, has a powerful practical basis as
> well. Sexual desires do not unite men but divide them. Though the broth-
> ers had banded together in order to overcome their father, they were all one
> another's rivals in regard to the women.
>
> (Freud, 1913a, pp. 143–4)

Because religion arose from human imagination – that is, man created God – it
has evolved in many forms since the totemic practices of primitive cultures. The
evolution of religion also had a cognitive dimension, demonstrated in the animistic and artificialistic beliefs characteristic of the early cognitive development
of young children (see Chapter 2). As man's cognitive processes evolved, allowing some to think abstractly and dialectically, so too did some, but certainly not
all, religious doctrines and argumentation about religion. Todd (2012) bemoans
the primitive anthropomorphic god that Dawkins (2006) attempts to demolish,
but presents counter-arguments about transpersonal, transcendent numinosity that
few can understand.

Freud's four works on religion, taken together, represent an elegant claim, but
can we be satisfied with argumentation alone? Science depends on observation, the
gathering of facts and the development of testable hypotheses. How can we test
Freud's assertions regarding the veracity of his theories of religion? Freud believed
that advances in the scientific understanding of our universe offered by scientists
such as Copernicus, Kepler, Newton and Darwin constituted devastating blows
to religious belief based on the cosmological argument. Other phenomena, such
as the vast troves of myths, legends and fairy tales that all have the same underlying thematic structure of the monumental struggle between good and evil, fought
between humans and a range of supernatural beings with the ultimate triumph
of good, suggest that man has a deep need to find order and justice in life, which
would otherwise appear capricious and without meaning. This is one reason that
religion has taken root and strenuously resists all assaults on its validity.

Freud believed that psychoanalysis inflicted the death blow to religion. Lest Freud appear too grandiose in this assertion, we should note that David Hume (1757) in *The Natural History of Religion* pre-empted Freud by 150 years in drawing the same conclusion that religion existed to provide a buffer against human misery and the acceptance of the finality of death. Similarly, Ludwig Feuerbach (1841) in *The Essence of Christianity* apprehended the fundamental thesis of Freud's theory – that God is a grandiose projection of man's own nature, purified and deified, motivated by the insatiable longing to be cared for in the way in which an idealized father would care for his child. Freud's contribution to these philosophical insights was to provide a psychology of religion grounded in the systematic introspective study of human nature.

There are two axiomatic themes transfusing Freud's major works on religion which we will briefly review here. The first is that sons 'kill' their fathers, either in reality or symbolically; the second is that sons, and indeed all children, have a loving relationship with fathers in infancy that they wish to replicate endlessly. The sequelae of these acts and experiences form the basis of religion. In *Totem and Taboo*, the sons killed the primal father; in *Moses and Monotheism*, the Jewish tribe killed its 'father', Moses, throwing the tribe into inconsolable guilt and remorse. Although both of these works represented a search for historical truth, Freud concluded that we have a predilection for accepting as true our deeply felt wishes, and hence our search for truth is flawed, as, inevitably, will be the outcome of such a search. Notwithstanding, Freud concluded that the ancestral father was later represented in the totem animal in subsequent generations, a representation that reinforced successive generations' identification with this father. The image (i.e., object representation) of the primal father that expressed itself as the totem animal is inherited trans-generationally in latent form, becoming manifest through social and cultural changes to the environment, both internal (e.g., cognitive development) and external (e.g., migration, the appearance of a new leader). Freud (1939) contended that Moses' idea of monotheism "signified the revival of an experience in the primeval ages of the human family which had long vanished from man's conscious memory" (p. 129). The totem animal, at first a surrogate of the father, morphed into 'God' at a later stage (Freud, 1913a). This single God of Moses was easy to accept because Moses was felt to be the primal father incarnate, just as Jesus was accepted as God incarnate thousands of years later.

We have, of course, no way of verifying Freud's theory. Hans Küng (1986) argued that although belief in God can be subjected to psychological analysis, this analysis can make no claim regarding the existence of God. The wish for God signals neither God's existence nor non-existence. Freud himself conceded that as history, his theory is open to criticism because it is not well grounded in historical fact. How can we know whether primitive man conceived of the totem animal in the manner described by Freud? Was he capable of ambivalent feelings and were these responsible for the murder of the primal father? Was he capable of experiencing guilt? What is the actual mechanism of transmission of primal man's representation of the primal father and their guilt and longing for the lost father to subsequent generations? Rizzuto (1979) has provided a scholarly evaluation of the complexities of Freud's psychoanalytic theory related to the origins of religion, and I refer the interested reader there for a detailed discussion. Despite the shortcomings in Freud's theories on religion, Rizzuto concluded that

> Freud's original formulation is essentially correct … [it] is one of his major contributions to the understanding of man – particularly of man as an object-related being, of man's lifelong use of early imagos and object representations, his dependence on object relations and his religiosity as an object-related activity.
>
> (Rizzuto, 1979, p. 28)

Put simply, an individual's conception of God is coloured by his cultural inherit-ance overlaid and mutated by personal experience, particularly the quality of the early caregiving environment. As Rizzuto (1979) summarized: "Freud insisted that God was nothing but the wishful emotional clinging to an exalted childhood father transformed into a supernatural being" (p. xix). It is noteworthy that the mother does not figure in Freud's theory of religion. In each of his applications and exten-sions of this basic precept of his theory, it is the father alone who figures: for example, the Father God emerged from the leader of the primal horde and the totem object; the Father God was pre-eminent in the religion of Moses and in the advent of Christ (the second Moses); and in the origins of Haizmann's and Schreber's psychoses (Meissner, 2009).

Freud's search was firmly directed towards understanding why people believe in God. He never explained why people do not believe in God, perhaps because he viewed non-belief as self-evident. He did make a passing reference to the issue that provides some clues: "a turning-away from religion is bound to occur with the fatal inevitability of a process of growth, and that we find ourselves at this very juncture in the middle of that phase of development" (Freud, 1927, p. 43). This is a fascinating question that awaits further elucidation. For example, what experiences in infancy presage non-belief? Could it be that some infants do not long for their fathers? Surely, at birth, all infants are equally helpless. What special qualities do non-believers share that prevent them from joining in the mass delusion of religion? We cannot assert that only naïve, ill-educated, intellectually limited or culturally indoctrinated individuals succumb to such beliefs, as our earlier discussion of the scientist-believers demonstrated, nor can we assert that only children who have had primarily positive, or for that mat-ter negative, parenting experiences are candidates for faith. Securely attached individuals might believe in God because their image of God is an extension of a much-loved earthly father. Insecurely attached individuals might believe in God as a compensation for the poor parenting they received from their earthly fathers. Conversely, they might believe in a punishing God who replicates the authoritarian fathering that they received from their earthly fathers; or they might not believe in God at all, arguing that if God existed, He would have intervened to stop the torment inflicted upon helpless children by excessively punitive fathers.

Perhaps the answer lies in developmental experiences beyond infancy. Freud's thesis regarding the splitting of the good and bad aspects of the actual father and the spiritual father may contain the kernel of an explanation as to why people do not believe in God. As they grow, children increasingly harbour resentment and hostility towards their parents which is at some point transposed onto a Deity. In this process, Freud believed that the image of a personal God that people derive from the image of the exalted father is also the same source upon which the image of Satan is formed (Freud, 1910). This father image, in turn, originated from two sources, according to Freud – the ancestral father of the primal horde and one's actual father. This is not too difficult to grasp – fathers are neither all-good nor all-bad and offspring therefore react to the father with opposing sets of emotions: on the one hand, affection and submission, on the other, hostility and defiance. This is why man's perception of and relationship with God has always been ambivalent. At first, God and Satan were one, just like the idealized human father, but both are eventually split – the 'good' father became God; the 'bad' father became Satan (Freud, 1923a). This splitting relieves individuals from acknowledging and processing their rage towards either their actual father or God the Father – it is more comfortable to project these feelings into a being that is the subject of universal and sanctioned hatred, thus splitting off those feelings that properly belong to one's 'real' father. In so doing, one fails to reach a mature, integrated stance that permits acceptance of the 'actual' father as both good and bad, and in so doing to relinquish the idealized father (God) who is all good and the denigrated father (Satan) who is all bad.

Like children's relationships with their real fathers, as they grow and develop, they increasingly resent paternal ('divine') authority and interference and perhaps entertain a wish that father (God) did not exist, thus allowing them freedom to behave as they want, or at least to make their own decisions about how to behave. This phase occurs in adolescence with one's real parents during the period of *Sturm und Drang* (i.e., the 'storm and stress' of adolescent rebellion against parental and other authority), a stage that is part of the natural process of separation and individuation that occurs throughout childhood (Erikson, 1959) which coincides with the time at which child believers in God begin to question and reject their faith. Children become increasingly independent of their parents and the influence of self-chosen models becomes ascendant. In this process of separation and individuation, letting go of parents may also signal a letting go of God, who is, after all, modelled on the image of the (fallen) 'exalted father'. Some psychoanalysts suppose that a psychoanalytic cure entails the relinquishing of belief in God because it signifies a relinquishing of infantile fantasies/neuroses and an embrace of the harsh realities of human existence without experiencing them as crushing (Fenichel, 1938).

There has been a barrage of criticism from scholars within a range of other disciplines regarding what they argue to be Freud's errors, generalizations and speculations.[2] This body of criticism is extensive and only a small sampling will be undertaken here. First, the criticism will be presented, followed by an attempted rebuttal, if I believe one to be justified. For a more detailed discussion of some of these criticisms, see Palmer (1997).

1. Freud's adoption of a primal horde theory, which states that the dominant male 'possesses' all the females and drives the young males, his competitors, out of the horde is not a universal social organization as claimed by Freud. Social primates exhibit wide variations in their social structures ranging from solitary members, mated pairs, isolated one-male groups and more-or-less democratic member collectives (Simonds, 1974; Zuckerman, 1932). Nonetheless, social structures can never be entirely 'flat' – there will always emerge a more dominant individual or groups of individuals who will try to subjugate the majority. Communism was a failed experiment because of the irreconcilable clash between human nature and the concept of absolute equality in the collective.

2. Totemism is not a demonstrable foundation of religion. Frazer (1910b) argued that because totems were not 'worshipped' they could not be deities. Although not universal, totems were a significant part of many primitive cultures. The key point belongs to Durkheim – the group was deified and 'worshipped' itself.

3. The universality of the presence of sexual aggression and sexual rivalry as the motivation for the murder of the primal father has not been demonstrated (Schmidt, 1931). I would argue that the sexual component of the rivalry is not essential for the theory to stand, just as I have argued elsewhere (Kenny, 2013) and below that Freud's proposed Oedipus complex is not essential to psychoanalytic theory generally (Kenny, 2014). Consider the biblical sibling rivalries between Cain and Abel, Isaac and Ishmael and Joseph and his brothers. None of these murderous rivalries had a sexual origin.

4. The problematic status of the Oedipus complex. The anthropological counterargument is that it is only possible, if indeed it exists at all, in a patriarchal and patrilineal society. A corollary in matriarchal and matrilineal societies has not been found. This is such an important issue, given its psychoanalytic roots, that I have dealt with it in a separate section, although my discussion will be psychoanalytic, not anthropological (see below).

5. Freud's so-called Lamarckian notion that psychological experiences may be trans-generationally transmitted, that is, a form of 'psychic inheritance', met with a great deal of early criticism, but is now finding support in the discipline of cultural neuroscience (Kitayama & Uskul, 2011). A cogent example is the secondary traumatization of the children of Holocaust survivors (Mendelsohn, 2006).

6. The anthropologist Bronislav Malinowski (1927) argued that if the killing of the father was the foundation of religion, it necessarily had to occur before culture, that is, in the 'prehuman anthropoid family'. Its absence in animal and prehuman collectives is argued to be a death blow to Freud's theory. This

argument fails to consider the causal role of collectivization and culture on individual behaviour and that individual behaviour is always contextually embedded, historically and socially. See, for example, Chapter 7, where I discuss the way in which group processes alter individual behaviour. Malinowski's preface to his book is worthy of psychoanalytic analysis – he bemoans the undue and wide-reaching influence of Freud's theories, even on himself, but he assures us that "pedantry will remain the master of passion ... and subsequent reflection soon chilled the initial enthusiasms ... with its chaotic arguments and tangled terminology" (Malinowski, 1927, p. vii). Malinowski concedes that he is indebted to Freud for the instruction he received in human psychology and for Freud's treatment of "sex and various shameful meanesses and vanities of man" (Malinowski, 1927, p. viii).

My thesis is that the details and nuances of the historical anthropology of the origin of religious belief are less important than we may suppose in grappling with the reasons for our need for God. I will argue that it is human nature, specifically the experience of infant helplessness, our need for a powerful father, the struggle to control (and be forgiven for) unacceptable impulses, our fear of death and our need to understand our place in the universe that drive our belief in God. This belief is expressed in diverse ways, just as we communicate in diverse languages, which are very different in both their oral and written codes. Just as language is hypothesized to have developed out of chance utterances of dominant individuals, whose genetic potential (possibly through a genetic mutation) activated the capacity for language development in isolated tribes (Deacon, 1997; Steels, 2009), so too did the various expressions of religiosity. However, the deep structure of language, called universal grammar, is the same across all languages (Chomsky, 2000); so too with religion – it is expressed in a multitude of forms and beliefs but all religions serve essentially the same purpose and contain the equivalent set of characteristic cultural markers outlined by Boyer and Bergstrom (2008). Indeed, there may well be parallel processes occurring in genetic evolution and cultural transmission. An analogy for the advent of specific cultural variants of religious beliefs and practices is the spread of alleles in a gene pool (Boyd & Richerson, 1985). Candidate cognitive and behavioural processes, such as, for example, cultural conformism, deference to leaders and imitation of powerful and successful members of the group, contribute to the instantiation and transmission of religious (and other cultural) beliefs and practices within social groups (Durham, 1991).

Lest we end this section showing only the irreconcilable differences between psychoanalysis and religion, it is perhaps worth noting that love is necessary for survival in both a psychological and a religious sense. Believers are told that God so loved the world that most theologies incorporate love into their doctrines, whether in the form of the promised redemption from original sin, or the gift of grace or reception into heaven or nirvana. In psychoanalysis, the foundational tenet is that the infant needs parental love to survive its own destructive and hateful impulses, which, without love, evolve into a tormenting and punitive superego, the contents of which are the introjections of parental superegos. Britton (2006) suggested that

God is the external representation of the superego. Using the story of Job from the Old Testament, Britton draws an analogy with psychological development in which Job represents the ego and God the superego. The emancipation of Job (ego) from God (superego) is achieved in Job's realization that he has a capacity and a right to form judgements about God's appallingly arbitrary and cruel visitations (demands and injunctions of the punitive superego) upon His faithful servant who has not deserved such brutal, unjustified treatment.

The role of the Oedipus complex in the origin of religion

Some antagonists to Freud's position on religion commit the 'genetic fallacy' in order to discredit his arguments. The genetic fallacy states that the truth or falsity of a proposition can be ascertained by specifying its origins. In Freud's case, the argument that Freud (may have) had an unresolved obsessional neurosis would lead to the conclusion that his argument that religion constitutes an obsessional neurosis of the masses is invalid. This is not a valid conclusion; it is possible that both propositions are true – that Freud was neurotic and that religion is a neurosis found in believers. It is interesting that Freud entertained various superstitions, was alert to 'omens', had more than a passing interest in clairvoyance, telepathy and thought transfer and engaged in numerology, at one point using its principles to calculate the likely age at which he would die (Palmer, 1997)!

Notwithstanding, Freud was opposed to any attempt that justified another life beyond the life on earth or any form of supernatural reality, and accordingly rejected the mysticism of Jung and occult practices which he condemned in "Dreams and occultism" (1933c) as the products of either unrestrained imagination or deliberate fraud. Freud formed the view early that religion represents a "mythological view of the world" that has abandoned the "reality-principle" and is "nothing but psychology projected into the external world" (Freud, 1901, p. 258), an obsessional neurosis comprising reaction formations[3] against the expression of forbidden (repressed) instincts.

A pertinent issue in this context is the question as to whether Freud's theory of religion needs the Oedipus complex. Would his theory of the origin and purpose of religion flounder if the Oedipus complex were either wrong or non-existent? Freud defends his attachment to this myth by his observation of its pervasiveness, if not universality:

> Rank has brought together a whole number of other heroic figures from poetry or legend, of whom the same story of their youth is told, either in its entirety or in easily recognizable fragments – including Oedipus, Kama, Paris, Telephos, Perseus, Heracles, Gilgamesh, Amphion, Zethos, and others.
>
> (Freud, 1939, p. 11)

Although much is made by subsequent scholars of the foundational importance of the Oedipus complex in Freud's theory of the origin of religion (e.g., Rizzuto, 1979), Freud in fact mentions the Oedipus complex on very few occasions in his major works on religion. Freud confirmed, I would argue incorrectly (see Kenny, 2013), the existence of the Oedipus complex using the case of "little Hans", a five-year-old boy who had a fear of horses (Freud, 1913a). In this case study, Freud concluded that Hans

> regarded his father … as a competitor for the favours of his mother, towards whom the obscure foreshadowings of his budding sexual wishes were aimed. Thus he was situated in the typical attitude of a male child towards his parents to which we have given the name of the "Oedipus complex" and which we regard in general as the nuclear complex of the neuroses. The new fact that we have learnt from the analysis of "little Hans" – a fact with an important bearing upon totemism – is that in such circumstances children displace some of their feelings from their father on to an animal.
>
> (Freud, 1913a, pp. 128–9)

The case of "little Hans" – his only child patient – is perhaps one of Freud's weaker analyses.[4] The link between Hans's clinical presentation and totemism is tenuous, if not dazzlingly fanciful. I have argued elsewhere that we need neither an Oedipus complex nor a displacement of Oedipal feelings towards a father onto an animal to understand Hans's psychopathology. (For a detailed critique, see Kenny, 2013.)

The Oedipus complex had its most complete airing with respect to the origin of religion in *Totem and Taboo*, in which Freud argued that children created "out of their filial sense of guilt the two fundamental taboos of totemism, which … corresponded to the two repressed wishes of the Oedipus complex" (Freud, 1913a, p. 143). The two prohibitions to which Freud referred in this passage are the laws protecting the totem animal and the prohibition against incest. There is only one mention in *The Future of an Illusion*: "Religion would thus be the universal obsessional neurosis of humanity; like the obsessional neurosis of children, it arose out of the Oedipus complex, out of the relation to the father" (Freud, 1927, p. 43), and one substantive reference in *Civilization and its Discontents*, as follows:

> We cannot get away from the assumption that man's sense of guilt springs from the Oedipus complex and was acquired at the killing of the father by the brothers banded together.
>
> …
>
> This conflict is set going as soon as men are faced with the task of living together. So long as the community assumes no other form than that of the family, the conflict is bound to express itself in the Oedipus complex, to establish the conscience and to create the first sense of guilt.
>
> (Freud, 1927, pp. 131 and 132)

Actually, the conflict expresses itself, in Freud's own words, "when men are faced with the task of living together" – not living specifically in a configuration in which the Oedipus complex expresses itself. Freud (1910) argued that

a personal God is ... nothing other than the exalted father. ... Thus we recognize that the roots of the need for religion are in the *parental complex*; the
almighty and just God, and kindly Nature appear to us as grand sublimations
of father and mother.

(Freud, 1910, p. 123)

This passage does not lend support to the causal role of the Oedipus complex
in our need for religion. Freud, in fact, names the process the 'parental complex',
terminology that appears more harmonious with other theories about the foundational role of early (non-sexual) relationships with both parents in a belief in God,
and, indeed, in the nature of that God. This passage is also unusual in that it offers a
role for the mother in the formation of religious belief, a role that is often absent in
Freud's essentially patriarchal theory of religion. Significantly, Freud's focus remains
almost exclusively on the role of the father-image on the son's conception of God;
Freud does not consider the process of belief acquisition in daughters.

Kenny (2013) and others (e.g., Fromm & Narváez, 1968; Lachmann, 2010)
have argued that there is little evidence for the existence of the Oedipus complex, at least not in its original Freudian form. See, for example, Jeremy Holmes, in
Kenny, 2014:

> I want to rewrite the Oedipus complex in attachment terms, to look at it
> from an evolutionary perspective, that is, a child's need for the parent is not
> the same as the parent's need for the child.
>
> ...
>
> Resolution [of the Oedipus complex] is the development of the capacity
> to tolerate a three-person relationship.
>
> (Holmes in Kenny, 2014, pp. 156 and 168)

However, neither Holmes nor I asserts that Freud's edifice falls if the Oedipus
complex either does not exist or is found to be particular rather than universal, or
have other non-sexual origins or interpretations. For example, today we understand
Freud's concept of Oedipal resolution as the capacity for interpersonal relatedness.
Freud's explanations for the origin of religion work just as well if the Oedipus complex were replaced with social learning theory (Bandura, 1977) and/or attachment
theory that attribute attachment rupture, a universal phenomenon (Bowlby, 1973),
rather than Oedipal rivalry as the source of rage and hate. In both social learning
and attachment theories, infants form non-sexual attachments to nurturing adults.
If nurturance becomes unavailable or is withdrawn, the child, threatened with a
loss of love, introjects or takes in the caregiver's behaviours, attitudes and attributes,
allowing the child to replicate self-rewarding experiences when the caregiver is
absent or withholding. This process in social learning theory is called identification.
Similarly, in attachment theory, when an attachment rupture occurs in infancy or
early childhood, the child experiences rage (and hate) towards his caregivers, guilt
about the rage and anxiety about the guilt (Davanloo, 1995, 2005). If these feelings

are not satisfactorily resolved, the child will become symptomatic in the way Freud describes, using a range of defences, in particular, splitting[5] and projection, to prevent the unacceptable feelings from breaking through into conscious awareness.

Contemporary psychoanalysis and religion

> God is dead. God remains dead. And we have killed him. Yet his shadow still looms. How shall we comfort ourselves, the murderers of all murderers? What was holiest and mightiest of all that the world has yet owned has bled to death under our knives: who will wipe this blood off us? What water is there for us to clean ourselves? What festivals of atonement, what sacred games shall we have to invent? Is not the greatness of this deed too great for us? Must we ourselves not become gods simply to appear worthy of it?
>
> (Nietzsche, 1882, section 125)

In addition to critiques arising from disciplines outside psychoanalysis, there are those coming from within, which cast a searing light onto the religious works themselves in order to identify the errors and gaps in Freud's reasoning (e.g., O'Neil & Akhtar, 2009). Akhtar (2009) complains that Freud's strident disregard for God had the effect of bracketing any psychoanalytic enquiry either in analysts themselves or in their patients, except to investigate the psychic meaning of adherence to a belief in an illusion. Such was Freud's conviction that psychoanalysis is an atheistic science, those professing religious beliefs were not accepted for psychoanalytic training in the early days of the 'movement'. Why, asks Akhtar, does Freud, the 'Godless Jew', have such a preoccupation with the subject and why does he debate with himself so vehemently (in the guise of an argumentative interlocutor) in *The Future of an Illusion*? Because, concludes Akhtar, this work is a battleground on which Freud plays out his opposing selves, and his ambivalence about God. Many of us who have devoted time to an examination of this question will empathize with Freud's conflicted stance and will feel less judgemental towards him than Akhtar. Or perhaps we will concur with Jung and Winnicott that the question of God's existence is not to be asked.

Akhtar juxtaposes Bion's concept of God with Freud's. Freud's God is, according to Akhtar, anthropomorphized – Freud demolishes a Judeo-Christian god who is 'up there'. In contrast, "Bion's God is everywhere. Freud's God is sculpted in human terms. Bion's God is painted in the watercolour of wisdom ... sings through the murmur of the wind and floats on the waves of rivers and oceans ... Bion's God is inescapable" (Akhtar, 2009, p. 5). These sentiments make for evocative poetry but what do they mean? How are they helpful conceptually? This view of God, and this hymn of praise to Bion (dare I declare it hero worship or hagiography?), is nothing other than nature deified. This naïve conception of God is characteristic of the natural religions of primitive cultures and very young children, hence not helpful in advancing any inquiry into the nature of God.

Contemporary psychoanalytic critiques of Freud's theory of religion can be subdivided into three main groups:

1. Those which are in agreement with Freud's central thesis that God is an illusion and atheism is the only defensible position (e.g., Beit-Hallahmi & Argyle, 1997; Fenichel, 1938). See, for example, De Mello Franco's (1998) summing up of this position:

    > The inference is that analysts start from a preconceived, *a priori* notion that religious behavior necessarily implies a primitive, neurotic concern to be … eliminated by interpretation, and that the nonreligious condition should not interest the psychoanalyst because it already represents liberation from "infantile illusions".
    >
    > (p. 114)

    This group frames the God–concept within psychoanalytic theory, interpreting the construct of a Heavenly Father in terms of "security-enhancing selfobjects" which offer continuity of feelings of safety and security at times of dread, for example when one is dying (Meissner, 2009, p. 216).

    Bomford (1990) has offered another psychoanalytic interpretation, arguing that God's attributes parallel the five attributes with which Freud characterized the Unconscious. These comprise the replacement of external by psychical reality (in God, omnipotence), timelessness (God is eternal), no negation (ineffability of God), displacement and condensation (God is indivisible) (see Table 2.3).

    A third subgroup views religion as important in developmental terms and for identity formation (e.g., Erikson, 1959). Man creates God by projecting his idealized self-image into an infinitely grandiose object, thereby preserving the best of both himself and his idealized parental imago.

2. Those critical of Freud's thesis that religion is illusory and a form of neurosis. There are professed psychoanalysts of faith who have redefined psychoanalysis as a form of religion or spirituality that serves both individual and communal needs (see, for example, Eigen, 2001; Jones, 2002; Kakar, 1991; Meissner, 1984; Rizzuto, 1979; Smith & Handelman, 1990; Spezzano & Gargiulo, 1997). They subscribe to the view that belief in God should be accepted as a matter of faith, "as an effable substrate of reality" (Kirshner, 2004, p. 74). Another exemplar of this stance is Eric Fromm (1964) whose humanism embraced Christianity:

    > Humanism, both in its Christian religious and in its secular, nontheistic manifestations, is characterized by faith in man, in his possibility to develop to ever higher stages, in the unity of the human race, in tolerance and peace, and in reason and love as the forces which enable man to realize himself, to become what he can be. [p. 69] … [T]he development of the universal is based on the fullest development of the individual.
    >
    > (p. 70)

3. Those who want to find middle ground between science and religion in general, and between psychoanalytic theory and religion in particular. At one end, they take a position of acceptance or tolerance of religious belief, combined with a perception that religion can exert a positive impact on the psychological well-being of believers. There is now, according to Blass (2006), "a pervasive tolerance of religious belief associated with its lying in the realm of personal participation that can never be questioned" (p. 28). Taking their cue from Winnicott's notion of transitional space and the value of illusion in infant development, the general theme in these middle roaders is that religion is a metaphor for experiencing and relatedness, an expression of the value of the illusion on which culture and creativity are based (Meissner, 2009). According to Winnicott (1965):

> [M]an continues to create and re-create God as a place to put that which is good in himself, and which he might spoil if he kept in himself along with all the hate and destructiveness which is also to be found there.
>
> (p. 94)

My own view is that any form of attempted rapprochement between psychoanalysis and religion involves a sleight of hand, in which both religion and psychoanalysis become transformed in ways that their founders would, in all probability, find unacceptable. In *A Godless Jew*, Peter Gay (1987) argues that had Freud been a believer, he would never have developed psychoanalysis. The major objection from both sides in any proposed armistice is the abandonment of truth claims, so let us explore this issue in a little more detail.

The concept of truth in psychoanalysis and religion

> [M]ost of what is real is not conscious, and most of what we are conscious of is not real, [it] is fiction and cliché.
>
> (Fromm, 1964, p. 75)

The search for truth has been a casualty in the efforts of contemporary theorizing to steer a middle course between religion and psychoanalysis. Some attempts at conciliation involve a redefinition of basic terms. For example, Symington (1994) offers definitions of religion in terms of morality and spirituality that are compatible with a denial of the existence of God. Eigen (2001) goes further than most in his conflation of religion and psychoanalysis. For example, he describes psychoanalysis as "holy" (Eigen, 2001, p. 42), "mystical" and "sacred" (p. 37), indeed, a "form of prayer" (Eigen, 1998, p. 11). These views sit in stark contrast to earlier psychoanalytic theorizing that considered analysis a success if the patient gave up his religion in the course of analysis (Fenichel, 1938), and to Lacan, who was adamant that religion and psychoanalysis were radically incompatible such that adherence to religion signified a failure of psychoanalysis. For Lacan, the struggle in analysis parallels the struggle in religion, which is to relinquish "the subject supposed to know" (1998, Book XI, p. 270) – the analyst in psychoanalysis and the God in religion – and to reclaim one's life.

Contemporary psychoanalysis and Western religion are both troubled by the question regarding the existence of God, a question that has been effectively quarantined by a significant number of psychoanalytic writers. Most contemporary psychoanalysts, true to the atheistic traditions of Freud and the early analysts, resile from organized religion, religious authority, theological dogma, fundamentalism and rituals, and indeed from making assertions about the objective truth of God's existence in their attempts to find the much-sought common ground, focusing on religious experience in a manner akin to natural religion – as a deeply personal and mysterious experience in which God is apprehended in personal terms as a matter of faith. Freud (1930) was alert to this tendency, particularly in philosophers, to transmute "the God of religion" into "an impersonal, shadowy and abstract principle" (p. 74). Blass (2006) also finds this absence of God in current attempts at conciliation misleading, indeed, dishonest, noting that in current psychoanalytic reasoning, contemporary religions are "not regarded as an expression of knowledge or truth pertaining to the nature of reality, the transcendent reality of God, but more as a kind of self- or relational experiencing within a realm of illusion" (p. 24). Illusion is a pervasive concern in psychoanalysis – we all harbour illusions of grandiosity and omnipotence that form the subject matter of psychoanalysis. In the same vein, some cling to religious illusions for psychological reasons pertaining to their life experiences, beginning in infancy. Psychoanalysis has no problem with religious illusions as long as they make no truth claims regarding objective reality. Psychoanalysis is, after all, centrally concerned with psychic, not objective reality. Thus, the problematic of truth claims is bracketed, and Freud's central thesis that religion is a distortion of reality is no longer a concern.

Freud's attempt to assign a proper place to religious beliefs was to assert an intermediate realm between objective truth and illusion – psychic reality – that is, a trace memory of a past reality which does not represent the actualities of the real world, but rather a distortion based on the primal nature of the trace memory. This is the locus of religious ideas, which are false propositions about a past objective reality. The propositions are false by virtue of the distortions that arise from the limits of human understanding and memory of both primal history and infant experience. This view is close to proponents of object relations theory, which is focused not on the origins or external reality of psychological disturbance but on the meaning of subjective experience coloured by infantile omnipotence and one's unique interchanges with the environment in search of wish-fulfilment. Across all religions, God is characterized by omnipotence and may well represent an idealized version of a primary object, a wish-fulfilling illusion.

From the outset, Freud (1930) urged honesty in our thinking about religion, and that no limits should be placed on the search for truth. Entering a psychoanalytic relationship with brackets around religious belief – rendering it unavailable for consensual validation or otherwise – is inimical to the project of psychoanalysis. Freud set an example in the expression of his unequivocal view that religion is an illusion. We need religion to explain the meaning of life to ourselves, but in so doing, we construct a convoluted and tortuous edifice that is both masochistic and non-inclusive. Freud compared us to the rest of the animal world, which does not ponder the imponderable. Rather, he exhorts us, like Voltaire, to return to a simpler life and simply "tend our gardens". Instead, we strive to program the pleasure principle and to avoid pain and unpleasure, aims that run counter to the "regulations of the universe" and ironically, the "plan of Creation" (Freud, 1930, p. 76). Stolorow (in Kenny, 2014), like Freud, urges more honesty in our apprehension of the human condition:

> [H]uman existence, stripped of its sheltering illusions, is inherently traumatising. In Heideggerian [terms], we might say we're always already traumatised. Because of our finitude and the finitude of those we love, trauma is built into the structure of our existence. Even if we haven't been previously traumatised, any trauma brings us face to face with the traumatising dimension of finite human existence itself.
>
> (p. 185)

Freud characterized religion as a mass neurosis that infantilizes and enslaves us; this is the price we are prepared to pay for evading the finitude of life, accepting our insignificance in a vast universe, and coming to terms with the reality of death. Religion stands between man and these realizations of what Freud referred to as manifestations of our feelings of infantile helplessness in the face of the overpowering forces of nature. The creation of gods provides some degree of perceived control over these forces and some degree of mitigation of man's pitiful state. The creation of an afterlife, for example, relieves us of our annihilation anxiety; the creation of a forgiving God assuages our guilt for wrongdoing. How comforting it is to believe that in the end, good deeds are rewarded, bad deeds are punished or forgiven if the sinner truly repents and that we can all look forward to an eternal life in a nirvana-like state where all suffering is banished. God often appears during times of great trauma. Impending death is a cardinal example. It has long been observed that many death-row inmates undergo religious conversion in their dying days. Because condemned prisoners have "extreme mortality salience – that is, they are aware of the exact date, time, place, and method of their deaths" (Johnson, Kanewske & Barak, 2014, p. 144), they have both a visceral dread and a strong denial of their impending end. Their last words reflect their attempts to manage the unthinkable; many find 'God' in this moment and through God a redeeming image of themselves. Whether God is cast in religious terms, as the protective, omnipotent Father or in psychoanalytic terms as the "security-enhancing selfobject" (Meissner, 2009, p. 216), God is repeatedly created and re-created to satisfy multifarious human need. Because we can necessarily only apprehend (intrapsychic) God-representations that constantly transmute to assuage our strivings and emotional longings, we have no way of apprehending God Himself. Meissner (2009) concluded that

the seemingly inherent contradiction between the concept of God as eternally infinite and changeless and the view of God as immanent, loving, and
acting within the world can be resolved [only] in terms of the symmetrical
tolerance of opposites in the logic of the unconscious.

(Meissner, 2009, p. 217)

Truth is not easily apprehended or acknowledged, either in our relationship with
ourselves or in relation to religion.

What is specific about psychoanalysis with regard to the construction of
history is the fact that, according to Freud, it is necessarily distorted; not
because we lack the necessary information to construct it objectively … but
because there is a more or less unconscious need in us to distort it; our desire
to construct history always involves a distortion … we are always liars, more
or less.

(Ludin, 2009, p. 5)

The same accusation can certainly be levelled against the historical construction of
religion. There is really a very small divide between Freud's assertion that religious
belief is based on wishful thinking and philosophers' and theologians' acceptance
that religious beliefs are based on hope (Pojman, 2003). What is hope other than
wishful thinking?

The other sources of religious knowledge are 'revelation' and the sacred texts,
both palpably flawed and fallible, based as they are on both wish-fulfilment and
projection, on the one hand, and rank human ambition for power on the other.
Recall, for example, the 'revelations' to God's representatives on earth during the
Catholic Inquisitions. Cursory reading of the Bible and the Qur'ān reveals the
imprint of the human hand, replete with inconsistencies, contradictions, precepts
that are contrary to declarations of faith and scientifically unsupportable assertions.
Take as an example the story of the Fall. The original Jewish story of the Fall and
the subsequently embellished Christian version differ in significant ways. The first
account in Genesis makes no reference to Satan, a figure that has loomed large
in every variation of Christianity since the New Testament. Yet in Genesis, there
was only a serpent, an instrument of God sent to tempt His human creations.
Subsequent Christian versions interpret the snake as Satan in concealed form and
all other human folly since as motivated by temptations from Satan (Colman, 1988).
Why do Christian religions need Satan? One possibility is that Satan and the coun-
terbalancing figure of Jesus Christ represent the split in ourselves between good and
evil and the split we enact on others, for example the good and bad mother, until
both aspects of self and other – the 'good' and the 'bad' – can be integrated. Another
related explanation might be that the original concept of God, known as Yahweh,
was as a wrathful, jealous and capricious God. In order to support the propagation
of a more merciful, benevolent God of the Christian texts, the wrath and jealousy

needed another home, which was found in the character of Satan. There are multiple examples of this kind of splitting in the Christian myth – the Deity was split into God (all good) and Satan (all bad); man was split by temptation and disobedience into sinner (unsaved) and repentant (righteous, saved); God split man into His 'chosen people' and the gentiles.

I have yet to see a credible, internally consistent theological argument on any aspect of faith claims. A sad example of the absurd is the work of Swinburne (1992, 1996), who performs complex cognitive gymnastics in his attempt to present a plausible set of propositions, but they fall horribly flat at every turn. In trying to account for the conceptual quagmire of disagreements (e.g., contraception, abortion, status of homosexuals, gay marriage, the role of women in the Church) about purported received ecclesiastical wisdom among those to whom God's word has been revealed, Swinburne (1992) resorts to pitiful assertions that some issues are "not fully open to divine inspiration" (p. 199) or, alternatively, should be viewed as metaphorical messages rather than being taken literally, which is a contradiction of a previous assertion that the Bible is the immutable word of God. Westphal (1998, p. 4) also attempts to defend religion against Freud, accusing Freud of engaging in the "hermeneutics of suspicion". By this, I think he means that Freud has not shown that religious beliefs distort reality; he merely implies it or tricks us into doubt. Westphal assumes that there is an objective reality to be known. Westphal's second criticism of Freud – his claim that religion is the universal obsessional neurosis – can be dismissed on semantic grounds alone. I believe that Freud was simply being literary and colourful in the use of this phrase. The only sound argument is based on the avoidance of the genetic fallacy. Just because religion contains our wishes does not *prima facie* prove that religion is illusory and a distortion of reality.

However, on a test of the logic of the possible explanations for faith, Freud is clearly ahead, despite controversies regarding the historical veracity of his account, the Oedipus complex and the assertion that religion is an obsessional neurosis of the masses. The demand from theists (e.g., Plantinga, 2000) that Freud prove that theism is false is unreasonable. Freud's theory does not pertain whether or not he addresses theistic arguments (e.g., ontological, cosmological, intelligent design), either to disprove them or to find them compatible with the psychoanalytic view of religion. However, if we accept that Freud's view of religion is plausible then theistic arguments can be subsumed under Freud's assertion that they are all examples of wishful thinking. I have already argued that the elements of belief all address a human fear (e.g., fear of death results in the wish for eternal life). Moreover, the demand that Freud produce a theory that is compatible with theism is likewise unreasonable. The burden of proof is clearly the responsibility of theists. Smythe (2011) rightly asserts that science is not required to develop theories for which alternative explanations are logically impossible; *ergo*, nor should Freud. The search for both necessary and sufficient conditions for causality, while possible in the physical sciences, is probably not achievable in the social sciences; *ergo*, we cannot impose such a requirement on Freud.

Freud has demonstrated that theistic beliefs are unlikely to be true, offering the elegantly simple explanation that we believe in God because we want to, and that the wish is so strong that we resist any challenges to the veracity of this belief. In this regard, we need to distinguish between causation and justification of religious beliefs. It is not beyond the realm of human cognition to accept that we hold beliefs that are unlikely to be true. Obviously, according to Freud's theory, this behaviour is another example of wishful thinking. Belief in God has no justification other than that we fervently wish God to be true, and we dread, like Nietzsche, the awful consequences of killing God.

Let us conduct a thought experiment. I ask readers who are believers in a Christian God to respond spontaneously to the same questions posed above with respect to the existence of a Hindu god. Of the thousands of gods in the Hindu pantheon, I will illustrate my point with Ganesha, the god with the head of an elephant, because he is universally worshipped by Hindus, Buddhists and Jainists. He has a detailed ancestry as the son of Shiva, a yoga god of the eternal cycle of creation, and Parvati. Ganesha is considered the "Lord of the Yoga" and all aspects of his idolatrous appearance, including the mouse which he uses for transportation and the ever-present dish of sweets, are linked symbolically to yoga principles. Ganesha is also a god for all seasons – he is a god of wisdom, a protector of knowledge, books and education, a bringer of luck and a remover of obstacles. Believers always consult Ganesha before undertaking any significant activity. His enormous girth symbolizes the universe, thus containing a paradox: earthly delights are not an impediment to spiritual insight. This is called, in the vernacular, having your cake and eating it! Ganesha's mother, Parvati, made him in much the same way that God made Adam, not from a rib but from the dust on her body. There are 90 known manifestations depicted in statues of Ganesha (Jansen, 2002). For example, his dancing pose "reveals the heartbeat of the universe and the underlying rhythm that unites all the existing manifestations" (p. 124). Is Ganesha more or less believable than the Christian God? Would a Christian worship Ganesha? If not, we must argue that the world's one billion Hindus are deluded, which demolishes any consensus arguments that might be invoked to support religious belief.

Colman (1988) offered an olive branch to both religion and psychoanalysis, suggesting that both the story of the Fall (of Adam and Eve) and the psychoanalytic account of infancy may represent versions of the same myth, expressed in terms acceptable to their respective flocks and historical time.

> [They] … are representations of an archetypal experience of 'original loss' necessary for the development of the self.
>
> …
>
> Archetypes may be regarded as inherent capacities, analogous to instincts, which are released or 'triggered' either at certain points in the developmental process or by specific environmental conditions. They contain opposite polarities which, in normal conditions, are mediated by interaction with the

environment. However, where the environment is not 'good enough' ... consciousness is flooded by archetypal images and fantasies in their unmediated, extreme forms. 'Heaven' and 'Hell' are one such pair of opposites which emerge – and are mediated or not – at the point of original loss.

(Colman, 1988, pp. 60 and 64)

To endure, both myths must make sense to an 'adult' self, either through a numinous experience or through the transference relationship with the analyst in psychoanalysis. During World War II, Fromm (1942) observed what he described as "a state of inner tiredness and resignation" (p. 181) in people. He attributed these feelings to "the moral corrosions of modern culture, in which true values go unaffirmed, and meaningless desires are fomented by the all-pervading, psychologically informed methods of advertising and the mass media" (Black, 2006, p. 8) which were put to such 'good' effect by the Nazis and communists. Of course, such techniques pervade Western capitalist cultures, where the senses are relentlessly bombarded through multiple forms of social media with messages to embrace the rank materialism being touted. Fromm argued that the pursuit of such empty goals creates dissatisfaction in those who cannot attain the materialist ideal, or a void within those who can but are not satisfied. Such people are 'ripe for the picking' by fundamentalist religions with their all-embracing arms of authoritarianism and propaganda promising 'specialness' and life beyond the mortal coil.

Different myths may guide us to the same truths; conversely, the same myth may reveal different underlying meanings (truths). Jung called these 'truths' archetypes. The myth of the Fall and the myth of infancy both seek answers, one religious and one secular, to the origin of human suffering, and hence evil. Jacoby (1985) made a similar argument, that is, that man's concept of paradise contains simultaneous grief over its loss because knowledge of paradise presupposes knowledge of its opposite. For those who have had good enough infancies, the opposite might simply be the mundane cares of our life on earth; for those who have not had satisfactory infancies, suffering takes on the character of hell – a relentless, unending, narcissistic wound inflicted by catastrophic loss or deprivation.

Perhaps religion and psychoanalysis represent similar strivings. Freud (1917) drew a parallel between the expulsion from paradise and the infant's separation from its mother, and the struggle to find salvation through religion or greater self-knowledge through psychoanalysis, using their respective tools of prayer or negative attention, and confession of sin or free association in the presence of an accepting other, either priest or analyst, who represents "the embodied supernatural" (Bollas, 1998, p. 31). We seek, either through religion or psychoanalysis, or some other means (e.g., psychedelic drugs), contact with the unconscious, the noumenal, the numinous, communication 'soul to soul' with another with whom we feel deeply attuned. This attainment of such contact, was, for John Keats (1884) "[a]lmost the highest bliss of human-kind, / When to thy haunts two kindred spirits flee". Perhaps one approaches the end of one's analysis as one approaches the end of one's life, hopefully with greater self-awareness, understanding and acceptance but still with a sense of the unknowability of the mystery of life.

Notes

1   A philosophy that asserts that physical processes (senses, neural impulses, chemical reactions) 'cause' mental processes (e.g., consciousness, cognition), that mental events are dependent upon physical processes and have no independent existence outside of these processes.
2   I am always struck by the tendency of critics to hold Freud to a very high standard with respect to the provision of 'proof' for his theories. Indeed, Freud was his own most exacting critic; many of his papers are addressed to an imaginary decrier who forestalls the criticisms he believes are imminent from unsympathetic readers.
3   Reaction formation is a (Freudian) defence mechanism that refers to "the exaggerated and compulsive character of a positive feeling or behaviour (e.g. affection, solicitude) which, by its very exaggeration and compulsivity betrays its very opposite (e.g. hostility, hatred). Freud viewed certain strong expressions of morality, shame and disgust as reaction formations and believed that reaction formation was an especially characteristic defence of obsessional neuroses" (Skelton, 2006).
4   The actual analysis was carried out by Hans's father. Freud supervised and interpreted the father's interactions with Hans.
5   Splitting: Melanie Klein proposed that one's objects (i.e., internalized significant others) are not objectively perceived or understood – they are frequently given exaggeratedly good or bad characteristics (i.e., they become part-objects). Children split their objects so that parental imagos are separately endowed in their child's imaginative play with wholly good and benign qualities and intentions, or wholly bad ones. Thus, splitting refers to the way in which objects come to be separated into their good aspects and their bad part-objects (Hinshelwood, 1991).

7

GROUP PSYCHOLOGY AND THE PSYCHOANALYSIS OF VIOLENCE

The power of the collective: social psychology and group behaviour

> *Certainement qui est en droit de vous rendre absurde est en droit de vous rendre injuste.*
>
> (Truly, he who can make you believe absurdities can make you commit atrocities)
>
> (Voltaire, 1765)

Freud (1913a) "[took] as the basis of [his] whole position the existence of a collective mind, in which mental processes occur just as they do in the mind of an individual" (p. 157). The foundational tenet of psychodynamic group therapy is that psychological development is socially mediated, that the mind and psyche evolve through contact with other people (Bion, 1961; Fonagy & Target, 2002; Stacey, 2003). Another tenet is that intrapsychic (within the individual) processes are observable in the communication and interaction between people (i.e., interpersonally) (Yalom, 1989). The final tenet, sympathetic with systems theory, is that groups possess an inherent structure subject to a unique set of psychological properties (Ashbach & Schermer, 1986; Bion, 1961; Foulkes, 1946). This occurs at the collective level, often unconsciously, and influences both group dynamics and the intrapsychic processes of group members. Freud (1921) explains the power and dynamics of group psychology and its social expression:

> Whoever be the individuals who compose it, however like or unlike be their mode of life, their occupations, their character, or their intelligence, the fact that they have been transformed into a group puts them in possession of a sort of collective mind which makes them feel, think, and act in a manner

quite different from that in which each individual of them would feel, think, and act were he in a state of isolation. There are certain ideas and feelings which do not come into being, or do not transform themselves into acts except in the case of individuals forming a group.

(Freud, 1921, p. 72)

Freud viewed taboos as a form of collective behavioural control that prevented individual members of a group from "gratifying ... repressed desire ... [and to prevent desire being] kindled in all the other members of the community" (Freud, 1913a, p. 72). Similarly, Freud viewed religious collectives as collective neuroses or delusions that spared its members from developing and struggling with their own individual neuroses (Freud, 1927, 1939). Freud also observed that individuals as members of groups, particularly during collective crises such as war, appear to lose their individual intelligence and acquiesce to the collective view which is less well morally and intellectually developed: "when it becomes a question of a number of people, not to say millions, all individual moral acquisitions are obliterated, and only the most primitive, the oldest, the crudest mental attitudes are left" (Freud, 1915, p. 288). Churches are collectives that operate in much the same way as taboos in tribal societies. People subscribe to particular religious or political orientations or doctrines in the way that tribes adhered to taboos, thus feeling themselves absolved of personal responsibility for the ethics and morality of the group to whose tenets they adhere and to the consequences of these tenets when enacted upon their enemies.

In a group every sentiment and act is contagious ... to such a degree that an individual readily sacrifices his personal interest to the collective interest. This is an aptitude very contrary to his nature, and of which a man is scarcely capable, except when he makes part of a group.

(Freud, 1921, p. 75)

Groups thus serve a very important, yet paradoxical, function. They allow us to deny our own base emotions (e.g., envy, jealousy, greed) while simultaneously permitting enactment of those same emotions, even transmuting the attendant feelings of rage and hostility into collective feelings of solidarity that arise from shared actions. Any shame that would accrue to the same acts performed as an individual can thus be abrogated and denied. It is these mechanisms that empower members of groups to disavow individual responsibility and to commit violence against others (Berke, 1996). This process takes many varied forms – tribalism, cultism, nationalism, fanatical patriotism and political and religious fundamentalism – but the same underlying psychological mechanism is apparent in each. The collective amplifies and disinhibits simmering antagonisms stimulated by fear, envy and hate that find a socially sanctioned outlet in collective action. In this way, the needs of the state and the self merge: "[n]ationalistic preoccupations with size (bigness), shape (borders and boundaries), inner content (racial purity) and outer appearance (prestige) mirror narcissistic concerns" (Burke, 1996, p. 338).

This is not to underplay the pervasive and desperate need of us humans to find meaning in our lives and to escape the intolerable idea that life is finite, insignificant and meaningless. The manner in which we engage in this timeless, transcultural quest for the transcendent numinous experience, and the diverse nature of the philosophical and religious doctrines that have emerged in this quest hardly seem limited by our collective imagination, which, at times, appears boundless. There are many current examples of the power of 'god' and 'god-substitute' collectives that remain potent in today's society. For example, "God is not dead to 1.1 billion Roman Catholics" (Todd, 2012, p. ix); evangelical churches are expanding and cults abound. Collective madness (*folie à beaucoup*) and all forms of collective action can occur with and without a belief in God, as long as there is a belief in some entity, whether human or supernatural, and the willingness of followers to submit to its doctrines and authority. Recall, for example, Jonestown and the cult of the People's Temple whose leader, Jim Jones, convinced 918 people to commit 'revolutionary suicide' by cyanide poisoning. God was evidently expunged by the doctrine of 'apostolic socialism' to which Jones subscribed and of which he assumed leadership.

Attachment theory (Bowlby, 1988) may shed light on the seeming pervasiveness of this phenomenon. In times of stress, uncertainty, loss and grief, people seek out their attachment figures for comfort and security. Figures who respond appropriately to the proximity-seeking of their friend or relative acquire the status of a secure base, from which the person can explore their options, regulate their distress and recover their psychological equilibrium. For some people, gods or spirits can simulate the processes observed in human attachment, as was evident in Christoph Haizmann and Daniel Schreber, who were discussed in Chapter 5. Relocating this attachment-seeking behaviour into religious contexts, we can see that people's need for a secure base is expressed in church-going and proximity-seeking to icons, who represent the idealized mother (the Virgin Mary), moral exemplars (Jesus and the saints) (Kirkpatrick, 2005) and the grandiose, narcissistic leaders of nations, to whom we shall now turn our attention.

The source of 'power' in the leader of the collective

[N]ations still obey their passions far more readily than their interests.

(Freud, 1915, p. 288)

Collectives have leaders. The mythology of the leader as hero, depicted in the writings of Heraclitus, Socrates and Plato, has found expression in all subsequent eras and cultures. Most of the religions of the world have a quintessential hero or prophet at the helm, for instance, Jesus, Buddha, Muhammad and the Dalai Lama. The intriguing question for students of human nature is what constitutes leadership quality, given the apparently vastly different characteristics of the world's leaders. One prominent theory is that most leaders possess some features in common, including narcissism, charisma and psychopathy. Narcissism, like Jung's archetypes, has both a bright and dark (shadow) side. Dark-sided narcissism, also called malignant narcissism, abounds in many of the world's leaders, both past and present. Hitler and Stalin were clearly malignant narcissists, who shared the following characteristics: interpersonal dominance, power-hunger, fearlessness, shallow charisma, shameless self-promotion, overconfidence, unilateral decision-making, deceit and pervasive disregard for ethical conduct, failure to learn from mistakes (or indeed to admit to mistakes) and grandiose self-interest. These characteristics are also descriptors of psychopathy and sociopathy (Watts et al., 2013). Recent research shows that narcissists are more successful at achieving positions of leadership, but those very high in narcissism do not make the best leaders because of their exploitative and tyrannical characteristics. Those low in narcissism do not fare well as leaders, either, because they may appear timid and indecisive; people with a moderate degree of narcissism make the best leaders because they balance self-confidence with a consultative style (Grijalva, Harms, Newman, Fraley & Gaddis, 2014).

Some narcissists who rise to high office are also intellectually gifted, which makes them good tacticians, such tactics usually serving self-interest. Robert Mugabe is a good example. Raised Roman Catholic and educated by the Jesuits, Mugabe trained as a teacher, and earned bachelor's and master's degrees in science and bachelor's and master's degrees in law from the University of London. Before he became corrupted by power, he was hailed as the champion of the black African struggle against white minority rule. He has the unusual distinction of having been awarded perhaps the largest number of titles, honours and honorary degrees internationally, and the ignominy of having them gradually withdrawn in response to his appalling abuse of human rights and disregard for the democratic process in Zimbabwe.

I put this question to four psychoanalysts in my book, *From Id to Intersubjectivity: Talking about the Talking Cure with Master Clinicians* (Kenny, 2014):

> Can you comment on how … people like Adolf Hitler, Joseph Stalin, Mao Tse Tung, Pol Pot, Papa Doc, Idi Amin, Muammar Gaddafi, Saddam Hussein – the list appears distressingly endless – rise to power and destroy their own people? How does that happen, and why does it happen repeatedly?

and received the following responses, first from Dr Ron Spielman:

> It's a frightening combination of an individual's powerful need to dominate and serve his own interests, and the population's need to be led by no matter how bad a father. A strong father is something unconsciously desired … [we] yearn for this – but … that … father is enacting some of the worst of our aggressions and destructiveness and hatreds and murderousness for us.
>
> (Kenny, 2014, pp. 134–5)

and this from Professor Allan Abbass:

> I think that among several psychosocial factors, unconscious rage and guilt
> drive much of the self-destructive and other-destructive conduct we see in
> the world today. I've seen many people go from harming to helping others
> when they have better anxiety tolerance and a better regard for themselves
> through working through underlying rage and guilt. It is obvious to me that
> this is a key factor.
>
> (Kenny, 2014, p. 251)

Spielman argued that institutions such as the Church and the armed forces serve the same function as strong leaders and that unless we have a sufficient amount of the right care early in life that allows us to develop our own minds, we will become and "remain vulnerable to group process, peer group pressure, party politics and cults" (p. 135). Haslam, Reicher and Platow (2011) offer a view of leadership that echoes Spielman. Effective leadership, they argue, does not emanate from psychological uniqueness, embodied in the notion of the 'great man' whose task is to motivate the passive or disillusioned masses to follow him, but from a leader's capacity to embody and promote beliefs that they share with others. Leaders are successful when their followers perceive themselves to be joined with them in shared goals; that is, a leader must be 'one of us' (Haslam et al., 2011, p. 2).

Leadership is more complex than a simplistic 'cult of personality' psychology, or being in the right place at the right time with the right message. It is about the capacity of leaders to identify with their followers as 'we'. The leader's actions become our actions, symbolizing what we would do if the positions were reversed. In this way, the leader assumes an archetypal quality and becomes the embodiment of a collective will. However, leadership entails more than the embodiment of shared goals and aspirations. As Spielman intimated, leaders also embody and act out our oft-denied murderous rage, which has its source in our feelings of envy, jealousy and greed. These feelings are played out at all levels of human intercourse, from the dyadic (e.g., between parent–child, siblings, husband–wife) to the macrocosm of international relations. These feelings arise because at some point early in development, children learn that they must relinquish at least some of their cherished individual wishes and fantasies (e.g., to have mother all to oneself and not having to share her with one's siblings) and embrace and adopt the collective principles of equity and fair play, which entail, paradoxically, the demand that there will be no favourites. Freud (1921) concluded that the emergence of *Gemeingeist* (lit. group spirit) has its origins in our primitive narcissistic envy that had to, out of necessity, be transmuted into a shared demand for equality and social justice. It is therefore not surprising that God's playing favourites with the Jews, His 'chosen people', has brought upon them the envious wrath of the rest of the world!

Hitler's anti-Semitism took root because he tapped into the anti-Semitism of the German people that dated at least as far back as the Reformation in the sixteenth century, when Martin Luther, a man filled with superstition, fear and hatred, particularly of the Jews, developed a strategy for annihilating them that Hitler implemented 400 years later. The difficult years between the two world wars provided fertile ground for Hitler's "willing executioners" (Goldhagen, 1996) to move from expressed hatred to the enactment of that hatred, at a time when the collective need for a heroic saviour to rescue them from their humiliation after World War I and the economic hardships that followed were at their height (Abel, 1986).

The quasi-numinous significance attached to 'archetypal' heroes, saviours or ideological figures such as Adolf Hitler (national socialism), Joseph Stalin (Marxism), Mao Zedong (communism), Robert Mugabe (one-party post-colonial politics) and Idi Amin (power by military coup) was acquired, not on the basis of their heroic nature or magnetic personalities but on the basis of the archetypal projection of rage, hate and envy by the collectives who followed them, in the name of their ideologies. These ideologies were, in effect, symbolic equivalents of religious doctrines, which also carried extreme penalties for dissenters, in the manner of the Church of the Middle Ages. They also take on the character Freud's *idées fixes* and paranoid delusions that are resistant to any reality-based challenge to their validity. Freud's (1921) depiction of the 'herd instinct' found its perfect embodiment in Nazi Germany under Adolf Hitler. Although the party machinery (i.e., the collective) performed the atrocities, in the case of Nazi Germany, against the 'enemies of the Nazi state' – the Jews, gypsies, mentally ill and physically and intellectually impaired – "behind the faceless mandarins and impenetrable group processes, there lies personal praxis ... the specific actions of ... aggrandizing, hate-filled personalities" (Berke, 1996, p. 336).

Berke (1996) draws a close parallel between rampant nationalism at the level of the state and malignant narcissism in the individual. Both involve the striving to implement a crazy ideology, a pathological self-absorption and hubris, and murderous aggression against those who have spawned their envy and rage. The history of nations is littered with the devastating outcomes of such processes. Nationalism has supported, indeed sanctioned unspeakable acts of mass murder.[1] Two brief examples will illustrate the arguments propagated here, both exemplars of a leader's madness enacted by an obedient collective (army) on a terrifyingly large scale.

Amongst many possible examples, I have chosen Cambodia under Pol Pot and Ukraine under Joseph Stalin. In the case of Cambodia, it took only four years (1975–9) for the communist Khmer Rouge to destroy the country and kill between 2.5 and 3 million of its citizens through forced relocation from cities to farms, deliberate starvation, unspeakable acts of torture and enforced overwork to the point of death. Intellectuals, those educated in Western universities, suspected capitalists and non-ethnic Cambodians, particularly the Chinese and Vietnamese, were taken out to what became known as the 'killing fields' and hacked to death with machetes. Books were burned, banks and hospitals were closed. Religion was forbidden and any Buddhists, Christians or Muslims who remained adherent were alike summarily massacred (Picq, 1989). Children whose parents were thought to be tainted with capitalism were removed to re-education camps, indoctrinated with communism and taught how to torture using animals. After training, children were assigned leadership roles in tortures and executions (Jackson, 1992).

Most people have heard of the Holocaust, a systematic attempt by Hitler to eliminate the world's Jewish population, and the atrocities that this word embodies. Fewer know about the Holodomor (Голодомор), a genocidal famine engineered by the Soviets under Stalin against the Ukrainian people between 1932 and 1933, whose aim was to punish farmers who resisted collectivization, to destroy the nation of the Ukraine and forever suppress any hope the people harboured for a country free from Stalinist rule (Dolot, 1985). A communist leader at the time (1934) explained the reason for the Holodomor: "Famine in Ukraine *was brought on* to decrease the number of Ukrainians, replace the dead with people from other parts of the USSR, and thereby to kill the slightest thought of any Ukrainian independence" (my italics) (in Danilov et al., 2004, vol. 3, bk. 2. p. 572) because Stalin was intent upon securing a unified Russian nation under his supreme command. Stalin was obsessed with his need for absolute control over the populace and the mechanism by which he gained control over the Ukrainians was forced collectivization through terror tactics, 'divide and conquer' ploys amongst different groups of peasants (e.g., deportation and execution of the Kulaks) and confiscation of their land and harvests, which resulted in mass starvation. By 1933, 25,000 people were dying of hunger every day. One quarter of Ukraine's population of around 10 million people perished within the two-year period of the Holodomor. Subsequently, there was vehement denial both within the Soviet Union and in the West that a famine had occurred. The West's denial allowed them to remain passive in the face of Stalin's genocidal madness because it suited their economic interdependence with the USSR to do so.

How do we begin to understand these atrocities and the leaders and followers who perpetrated them? The historian Paul Johnson (1987) observed that men like Hitler and Stalin are guided by "personal prejudices of the crudest kind and by their own arbitrary visions" (p. 376). Pol Pot wanted a self-sufficient agrarian communist economy, free of Western influence; Hitler wanted an ever-expanding, racially pure Aryan nation, cleansed of Slavs, Jews, gypsies and the infirm; and Stalin wanted supreme dominion over a subjugated republic of disparate nations. All voraciously pursued power and revenge by manipulating the people into the collective pursuit of a hateful form of nationalism, founded on "fanatical patriotism, mass identification with narrow, excessive, unreasoning, boastful beliefs in the right and might of one's country over others, all in order to annihilate envious hungers and conditions of consuming impotenc[e] … and terrible fragility" (Berke, 1996, pp. 338, 340). These atrocities constitute an extreme collectivized expression of envious self-assertion that over-values self (one's nation or race) and devalues others (other nations and races). Hitler tapped into the German myth, nowhere better expressed than in Wagner's operas, and taken up in *Mein Kampf,* that Germans were the 'chosen people' and that Aryans were superior to all other races. How enraged he must have felt that he had competition for this title from the Jews, who were a cultured and successful people. His envy was akin to a malignant form of sibling rivalry that precedes intra-familial homicide in families consumed by envy and rage.

Group processes

> We need to know about the social conditions which have educated original
> activities into definite and significant dispositions before we can discuss the
> psychological element in society. This is the true meaning of social psych-
> ology. ... Native human nature supplies the raw materials but custom fur-
> nishes the machinery and the designs. ... Man is a creature of habit not of
> reason nor yet of instinct.
>
> (Dewey, 1922, p. 125)

In this section, I will discuss five iconic experiments in social psychology that elucidate some of the powerful dynamics of group processes and which show how individuals abandon their personal ethics to conform to group norms and expectations.
This will be followed by a discussion of cultic phenomena, with special reference
to Christian and Islamic fundamentalism.

Stanley Milgram: a study of obedience

In the 1960s, Stanley Milgram (1963, 1965a,b, 1974) conducted a series of experiments to test the limits of obedience to authority, including what people would
do in a situation in which they were instructed to physically harm, possibly to the
point of death, a complete stranger, on the basis that the person had been instructed
to do so by a prestigious authority figure. Milgram wanted to understand how
otherwise normal individuals could engage in horrific acts such as the genocide
of the Armenian population by the Ottoman government in 1915, and the Jewish
people during World War II.

Milgram's participants were informed that the study was investigating memory
acquisition. Pairs of participants were assigned to the roles of teacher and learner.
Teachers were seated in one room, learners in another. Learners, unbeknown to
the 'teachers', were confederates of the researcher. The teacher was instructed to
deliver electric shocks of increasing voltage whenever the learner made an error in
the memory task. As the voltage increased to a maximum of 450V, and as the cries
of pain and anguish increased in the learning room, some of the 'teachers' expressed
concern and exhibited distress about the harm that such high voltage would inflict
on the learner. However, they were encouraged to continue with the task, with the
experimenter becoming increasingly insistent if the teacher continued to express
reluctance. Milgram reported that 62.5 per cent of 'teacher' participants completed
the experiment – that is, inflicting the highest-voltage electric shock and conse-
quently believing that they had delivered a potentially fatal electric shock to the
learner. (In reality, there was no electric shock; confederates were trained by the
experimenter to respond as if they were receiving electric shocks.) These studies were recently replicated, with some adjustments to the method in order to
meet ethical standards (Burger, 2009). Results showed that rates and patterns of

obedience were only slightly lower than those found by Milgram 50 years earlier. Men and women demonstrated equal rates of obedience.

Milgram conducted this basic experiment with a number of variations. In one (1965a), there were two teachers – one who administered the memory task (a confederate) and one who administered the electric shocks (genuine participant). If the genuine participant was the sole teacher, s/he was much more likely to complete the experiment. If the confederate refused to continue, the genuine participant was much more likely to do the same, that is, was more likely to defy the authority figure of the researcher. Reactions of genuine participants were also influenced by experimenter instructions. For example, the representation of defiance of authority as normative produced decreased obedience.

There has been much subsequent debate about how to interpret the results from Milgram's experiments. Were participants blindly obeying orders (i.e., subjugated to authority) or were they identifying with a leader and a cause that rendered them able to inflict harm (and do what under any other circumstance they would consider to be wrong) because they believed in the righteousness of the 'bigger' cause? Neville and Reicher (2013) argued that the divide between ordinary people and evil psychopaths is much narrower than we would like to believe, because evil acts are potentiated by circumstance. Milgram showed this by varying different parameters in the basic paradigm. For example, Milgram sometimes issued orders in an authoritarian way to urge reluctant participants to continue (e.g., "You have no choice, you must go on"). For others, he asserted the scientific value of the experiment and that the participants would be contributing to knowledge if they completed the experiment. Many more participants discontinued in the former than the latter condition. If the scientist stood in the room dressed in a white coat, 65 per cent of participants continued to deliver what they believed to be lethal doses of electric shock to learners. These variations in compliance suggest that people do not act like 'zombies' (i.e., blindly obey) in relation to authority. However, they are clearly in conflict between two tendencies – the first to comply with authority and the second to help the 'victim'. The question becomes, "How do people decide?" In a reanalysis of Milgram's data, Haslam et al. (2011) found that one determining feature was the degree to which participants identified with the authority figure as a scientist who was working for scientific advancement. If the experimenter was not represented as a scientist, compliance was much lower. If there were two experimenters present who argued, compliance also became lower. Another influencing factor was the degree to which identification with the 'learner' was encouraged or discouraged. If the 'learner' was in another room, compliance was higher because the harm being inflicted was at a distance. This explains why people are not sympathetic to asylum seekers. Their pain and loss have occurred at a distance and is hidden from immediate sight, making it easier to villainize those seeking to take from the incumbents.

One of the key findings of these and other similar subsequent studies is that people will inflict harm, not because they are unaware of doing wrong, but because they believe in the value and rightness of the higher cause – it becomes a means–end argument in which the means justifies the end. Haslam et al. argued that the people we should most fear are not 'zombies' – those who blindly obey their authority figures – but zealots, who are committed to ignoble causes and who perversely justify their actions in terms of their cause. Osama bin Laden springs immediately to mind.

Albert Bandura's Bobo doll experiment: a study of aggression

Albert Bandura (1977) was a social psychologist who wanted to understand the origins of aggressive behaviour in very young children, in particular, whether aggression is learnt through the processes of observation and modelling as well as through direct reward for aggressive behaviour. To interrogate this question, Bandura, Ross and Ross (1961) developed the Bobo doll experiment. This involved 72 children, aged between three and six years, who were attending a university child care centre. Children were divided into groups, one of which was exposed to an adult model interacting aggressively with the Bobo doll – hitting, punching and kicking the doll, with these acts being accompanied by aggressive verbalizations – while the other group observed an adult model interact in a non-aggressive, socially appropriate manner towards the Bobo doll. Bandura predicted that children who observed an adult behaving aggressively would be more likely to act aggressively towards the Bobo doll even when the adult model was not present. The groups were subdivided by sex, so that Bandura could ascertain whether children were more likely to imitate a same-sex model. The children were then removed into a time-out situation for 10 minutes to increase their frustration, after which they were taken to a playroom containing both 'aggressive' and 'non-aggressive' toys as well as the Bobo doll, where they played for 20 minutes while being observed by expert raters through a one-way screen. Results indicated that children who were exposed to the aggressive model imitated the aggressive behaviour they had observed even in the absence of the adult whom they had witnessed behaving aggressively. This phenomenon is called delayed imitation. Children in the non-aggressive group actually behaved less aggressively than those in a control group who had no exposure to either an aggressive or non-aggressive adult model. Boys were sensitive to the sex of the model. Boys observing an aggressive male model were more aggressive than those observing an aggressive female model. Boys who had observed an opposite-sex model behave non-aggressively were more likely than those in the control group to engage in violence. Further, boys were more likely to imitate the physical acts of violence, while girls were more likely to imitate the verbally aggressive statements that accompanied the violent acts. Overall, boys behaved more aggressively than girls. In a subsequent study, Bandura (1965) showed that these effects were enhanced or diminished depending on whether the adult model was seen to be rewarded for their aggressive or non-aggressive behaviours. Taken together, these studies showed unequivocally that observation and imitation are powerful modes for the social transmission of behaviour. It is only a small step to understand how the Bobo doll becomes the infidel for newly recruited jihadists.

Philip Zimbardo: the Stanford prison experiment

Philip Zimbardo, a former classmate of Stanley Milgram, expanded on Milgram's work in the prison setting. He and his colleagues (Haney, Banks & Zimbardo, 1973) wanted to understand how behaviour changes if one becomes either a prisoner or a prison guard in a simulated prison environment. In broader terms, this was an investigation into the situational determinants of behaviour, with the prison situation the exemplar in this study. This experiment is highly significant in helping us to understand what Zimbardo (2007) later called the 'Lucifer effect', which is the observation that good people are capable of doing very bad things under certain circumstances. In the course of a six-day experiment (originally designed as a two-week experiment) at Stanford University, researchers set up a simulated prison, comprising three standard-size prison cells housing three prisoners each, a 'solitary confinement' room and a prison yard. They selected 24 from a group of 70 volunteer, white, male undergraduate students who met inclusion criteria (no criminal record, psychologically and physically healthy). Some had been conscientious objectors to the Vietnam War. Volunteers were randomly assigned to become a prisoner or a prison guard. Prisoners lived in (i.e., spent 24 hours per day for the duration of the experiment in the simulated prison). Prison guards worked in three-person teams for eight-hour shifts, after which they resumed their normal outside life until rostered onto their next shift. The behaviour of both groups was video-recorded. The experiment had to be curtailed because the prison guards became hostile, abusive and dehumanizing towards prisoners and prisoners became initially stressed and anxious and then depressed and passive. The guards were most abusive at night, because they thought there was less chance of detection (Haney & Zimbardo, 1998). Of great import, Philip Zimbardo, who acted as the prison warden, became desensitized to the abusive behaviour of the prison guards. His graduate student raised the alarm, expressing grave concern about the ethics of continuing the experiment. This experiment demonstrated how power and authority can corrupt normally decent, moral human beings. Today, an experiment of this nature would not pass an Ethics Committee, so it cannot be replicated. Sadly, though, we have real-world examples of this process being played out, for example, in the Guantanamo Bay and Abu Ghraib prisons and, more recently, in refugee detention centres.

The shocking realization emanating from this and similar subsequent experiments was how readily situational factors can undermine a lifetime of prosocial socialization training, especially in situations that institutionalize people. Paradoxically, the worse prisoners were treated by the guards, the more prisoners expressed their intention to harm others, a process known as identification with the aggressor (Ferenczi, 1933; A. Freud, 1936). This can occur when people are overwhelmed by inescapable threat, in a bid to survive. The threat can be extreme, as experienced by people who have been kidnapped or mistreated in prison or as a member of a cult, but also is attendant upon less dire circumstances that include emotional abuse, abandonment, isolation or subjugation (Frankel, 2002).

Haney and colleagues (1973) concluded that a 'pathological' situation and not pathological individuals was responsible for the dramatic changes in the behaviour of both prison guards and prisoners. This study has practical implications for understanding how commission of crime can be situationally determined and how prisons are not institutions conducive to rehabilitation. On the global stage, this study helps us to understand how power corrupts leaders. Robert Mugabe, for example, was lauded as a great reformer when he first took power in Zimbabwe; he is now considered a monster. Power has corrupted him completely to the point where, like Philip Zimbardo, he is incapable of the type of self-reflection that would allow him to see his behaviour in the light of those whose lives he has irreparably damaged or destroyed.

Solomon Asch: conformity

Another social psychology experiment is pertinent to our current discussion and may assist us to understand why billions of people subscribe to religion or engage in other conformist behaviour within a group that they would otherwise not perform as an individual. I am referring to Solomon Asch's (1956) conformity experiments. Conformity is a form of social pressure that describes a behavioural tendency to comply with the implicit rules of a group to which an individual belongs, even if such norms are contrary to one's own beliefs. Asch set up an experiment in which participants were asked to judge the length of lines. One genuine participant was included in a group of eight, the other seven of whom were experimenter confederates. At the beginning of the experiment, each participant (male college students) was asked individually to state aloud to the group which line on one card matched the length of one of three lines on a second card. In 12 of 18 trials, confederates deliberately chose the wrong line. One third of the participants conformed to the majority's clearly incorrect answer; 75 per cent conformed on at least one trial, while 25 per cent never conformed. By comparison, in a control where there were no confederates and the participant was tested individually, wrong answers occurred less than 1 per cent of the time. A number of variables influenced the degree of conformity; one or two confederates had almost no effect, while three or more dramatically increased conformity. When one confederate gave the correct answer, the participant was less likely to conform to the group, because he had an ally.

During debriefing, most of the participants reported that they knew that they were choosing the incorrect answer but decided to conform to the group to avoid possible conflict, ridicule or exclusion from the group. Asch concluded that three main influences on conformity were operating – normative influence (wanting to fit in with the group), informational influence (believing that others know more than you, particularly if they have high status) and social support (having an ally in the group).

In a re-examination of Asch's studies, Bond and Smith (1996) found that conformity, while still present, has decreased since the 1950s. However, when conformity is assessed in a cultural context, within countries that are either individualistic or collectivist, they found that collectivist countries showed much higher levels of conformity than individualistic countries.

Irving Janis: groupthink

Groupthink, a term coined by social psychologist Irving Janis (1972), is an extreme form of conformity in which people are prepared to keep the peace at all costs. It tends to occur more in homogeneous groups, when a powerful and charismatic group leader is insistent on the preferred course of action, when the group is under severe stress, where significant moral dilemmas are part of the decision matrix and where objective outside experts are not called upon. The consequences of groupthink include the illusion of invulnerability, collective rationalization, stereotyping of 'out'-groups, self-censorship, belief in the inherent morality of the group, poor information search, incomplete survey of alternatives, failure to appraise the risks of the preferred solution, selective information processing and conflation of ethics and expedience (Turner & Pratkanis, 1998). Polarizing good (us) and evil (them) relieves groupthinkers of feelings of shame and guilt, particularly if the group decision violates their personal moral code (Janis, 1972). Groupthink provides one level of explanation for actual or potential political and military catastrophes that include Pearl Harbor, Nazi Germany's decision to invade the USSR in 1941, the Bay of Pigs, Watergate, the escalation of the war in Vietnam and Israel's lack of preparedness for the 1973 war (Turner & Pratkanis, 1998).

You will be able to discern all of these social psychological processes in cults, discussed below, and in fundamentalist organizations of all kinds, to be discussed in Chapter 8.

Cultic phenomena

A cult "is a form of worship with specific rites and ceremonies in which excessive devotion is paid to a particular person or belief system, creating a closed group environment, everything within which is deemed good and everything outside bad" (Allen, 2007, p. 100). As you read this section, it would helpful to keep in mind that a cult is an 'institution' similar to a prison and the factors that applied in the Stanford prison experiment may also apply within cults. A good example of a cult is Wahhabism, a precursor of Islamic fundamentalism. It was characterized by unquestioning belief in one man's reading of the Qur'ān; absolute devotion to the leader (who was both the religious and military supremo); 'us and them' mentality; a belief in millenarianism (the end of the world is imminent, at which time Islam will triumph); acceptance of *jihad*[2] as one's sacred duty; recruitment of vulnerable young men, isolating them and subjecting them to long periods of religious indoctrination whose aim is the attainment of the status of *shahid* (martyr), the end goal of all *jihadi* (Allen, 2007).

Cults are not just the province of developing, war-torn or fundamentalist countries. Langone (2001) estimated that between 2 and 5 million Americans have been involved in cults. Cults attempt to sever family and other social ties in order to attach the new member to the cult. For this reason, cultic language is often steeped in familial terms; the cult leader becomes the true father to his cult family. For example, the Reverend Sun Myung Moon, founder of the Unification Church, referred to himself and his wife as the 'True Father' and 'True Mother' (Whitsett & Kent, 2003). Another cult called itself 'The Family' (Kent, 1994). Cult members often have their names changed as a further strategy to sever their former ties and to disconnect them from their pre-cult lives. Individuality and independence are forbidden and violations of those wishing to retain their own mind are often severely punished. Induction often involves rituals of denigration, public confession, purification and intensive indoctrination, methods used in communist China to break the spirit of the 'bourgeois' and 'capitalists'. These and other methods are used to resocialize new members into cultic norms, which Davis (2000) described as an "ethic of radical obedience" (p. 249). Cults are a little like human psyches; they divide the world into good (cult) and evil (non-cult), a process that involves the psychic defence of splitting, discussed elsewhere. Cults also evince other psychopathology, including primitive narcissism and grandiosity, cult members perceive themselves above or outside social norms, laws or any sanctions imposed from without. Cult members are answerable only to the cult leader, who is the embodiment of a deified higher authority, and who is the final arbiter on questions of morality.

Many cults have an apocalyptic narrative at their core, that is, a vision of a final reckoning, a monumental battle between the forces of good and evil, a belief that cult members' lives are irrevocably set on a path of either self-destruction, in which the cult must be destroyed, or conflagration, in which all others except the cult will be destroyed. The Jonestown and Waco cults are examples. Such cults share this apocalyptic vision with historical movements and nationalistic 'religions', in particular, fundamentalist and terrorist organizations. Stolorow (2007) argued that this 'resurrective' ideology, and its attendant rhetoric of evil, is both an attempt to retreat to and retrieve an earlier, less problematic existence before trauma shattered innocence and a naïve belief in an ordered and meaningful existence.

Cults also evince the quality of Manichaeism – an ancient religious philosophy originating in Persian-controlled Mesopotamia (Brown, 1969) – that defines movements in terms only of good and evil, and which simplistically reduces complex issues into these basic terms. As a political philosophy, it shares with Tajfel's (1978) theory an uncontroversial division between one's own virtuous 'in'-group and the other's evil 'out'-group. For example, Ronald Reagan described the USSR as the "evil empire", with the implication that the USA was the virtuous empire. The post 9/11 rhetoric in America also had this Manichaeistic quality. President George

Bush told American citizens that they could take only one of two positions – for or against the war on terror. Bush was seeking a mandate from the populace for the employment of all means, including violence and terrorism, to apprehend those who were responsible for inflicting a catastrophic rent in the fabric of American society, exposing its vulnerable underbelly, its humiliation over an attack on its own soil and shame at having been caught unprepared. Abu Ghraib and Guantanamo Bay were products of this rhetoric, inflicting upon selected offenders or scapegoats (when genuine offenders such as Osama bin Laden could not be apprehended) the same rent in their psyches, humiliation and shame for which the American government, rightly or wrongly, held them responsible.

The psychoanalysis of violence

> I call revolution the conversion of all hearts and the raising of all hands on behalf of the honour of the free man, the free State which belongs to no master, but which is itself public being, which belongs only to itself.
>
> (Marx, 1843, p. 558)

At what point does violent rhetoric transmute into violent action? To understand the triggers, we must understand the "symbolic and emotional logic that underlies ritualized acts of religious and political violence that otherwise seem senseless and irrational" (Gorski & Türkmen-Dervişoğlu, 2013, p. 199), in much the same way that we needed to understand what motivated the psychotic delusions and hallucinations in Christoph Haizmann and Daniel Schreber in order to render them comprehensible.

To understand violence, we must examine it from multiple perspectives at both the personal (individual) and collective (group) levels. Without this dual perspective, we can never understand why some people become unthinking adherents of cults, sects or social or political movements or causes that promote and reinforce violence, while others resist such participation. The aim of this section is to explore the factors that potentiate participation in violent acts upon individuals, social or cultural groups or countries, first by exploring the particular experiences of individuals and then by showing how specific individual psychologies fit hand-in-glove with groups espousing violent solutions to conflict.

Origins of interpersonal violence

One of the ideal outcomes of development is the capacity to mentalize, that is, to understand that I and others have minds with feelings and thoughts that are connected in some way with external reality (Fonagy & Target, 1996a,b). In the course of development, the child initially believes that there is an exact correspondence between inner and outer reality, that is, they operate from the stance of 'psychic equivalence' in which thoughts have equal weight with actions. This is why young children believe that the monsters of their nightmares are actual monsters that need to be chased from their bedrooms in the dead of night. The other developmental cognitive process that occurs on the road to mentalization is 'pretend mode', which is a function opposite to psychic equivalence. In pretend mode, the child believes that his/her thoughts and feelings have no impact on external reality. These two modes are mirror images – psychic equivalence is too real and pretend mode is too unreal. Both are divorced from the real world and the function of the ego. These modes are developmental processes that precede the capacity for reflection and mentalization, that is, the understanding that thoughts and feelings are mental states that might or might not have an impact on the real world (Bateman & Fonagy, 2004).

The capacity to mentalize grows out of children's primary attachment relationships, through which they learn that internal experiences and affect states are meaningful to their parents, who are able to respond appropriately to soothe, play with or feed their child. When the child is deprived of such a relationship, s/he fails to develop a sense of an agentic self, a deficit commonly identified in violent individuals. This failure creates a feeling of profound neediness and inability to progress one's cognitive and social development past psychic equivalence and pretend mode. Such individuals are incapable of distinguishing fantasy from reality, and psychic from physical reality (Fonagy & Target, 1997; Freud, 1911b).

Psychological trauma (i.e., physical, sexual and emotional abuse such as repeated misattunement, denigration or humiliation) is a significant precursor of violent behaviour (Johnson, Cohen, Brown, Smailes & Bernstein, 1999). If such trauma is perpetrated on young children by an attachment figure, children will remain mired in these early forms of cognitive processing and will fail to develop the capacity for mentalization. A failure of mentalization includes a failure to mentalize one's own emotions, so these remain unprocessed and often terrifying. One such emotion is murderous rage engendered out of the profound narcissistic injury experienced when a child has been chronically misunderstood, abused, abandoned or humiliated. Because such feelings are experienced as alien to the self, the individual evacuates these feelings by projecting them into the environment, into others or into their interpretation of situations. The other psychological process that occurs in those who have been abused is identification with the aggressor (abuser) (Ferenczi, 1933; A. Freud, 1936), in order to develop or restore a sense of personal control over one's thoughts and behaviours and the external environment. This process is perhaps close to how the Palestinians in the Middle East are currently feeling, and may assist us to explain suicide bombing, which I discuss in the final chapter of this book.

Fonagy (2001) argues that there are three processes that link violence to a failure of the development of the capacity for mentalization. First, there is a failure to make the link between action and intention, due to the failure to develop a sense of agency. In fact, the major religions discourage the development of a sense of autonomy and agency in its followers. Pious Muslims, for example, will intone the words *in shā Allāh* ('if Allah wills') prior to enacting any personal intention in recognition that God is at the controls of one's life and the actor is merely a puppet in the hands of the divine mover (Robinson, 2003). Second, there is incapacity to predict or appreciate the possible consequences of one's behaviour. Third, feelings and thoughts are often not felt to be real or meaningful; they can be repudiated, dissociated and changed, thereby allowing violent perpetrators to reinterpret their violent acts as justified and acceptable.

While it is important that we understand the antecedents of personal violence, that is, the processes or deficits within the individual that potentiate the enactment of a taboo, we also need to view violence from other perspectives, including the social, cultural, ethnic, political and economic, that come into play when violence erupts between groups. It is to these collective factors to which we will now turn our attention.

Religious-nationalist violence

> Monotheism … this rigid consequence of the doctrine of one normal human type – the faith in one normal god beside whom there are only pseudo-gods – was perhaps the greatest danger that has yet confronted humanity.
>
> (Nietzsche, 1882, p. 144)

Religious nationalism is a social movement that claims to speak for the nation which is, itself, defined in religious terms (Rieffer, 2003). In the past 40–50 years, there has been a catastrophic upsurge in global violence that has a religious-nationalist-ethnic origin that exceeds most other periods in history (Fox, 2004). What factors can account for this appalling state of affairs? Gorski and Türkmen-Dervişoğlu (2013) argue that this is a complex question that cannot be adequately answered by unitary theories, whether macro-cultural or micro-rationalist, that explain ethno-religious violence in terms of "greed, grievance and guns" (p. 194), because both theories fail to take account of the symbolic meaning of violence.

Historically, nationalism emerged as part of the modernist project, which was underpinned by secularization, such that nationalism was perceived to be an 'enlightened' replacement for religion. The causes of the rise in religious nationalism in recent times have variously been attributed to the collapse of communism in Russian and Eastern Europe, the failure of secularism, as a reaction against colonialism (e.g., Buddhist, Hindu, Islamic and Sikh nationalism), disillusionment with Western secular democracies, the encroachment of Western secularization through globalization or the search for ontological security in an unstable, uncertain world (Gorski & Türkmen-Dervişoğlu, 2013). Others have argued that the "Judeo-Christian discourse of chosen peoples and elect nations" has provided the "cultural template for Western nationalism" (Gorski & Türkmen-Dervişoğlu, 2013, p. 195) and, hence, that religion has exerted a fundamental influence on the formation of nation states throughout history, with other states searching for their own discourses (Smith, 2003).

The language of recent nationalist movements has often been couched in religious terms. For example, Poland has been depicted as the "Christ of Nations", resurrected from the dead after communism (Zubrzycki, 2006); Serbia has taken on the identity of a "the crucified nation" and Moscow that of the "third Rome" (Gorski & Türkmen-Dervişoğlu, 2013, p. 195). Parallel and stronger religious identity formation has occurred in the East – in Israel, Palestine, Saudi Arabia, Iran and Pakistan, for example. Friedland (2001) notes that unlike the Christian New Testament, the religious works from the East, such as the Qur'ān and the Torah, not only prescribe individual behaviour and the nature of the relationship that individuals must have with God, but also have a socio-political dimension addressing how believers must live and act together in community. The impact of local pressures, cultures and histories must not be understated in our attempts to understand the particular expressions of religion in these religious nations. The 'Christianities' of the African nations look vastly different from those in Western Europe, imbued as they are with primitive cultural characteristics that include polytheism, magic, witchcraft, sorcery, animistic rituals, animal slaughter and hysteria (e.g., frenetic dancing, falling into trances, *inter alia*). Heightened local religious expression has also emerged in reaction against particular socio-political forces, such as increasing attempts at secularization in Iran and Turkey. Extremist fundamentalist groups, such as Hizb'Allah, can also become 'mainstream' and morph into a religious–nationalist entity embraced by the majority of the population (Saad-Ghorayeb, 2002).

Some thinkers, including David Hume (1757),[3] have been persuaded that monotheistic Christian religion, with its doctrine of the 'chosen people' and the denigration of the non-chosen, sowed the seeds for religious violence that crystallized in the holy wars and *jihads* that continue today (Schwartz, 1997). It would constitute an over-simplification to ascribe the cause of all wars to Christian monotheism. One has only to examine the histories of polytheistic nations such as India, Pakistan and Sri Lanka to uncover their long histories of violence. If we cannot lay blame at the feet of particular religious beliefs such as monotheism or polytheism, does religion itself, regardless of its ilk, predispose to violence? Perhaps, but probably not more so than the abominable atrocities perpetrated on those who had the misfortune to live in godless totalitarian states during the assurgency of fascist and communist ideologies. Wars have also been waged for reasons other than religion – the rank pursuit of profit, power and territory come immediately to mind. We need to return to the central thesis of this book for an answer: that is, violence has its roots in human nature. Man's violent impulses, hate, envy, greed and rage must find expression, whether it be through a monotheistic or polytheistic religion, a political ideology or a cult. When such impulses need discharge, violence is a possible response that restores equilibrium when the precarious balance between the individual and collective good has been disturbed.

Of course, there are also sociological arguments for religious–nationalist violence. Consider, for example, social identity theory (Tajfel, 1978). In developing this theory, Tajfel, a Polish Jew who lost almost his entire family in the Holocaust, was trying to understand how such an event could occur. The theory states that a person's social identity is based on his/her group member-ship, and group membership provides a sense of belonging and place in the social world. In order to enhance our self-esteem, we enhance the status of the group to which we belong. Nothing could be more prestigious than belonging to the group of 'chosen people', whatever their ilk; in Nazi Germany, mem-bership of the Gestapo and Hitler Youth. In enhancing the status of our own group, we reduce the prestige and status of 'out'-groups and non-members of our 'in'-group. Such processes motivate horrific acts of war and genocide on a large scale, as occurred with the Jews, and torture, victimization, dehuman-ization, violence and bullying on an interpersonal scale. Given that Western civilization has always felt uncomfortable with its aggression, hate, envy and sexuality, how do 'in'-groups maintain the status quo? Answer: by punishment for transgression, which increases the solidarity of the group and adherence to group norms, functioning in much the same way as totemism in primitive cul-tures. Rituals of purification, sacrifice and penitence, which have nowhere been on starker display than in the extreme ascetic enactments of medieval monks who engaged in appalling acts of self-mutilation (e.g., castration, flagellation), deprivation, poverty, silence and celibacy (Robinson, 2003), served a dual role – first, to enhance adherence to doctrine and its social expression; second, to dif-fuse aggressive and sexual impulses. Further, in order to avoid reprisals, groups will often scapegoat one of their members – usually a marginalized and weaker member – into whom is poured the envy and hostility of the whole group. This process restores group harmony through the vicarious relief and dissipation of the group's destructive impulses (Girard, 2011).

More recent approaches have applied game theory, incorporating both physical and human capital, as a basis for understanding civil war. Azam (1995) proposed that minority ethnic groups will cooperate with a majority government if they feel protected and if resources are distributed in an equitable manner. However, civil war involves the killing of one's own kind, called "within-species killing" (Grossman, 1995). Overcoming humanity's deep aversion to killing its own kind requires the demonization (i.e., amplifying negative characteristics and other dif-ferences) of its enemy, a process that Freud recognized as projection and Klein as projective identification and which sociologists and social psychologists under-stand to be a function of group processes. Further, the importance of the sym-bolic in religious-nationalist wars has often been understated; the desecration or perceived desecration of (religious) symbols will trigger violence even when pol-itical and material interests will not be served (Kaplan, 2007). The reaction to the desecration of the symbol could well represent a displacement onto a shared image or symbol of feelings of personal desecration of self that could not otherwise be expressed or assuaged. Recall the outrage among Muslim groups in Denmark when 12 cartoons depicting the Islamic prophet Muhammad were published in a Danish newspaper in 2005. These cartoons sparked violent demonstrations and riots internationally in which 200 people were killed, as well as attacks on Christian churches and European embassies of countries that supported free speech and who refused to sanction the Danes.

Bourdieu (1972) attempted to integrate macro-cultural and micro-rationalist theories of religious violence by proposing that the social field in which it occurs represents simultaneously both objective (e.g., economic, cultural and social) and subjective forms of capital, termed 'habitus', which comprises personal property, skills, cognitive appraisals and perceived social value that are assessed relative to the prevailing objective forms of capital. Collective identities, whether based on class, ethnicity, culture or politics, increase or decrease in salience as social conflict increases or decreases between competing collective identities. Thus, these 'categories' are not fixed structures but fluid processes that represent relations between prevailing social forces that may be symbolic expressions of felt inequality or injustice as much as expressions of dissatisfaction about disparities in material wealth. These collective rituals, such as the outpouring of Muslim outrage against the Danish cartoons, regenerate intra-group solidarity and restore esteem following perceived or actual humiliation by another collective, in this example, mainstream Danish society. The focus of action on the symbolic leader of the tribe, in this example, Muhammad, renders the cause meritorious in a way that retaliation against a personal slight does not. Collective outrage empowers both individual and group simultaneously and those who participate become members of a powerful 'in'-group, in this case, outraged Muslims who are defenders of their faith and loyal soldiers of their leader as opposed to a marginalized minority in a Western culture. Thus, civil wars and their precursors (demonstrations, riots) provide a political pretext for settling both personal and collective scores; private motives find public justification and in so doing, the righteousness of the personal grievance is reinforced.

> The lust for revenge is like a howl of rage against the narcissistic damage done to the self ... [it is] released by catastrophic loss to compensate for feelings of helplessness, pain and terror. The wound that will neither heal nor become healing is thus a sense of self which has suffered a fundamental assault at its core.
>
> (Colman, 1988, p. 77)

This brief discussion has highlighted the importance of religious ideologies in the generation of nationalism; the formation of national identities along religious lines (Jews, Catholics, Muslims, Hindus); the use of a pseudo-religious rhetoric in nationalistic sloganeering; and the embeddedness of the personal motive in the action of the collective through psychic mechanisms described in the psychoanalytic literature – projection, dehumanization, demonization, displacement and identification with a leader (often also an aggressor). All of these intrapsychic processes need to be added to current theories of political action and religious group membership in order to gain a fuller understanding of the genesis of religious conflict.

There are uncanny resemblances between the Satan myth, psychoanalytic theorizing and the world's religious conflicts. Colman (1988) described how these processes operated in the original narrative – the clash between God and Satan:

> The point about this kind of interaction is that it is reciprocal: each side sees in the other the mirror-image of their own unrecognized self, and this serves only to confirm their belief that the other is the true aggressor. In the same way ... God and Satan can be seen as dual aspects of the same being; that attempting to destroy the other and feeling destroyed by the other (Satan's position) is the same as feeling destroyed by the other and attempting to destroy the other in retaliation (God's position). Thus the angel in pain is the God whose omnipotence has been wounded and who seeks revenge – hence the ferocity with which Satan is driven out of Heaven.
>
> ...
>
> In situations of catastrophic loss, the individual ... may resort to ... [the expression of] envy and revenge as a defence against the unbearable pain of irredeemable loss.
>
> (pp. 77 and 78)

The clash of civilizations

Huntington (1993) selected a different unit of focus to try to explain religious/ nationalist conflict, but, at its base, the two theories are not incompatible. He argued that the 'fault lines' drawn between nations were neither economic nor ideological, but cultural. These ignite not conflict between nation states, but between civilizations, which he defines as 'cultural entities' that operate at the level of the village, geographic region, ethnic group, nation and religious group. Civilizations subsume nation states – we speak of Western civilization (Europe and North America), Latin American civilization (all of the nation states in South America) and Islamic civilizations (the nation states in the Middle East). Huntington (1993) identified eight major civilizations – Western, Confucian, Japanese, Islamic, Hindu, Slavic-Orthodox, Latin American and African. Differences between civilizations are 'real' compared with the sometimes arbitrary differences between nations. The differences between language, history, culture and religion give rise to fundamental differences in how individuals perceive, act and relate to others at the micro level of the family and the macro level of society.

For example, in Western culture 'the squeaky wheel gets the grease', while in Japanese culture 'the nail that protrudes will be pounded down'. These two axioms capture an essential difference in social norms between Western and Japanese civilizations. Some cultural neuroscientists invoke the brain's characteristic neuroplasticity as a key element in the development of cultural norms. For example, Tibetan monks who practise intense meditation show a very different pattern of brain activity in the gamma waves from novice meditators. Individuals charged with navigating their way around the planet, whether primitive hunters returning to base camp or London taxi drivers, show increases in hippocampal size because the hippocampus is involved in spatial orientation (Kitayama, 2014). Cultural practices and values thus become inscribed in our neurons over time and become enmeshed in our brain activity. Of great interest is the value placed by certain cultures on emotional expression. In Western cultures, emotional expression is valued and encouraged, while in Asian cultures, the reverse is true, which places a much higher value on social cohesion and harmony than on individualism. These cultural differences are embedded in the neurons. When European-Americans were asked to suppress their emotional reaction in response to an emotionally arousing stimulus (e.g., a dead body), they were able to suppress the outward display of emotion, but brain activity indicated that an emotional reaction was occurring. Activity in the frontal regions of the brain indicated that participants were experiencing conflict over the suppression of their emotions. For Asians, not only were they able to suppress an outward display of emotion, their brain activity showed a momentary response followed by dissipation of brain activity and there no was no conflict in the frontal regions (Kitayama & Uskul, 2011).

Contacts between civilizations can either enhance 'civilization-consciousness' and tolerance or amplify differences and animosities. Huntington (1993) argued that globalization has weakened the unique identities of and boundaries between nation states, and fundamentalist religions stepped into this breach in all of the major faiths, including Christianity and Islam. This process of religious resurgence has been described as the "desecularization of the world" (Berger, 1999), and is understood to meet unmet needs for identity, security and belonging. Parallel social processes are also in evidence in, for example, the reindigenization of first-nation people and the re-Asianization of Japan, which may serve the same psychological needs as desecularization. Notwithstanding, divisions along religious lines are more powerful than other social and cultural distinctions. As Huntington (1993) quips, "A person can be half-French and half-Arab and simultaneously a citizen of two countries; it is more difficult to be half-Catholic and half-Muslim" (p. 27). Thus, with the collapse of ideologies such as communism and fascism and the failure of non-Western civilizations to embrace the Western values of democracy and liberalism as universal, people are lining up behind religious ideologies to assert their identities and to find a psychological and metaphysical home.

The clash of Christianity and Islam

> I will surely bless you and make your descendants as numerous as the stars in the sky and as the sand on the seashore. Your descendants will take possession of the cities of their enemies.
>
> (Genesis 22:17)

We are here concerned with a very particular clash of civilizations – that between Christianity and Islam. The verse from Genesis is ambiguous. To whom is God referring? To whose descendants? Who is the enemy? In order to understand the current state of affairs between these two religions let us pause a moment to consider Islam's 1,300-year history. The figure of Abraham is often invoked as the common origin of that group of faiths known as the Abrahamic religions – Judaism, Christianity and Islam. Abraham has also been assumed to be the common ancestor, the founding father, of all peoples practising these faiths; they are referred to as the 'children of Abraham'. Abraham is described as a great prophet in the Qur'ān, and claimed therein to be a Muslim (Islam believes that every human is born Muslim – an odd claim since they were the last of the three Abrahamic religions!). He is also considered to be Jewish by the Jews. God chose Abraham to found a nation of the chosen in order to ensure the worship of the one true God until, according to Christians, the coming of Christ.

The Abrahamic religions share in common a belief in one God (monotheism), that the divine word of God was revealed through God's appointed messengers, that the world was created by God (creationism) and that there is life after death; that is, the soul survives the physical body (immortality) and resides in either hell or heaven (paradise). There are also differences: Islam perceives Jesus as one of God's prophets; Judaism believes that Jesus was a false prophet; while Christianity views Jesus as the Son of God and the saviour of the world. The former two religions deny the resurrection of Jesus, in contrast to Christianity, yet Islam believes, along with Christianity, in the second coming. Muhammad, God's prophet in Islam, purportedly believed that Jesus was a prophet, but that to make him divine was tantamount to pagan magic (Nafissi, 2005). With respect to human nature, both Islam and Judaism ascribe equality to man's predilections to do good or evil, in contrast to Christianity, whose doctrine of 'original sin' places man's propensity for evil in the foreground, against which he must fight throughout his life. When it comes to tolerance of the other, Islam believes that Jews and Christians should be respected as 'people of the Book' but of only limited revelation; Judaism views both Islam and Christianity as false interpretations and (unwarranted) extensions of the Jewish faith, while Christians view Islam as a false religion and Judaism as a true but incomplete religion. Freud has this to say about Islam and Judaism:

> The case of the founding of the Mahommadan [*sic*] religion seems to me like an abbreviated repetition of the Jewish one, of which it emerged as an imitation. It appears, indeed, that the Prophet intended originally to accept Judaism completely for himself and his people. The recapture of the single great primal father brought the Arabs an extraordinary exaltation of their self-confidence, which led to great worldly successes but exhausted itself in them. Allah showed himself far more grateful to his chosen people than Yahweh did to his. But the internal development of the new religion soon came to a stop, perhaps because it lacked the depth which had been caused in the Jewish case by the murder of the founder of their religion. The apparently rationalistic religions of the East are in their core ancestor-worship and

so come to a halt, too, at an early stage of the reconstruction of the past. If it is true that in primitive peoples of today the recognition of a supreme being is the only content of their religion, we can only regard this as an atrophy of religious development and bring it into relation with the countless cases of rudimentary neuroses which are to be observed in the other field.

(Freud, 1939, pp. 92–3)

Abraham was born 4,000 years ago in the city of Ur, which was at that time part of ancient Mesopotamia, now Iraq. His birthplace is considered holy by the Sumerians, the world's oldest civilization, which had laws, literature and art. However, the Sumerians worshipped 5,000 gods! Abraham is buried in Hebron, which is currently part of the disputed Palestinian territories. In Genesis 12, God commands Abram (Abraham; in Hebrew *ab-raham* means 'father of the womb' = 'ancestor of the tribe') to leave his home (Ur) and travel to a land – the land of Canaan, now Israel-Palestine – that God would reveal to him in due course. Abraham wanders the earth for the next 100 years in the region now called the Middle East, from Turkey to Israel-Palestine. God promised Abraham many descendants, as his name implied, but by the age of 86 years, he still had no children. His wife, Sarah, who was 70 and had remained barren, gave Hagar, their servant girl, to Abraham as recompense, and together they had a son, Ish'mael. At some proximal point, Sarah herself becomes divinely impregnated (why God waits so long to bless her with a child is a mystery) and she gives birth to a son, Isaac. Riven with jealousy of the much younger Hagar, and now having produced an heir for Abraham, Sarah pressures Abraham to send Hagar and Ish'mael into the dessert, where she hopes they will perish. Not so – God saves them and Ish'mael subsequently becomes the Father of the Arab peoples. Is it coincidence that Maryam, the Christian concubine of Muhammad, gave the Prophet a son, Ibrahim, late in his life? Perhaps it was Muhammad's attempt to redress a wrong – that of an elder son not being given his birthright (Kobrin, 2003)? Giving his son the same name as his Jewish father-equivalent may have been part of this attempt at redress, rendering his son the "fantasy patriarch for both Muslims and Jews" (Kobrin, 2003, p. 218). Ish'mael is honoured as a forefather of the Prophet Muhammad.

In Genesis 22, and also in the Qur'ān, we learn that God tests Abraham with the demand that he sacrifice his only remaining son, Isaac, as a burnt offering. Isaac is saved when God realizes the blind obedience of Abraham. This version is by no means unproblematic, with other sources stating that Abraham did in fact sacrifice his son, as child sacrifice to various gods was common at that time. There are other pre- and post-Abraham mentions of child sacrifice in the Bible. An example of a pre-Abrahamic account is Exodus 4:24–26, in which there is a bizarre tale of God inexplicably trying to kill Moses, an attempt thwarted by his wife, who cuts off the foreskin of their son and with a "magical incantation", intoning Moses as a "bridegroom of blood by circumcision", wards off Yahweh's murderous rage. This event is the apparent basis for the Jewish practice of male circumcision. A post-Abraham account can be found in 2 Chronicles

28:1–3, which tends to reinforce the version that Isaac was indeed "sacrificed". When social attitudes to child sacrifice changed – in Chronicles, the practice was referred to as "an abomination of the heathen" (today we would call this unholy ritual infanticide), so too did the biblical and Qur'ānic stories about Abraham (Friedman, 2003). The Qur'ānic sacrifice story gilds the lily even further than the Bible, stating that Isaac told his father he was prepared to be sacrificed if that were the will of God (see Qur'ān, 37:101–107)! In Islam, Abraham's sacrifice (or otherwise) is commemorated each year through animal sacrifices during *Eid ul-Azha*. A more sinister current incarnation of this practice occurs in the form of indoctrinating young children for the purpose of producing suicide bombers, an issue I will address in the final chapter.

The story continues that God was so impressed by Abraham that he promised to bless him and multiply his seed: "all the nations of the earth will be blessed through your seed because you listened to my voice" (Genesis 22:15–19). This passage may suggest that God was replacing the seed he had in Isaac but lost at God's instigation. If we assume that Isaac survived God's narcissistic capriciousness, as in redacted biblical history, he became the Father of the Jewish people. There are many parallels between the Christian and Muslim accounts of their early history, but with some major adjustments. For example, Muslims claim it was Ish'mael and not Isaac who was going to be sacrificed!

Lineage is traced from Abraham to his two sons, Isaac and Ish'mael, to his grandson, Jacob, and great-grandson, Joseph, who, being the favoured child and thereby stimulating severe sibling rivalry amongst his brothers, is sold by them into slavery in Egypt, where his leadership qualities and eloquence allow him to persuade other Israelites to follow him back to Canaan. The lineage is then lost; the next significant figure is Moses, who, according to the Exodus story, leads the enslaved tribe out of Egypt. It is Moses' successor, Joshua, the mastermind of the Jewish assault on Canaan, who, upon victory, changed the name of the land to Israel.

I cannot imagine a worse foundation for the establishment of a situation in which different tribes (siblings) must cohabit. Abraham's was a profoundly dysfunctional family. It contains within it the tragedy of unresolvable sibling rivalry that we witness today in Israel and Palestine. I am struck by the repetition of this theme – the theme of God as Father favouring one of his children over another, as he did with Cain and Abel, with Isaac and Ish'mael and with Joseph and his brothers. God, through Abraham, instigated a deadly rivalry between his two sons that has endured to the present day. The Jewish settlers believe that God gave them this holy land; the Palestinians counter-argue that Abraham is also their founding father and that they have an equal right to the land. God told Abraham, "I will make you a great nation and all the families of Abraham will be blessed" (Genesis 12:2). More specifically, God promises Abraham, "behold, I have blessed [Ish'mael], and will make him fruitful, and will multiply him exceedingly; twelve princes shall he beget, and I will make him a great nation" (Genesis 17:20).

It is not difficult to see how the fundamentalist banner – "Kill yourself for God" – has taken hold in the Middle East. This bitter battle for the same tiny piece of land embodies the Abrahamic story today – one of bitter conflict, rivalry and murderous rage. Abraham died in Hebron. The two brothers, Isaac and Ish'mael, met there to bury their father. It remains a holy place where both Jews and Muslims come to worship God and to honour Abraham.

Notes

1   Examples include the My Lai massacre during the Vietnam war, the massacres in Bosnia, Rwanda, the Sudan, Syria and Libya, and other forms of destructive behaviour such as suicide bombing (Atran, 2003) and the abuse of military detainees and suspected terror-ists (Fisk, Harris & Cuddy, 2004). Its newest manifestation is in evidence in the Islamic State (IS) movement that has gained so much traction in the Middle East in recent times.
2   Originally referring to a 'spiritual struggle', the word *jihad* now takes the meaning 'holy war'.
3   In *The Natural History of Religion* (Hume, 1757) argued, like Freud, that polytheism preceded monotheism and that polytheism was preferable because it resulted in greater tolerance of divergent views, while monotheism, the dogma of the Inquisitions, results in denigration of the faiths of 'non-believers' and persecution or worse for non-compliance with worship of a single Deity.

8

TERROR THEOLOGY AND FUNDAMENTALISM

> Fundamentalism is ... literalism in interpreting the scriptures of any religious
> tradition as history rather than as mythology and metaphor expressing uni-
> versal or archetypal themes of timeless significance for humankind's under-
> standing of its origins, future destiny and significance in cosmology.
>
> (Todd, 2012, p. 3)

Terror theology is a wellspring of immense shame and horror for humankind for its
motivation of countless acts of wanton destruction, mindless violence, mass murder
and genocide. Although the 'faces' of terror theology and fundamentalism may look
very different across nations, religions and centuries, the underlying psychic mechanisms that drive it are remarkably similar, as I will demonstrate later in the chapter
with both Christian and Islamic exemplars. Armstrong (2000) describes fundamentalism as an "embattled form of spirituality" that is reactive to a perceived crisis, for
example imminent annihilation, contamination by a secularized, materialist culture,
an excess of democracy and personal freedom, modernity or science, necessitating
a "a cosmic war between the forces of good and evil" (p. ix). I would add that the
embrace of fundamentalism is enabled by two processes: first, social pressures that
homogenize minds, processes that were discussed in the previous chapter; and second,
relatedly, a failure of introspection, that is, an unwillingness or incapacity to think for
oneself, a denial of a space within for self-reflection that occurs in a situation in which
external reality is so chaotic and destructive as to overwhelm one's emotions and ability to think because one's capacity to bear the anxiety or distress of one's situation has
been exceeded. Stolorow calls this type of experience "horror" (Kenny, 2014).

Who is vulnerable to the fundamentalist message? Although it is rarely possible
for academics to get close enough to members of cults prior to their joining or while
they are active members to undertake a detailed assessment of prospective members' psychological development and motivations for joining such organizations, it

is probable that those who have had unsatisfactory attachment experiences early in life, and who grow up with low self-esteem, unresolved emotional pain, identity diffusion (i.e., no clear sense of who one is or where one belongs) and a sense of alienation from self and others are likely to be attracted to such organizations because they are searching for remedies for the psychological traumas they have experienced. Thus, the disenfranchised, the embattled, the denigrated and rejected, the deprived and needy, the traumatized and dispossessed, the envious and rageful are all fair game for the message of fundamentalist religious and politico-religious ideologies, particularly at times of heightened *anomie*, when the established values of a society are called into question (Galanter, 2013). Why? Membership of a fundamentalist group reverses these intolerable feelings. Fundamentalist ideology bolsters group self-confidence. Fundamentalism turns 'out'-groups into 'in'-groups that empower, enrich and 'feed' their members. Adherents are no longer denigrated and alone, but exalted as a select and chosen few. Fundamentalists become warriors with a simple message of salvation that is found in a naïve and literal interpretation of ancient sacred texts. Gone is the hopelessness and uncertainty of life; the path is straight, the goals are clear. However, to partake in this nirvana, one must relinquish one's 'self', one's individuality, one's 'mind' in order to render blind obedience to the collective ideology, which, in the situation under discussion, is terrorism, an institutionalized form of violence at the heart of politico-religious fundamentalism. Egypt's Muslim Brotherhood (*al-Ikhwan al-Muslimun*), whose motto is "Islam is the solution", is a cogent example. Another is America's Patriots, who have eschewed mainstream society (because mainstream society has eschewed them), and chosen to live in isolated communities where they develop and propagate their messages of bigotry, divisiveness and hate (Neiwert, 1999).

At their core, acts of fundamentalist terrorism must breach a (hopefully) insurmountable barrier for most members of a civilized society – the prohibition against the taking of life, particularly the lives of one's own countrymen, innocents and children. Yet, we know that these heights have been scaled and breached repeatedly in the course of history. What factors make this possible? A number of candidate factors come to mind. First, many atrocities like genocide and random suicide bombing are characterized by the (perceived) need for purification; the term 'ethnic cleansing' carries this meaning, as did Osama bin Laden's call for a return to the values of Islamic ancestors, to cleanse humanity of the impure and corrupted values of the West. Conversely, during the nineteenth and twentieth centuries, the West described as the 'yellow peril' the mass immigration of East Asians. During World War II, the Allies donned the mantle of a holy mandate to stop the 'yellow peril' from invading and destroying white civilization. It follows that those who must be cleansed are necessarily impure and indeed evil, and the cause – to rid the world of this contamination – is sacred, sanctioned and supported by God (Allah).

The defence of splitting makes the polarization between 'us' ('in'-group, all good, doing God's will) and 'them' ('out'-group, all bad and doing the work of Satan) possible. In order to override one's basic human decency with respect to others, we must "sever the bond of sympathetic imagination which constitutes the fellow-feeling that makes behaving badly unacceptable" (Young, 2001, p. 26), thus allowing us to view the other as inhuman, subhuman or dehumanized. During war, for example, our enemies cease to be our fellow human beings; they become infidels (e.g., in the Crusades and other 'holy' wars), savages (e.g., indigenous groups such as the American Indians and Australian Aborigines), brutes or beasts (e.g., German soldiers), vermin (e.g., Hitler's characterization of Jews), monkeys (e.g., Japanese soldiers), gooks (Viet Cong) and cockroaches (victims of the Rwandan genocide). Once the dehumanization process is complete, Arendt (1963) describes how evil becomes banal and everyday, using as an example the 'just-another-day-at-the-office' model through which Nazis like Adolph Eichmann organized administratively the deaths of millions of Jews.

In this chapter, we will explore what makes it possible for individuals and nations to torture and kill one another in the name of a higher cause, an ideal or a religion. We will first examine the atrocities perpetrated in the name of religion, beginning with a discussion of atrocities through the ages. This will be followed by an account of Islamic extremism and atrocities perpetrated in the name of Allah. Finally, I will attempt a psychoanalytic explanation of what motivates humans to think and behave in such extreme ways.

Before doing so, however, I would like to make a disclaimer that any analysis that focuses on only one cause is at best naïve and, at worst, deceptive in its fundamentalism and simplicity. This is the case with those who would attribute all of the tribulations of the Middle East to Islamic fundamentalism. Undoubtedly, like all wars, there are multiple determinants, with socio-economic struggles and nationalist movements among the many that could be cited. Most Muslim societies that are currently in conflict have in common disparities in wealth between the ruling classes and the people, corruption in government and the military and the absence of a 'voice' for the majority, whose anger and frustration are offered no safe outlets and have finally breached the banks of top-down control. When these conditions prevail, eruption of a class struggle is rendered inevitable.

While social crises were, previously expressed in terms of Marxist class struggles, these same forces express themselves in the Muslim world in terms of Islamic fundamentalism. I will necessarily, in the remainder of this discussion, focus on the psychological issues, as opposed to the social, economic and political factors that are also major players in the current tragedies in the Middle East. For example, the support of the USA for Israel is never far from reigniting Muslim hatred of the West, the USA in particular. A perceived central driving force for the current agitation is the belief that the ruling classes in some Muslim nations are too Westernized and thus insufficiently Islamic, which provides a strong religious foundation for the unrest. However, Hasan (2003) argued that this distinction is merely rhetorical and points to "the absurdity of any Western attempt to eliminate fundamentalism in Afghanistan, Iran or elsewhere. If fundamentalism [were] essentially a Marxist movement ... only successful economic development and a consequent alleviation of class inequalities in Muslim societies ... will end it".

Facts and figures on the world's religions

Before we embark on this most difficult discussion regarding the intersection between religion and our human natures, we need to situate religion in our modern world, to understand its place and importance in our lives. Let us start, then, with the most fundamental enquiry: how many people around the world believe in God? Table 8.1 provides estimates of the percentage of the world's population that subscribe to the major religions.

Christianity boasts an estimated 2.2 billion adherents. In the United States of America, 78% describe their religious affiliation as Christian. In Austria, 80% are Christian; in Brazil, 89%; in Bolivia, 94%; in Argentina, 85%; in Russia, 73%; and in Australia, 67% nominate their religion as Christian. By contrast, in China, only 5% of the population describes itself as Christian, with the largest group (52.2%) nominated as 'unaffiliated'. In India, 2.5% of its population is Christian, with 80% (close to 1 billion people) describing their religious affiliation as Hindu.

The world's second largest religion, Islam, has an estimated 1.57 billion followers. The concentration of Muslim countries – Algeria, Bahrain, Egypt, Iran, Iraq, Jordan, Kuwait, Lebanon, Libya, Morocco, Oman, Palestine, Qatar, Saudi Arabia, Sudan, Syria, Tunisia, Turkey, United Arab Emirates and Yemen – in the Middle East may have contributed to the popular but erroneous perception that the majority of Muslims live in the Middle East. In fact, the majority (more than 60%) of the world's Muslims live in Asia. The remainder are located as follows: 20% in the Middle East; 15% in Sub-Saharan Africa; 2.4% in Europe; 0.3% in the Americas; and 2.3% other. One fifth of the world's Muslim population, an estimated 317 million, live in countries where Islam is a minority religion. In Israel, for example, 15% of the population is Muslim – they are known as Israeli Arabs. Five countries – India, Ethiopia, China, Russia and Tanzania – are home to 75% of minority Muslim populations. Hindu India has the third largest Muslim population of any nation (161 million), but in India, this represents only 14% of the population. Within the Muslim population, approximately 10–25% is Shi'ite, of whom 80% live in Iran, Pakistan, India and Iraq. These figures, produced by the Pew–Templeton Global Religious Futures Project (2010), challenge the popular notion that most Muslims are Arabs. Further, it highlights how the mix of religion, politics and social class creates volatile environments where tensions between groups erupt from time to time into street violence, bloodshed, riots and *coups d'état*. The Pew Research Center's Forum on Religion & Public Life (2011a) has forecast an increase of 35% in the Muslim population over the next 20 years (an increase from 1.6 billion in 2010 to 2.2 billion by 2030). This represents a projected twofold increase over non-Muslim populations.

Figures from the Pew Research Center's Forum on Religion & Public Life (2011b) showed that in 2010, 37% of countries globally placed high to very high restrictions on religious practice, an increase of 8 percentage points since 2007. These 37% of countries housed 75% of the world's population, an increase from 68% since 2007. Government restrictions on religion were assessed using the 10-point Government Restriction Index (GRI), which measures government laws, policies

TABLE 8.1 Percentage of world population by religious affiliation

Religion	Percentage of world population	Number in billions (b) or millions (m)
Christians	31.5	2.2b
Muslims	23.2	1.6b
Unaffiliated	16.3	1.1b
Hindus	15.0	1.0b
Buddhists	7.1	488m
Folk religionists	5.9	405m
Jews	<1.0	13.8m
Other	<1.0	58.1m

Source: Pew–Templeton Global Religious Futures Project (2010).

and actions that restrict religious beliefs or practices, including efforts by governments to ban particular faiths, prohibit conversions, limit preaching or give preferential treatment to one or more religious groups. The 10-point Social Hostilities Index (SHI) assesses acts of religious hostility by private individuals, organizations and social groups, including mob or sectarian violence, harassment over attire for religious reasons and other religion-related intimidation or abuse. Government restrictions were influenced by increases in crimes motivated by religious hatred; however, the converse was also true – increasing government restrictions on religion resulted in increases in crimes motivated by religion.

The SHI and GRI were closely associated. Increases in the GRI were associated with increases in SHI. Countries with government restriction scores that have increased from 2007 included Indonesia, Maldives, Afghanistan, Tunisia, Syria, Russia, Yemen, Azerbaijan, Algeria and Belarus. Countries with GRI scores that have decreased since 2007 included Egypt (to 2010, but by 2012 GRI scores would have increased), Saudi Arabia, Iran, Uzbekistan, China, Myanmar and Vietnam.

In the name of God: Christian fundamentalism

You find as you look around the world that every single bit of progress in humane feeling, every improvement in the criminal law, every step toward the diminution of war, every step toward better treatment of the coloured races, or every mitigation of slavery, every moral progress that there has been in the world, has been consistently opposed by the organized churches of the world. I say quite deliberately that the Christian religion, as organized in its churches, has been and still is the principal enemy of moral progress in the world.

(Russell, 1957, p. 9)

These words might sound like hyperbole from an avowed atheist, but a moment's reflection will yield a great deal of evidence for the veracity of Bertrand Russell's statement. When we see the words 'terror theology' and 'fundamentalism' we, in the West, immediately associate them with Islamic extremists. While it is true that there are very disturbing trends in the Middle East and around the world in which extremist Islamist groups wage holy war and commit unspeakable atrocities against 'infidels', terror theology has also had a long and shameful history in Christianity, as we will soon discover. In their extreme forms, monotheistic religions are intolerant, divisive and terrifying. If there be only one right way, every other way is wrong. If adherents are good, chosen, saved, others are evil, unchosen, unsaved. The Romans fed Christians to the lions because they mistook Christian intolerance for sedition (Lefkowitz, 2003). Let us examine four examples of Christian terrorism from different periods in history – the brutal murder of Hypatia of Alexandria, the atrocities committed by the Catholic Church during the Counter-Reformation, the various misuses of Christianity in the modern world and the appropriation of God in times of war.

Hypatia of Alexandria

Hypatia was a pagan (i.e., non-Christian) philosopher, mathematician and astronomer who lived in Alexandria, Egypt in the third and fourth centuries CE. She is thought to have been born around 350; she was brutally murdered by Christians in 415 CE. Throughout her adult life, Hypatia was a highly respected scholar and a popular teacher. In 400 CE, she became Director of the Museum of Alexandria, which was the centre of Greek intellectual and cultural life, and which housed the great library of Alexandria. This period was a time of great tension between the pagan Orestes, governor of Alexandria, and the Christian bishop, Cyril, who had expelled all the Jews from the city. When Orestes objected, Cyril despatched his monks to murder Orestes. Cyril objected to Hypatia for many reasons, not the least of which for her non-Christian beliefs, her 'heretical' teachings at the Museum (Hypatia, n.d.), her friendship with Orestes and the fact that she had risen above her status as a woman, was independent and moved in high circles that were usually the province of men. Such was Cyril's rage and jealousy that he publicly denounced Hypatia, inciting a mob led by his fanatical monks to murder her. It is worthy of note that Cyril, who dispensed with his enemies by murdering them, was later declared a saint! Socrates Scholasticus recorded the horrific event in his *Ecclesiastical History* (VII.15), as follows:

> There was a woman at Alexandria named Hypatia, daughter of the philosopher Theon, who made such attainments in literature and science, as to far surpass all the philosophers of her own time. Having succeeded to the school of Plato and Plotinus, she explained the principles of philosophy to her auditors, many of whom came from a distance to receive her instructions. On account of the self-possession and ease of manner, which she had acquired in consequence of the cultivation of her mind, she not infrequently appeared in

public in presence of the magistrates. Neither did she feel abashed in coming to an assembly of men. For all men on account of her extraordinary dignity and virtue admired her more. Yet even she fell victim to the *political jealousy* which at that time prevailed. For as she had frequent interviews with Orestes, it was calumniously reported among the Christian populace, that it was she who prevented Orestes from being reconciled to the bishop. Some of them therefore hurried away by *a fierce and bigoted zeal*, whose ringleader was a reader named Peter, waylaid her returning home, and dragging her from her carriage, they took her to the church called Caesareum, where they completely stripped her, and then murdered her with tiles [oyster shells]. After tearing her body in pieces, they took her mangled limbs to a place called Cinaron, and there burnt them. This affair brought not the least opprobrium, not only upon Cyril, but also upon the whole Alexandrian church. *And surely nothing can be farther from the spirit of Christianity than the allowance of massacres, fights*, and transactions of that sort. This happened in the month of March during Lent, in the fourth year of Cyril's episcopate, under the tenth consulate of Honorius, and the sixth of Theodosius [AD 415]. [My italics]

(Socrates Scholasticus, 2001, p. 165)

Compare Socrates' account with that of John, Bishop of Nikiu, written more than 300 years later:

And in those days there appeared in Alexandria a female philosopher, a pagan named Hypatia, and she was *devoted at all times to magic*, astrolabes and instruments of music, and *she beguiled many people through Satanic wiles*. And the governor of the city [Orestes] honoured her exceedingly; for *she had beguiled him through her magic*. And he ceased attending church as had been his custom. ... And he not only did this, but he drew many believers to her, and *he himself received the unbelievers at his house*. ... And thereafter a multitude of believers in God arose under the guidance of Peter the magistrate – now this *Peter* was *a perfect believer* in all respects in Jesus Christ – and they proceeded to seek for *the pagan woman who had beguiled the people of the city and the prefect through her enchantments*. And when they learnt the place where she was, they proceeded to her and found her seated on a (lofty) chair; and having made her descend they dragged her along till they brought her to the great church, named Caesarion. Now this was in the days of the fast. And they tare off her clothing and dragged her through the streets of the city till she died. And they carried her to a place named Cinaron, and they burned her body with fire. And all the people surrounded the patriarch Cyril and named him "the new Theophilus"; for he had destroyed the last remains of idolatry in the city. [My italics]

(1916, LXXXIV.87–8, 100–3)

In this account, we see the typical accusations and denunciations that appear time and again in Christian writing, beginning with the Bible, in which unbelievers are characterized as evil, possessed by Satan or having satanic powers and who must be hunted down and destroyed lest they corrupt the righteous. Freud would describe such assertions as symbolic products of the accuser's own nature which he projects into hated, threatening or feared objects. Bishop John's account is clearly irrational, neither scholarly nor dispassionate, and oozes venom and hatred of Hypatia, who was, in his view, an unworthy pagan woman, an unbeliever who practised magic, was in cahoots with Satan, through whom she "beguiled" others, and who entertained unbelievers. Bishop John was none too Christian a character himself; he was deposed from his office as Administrator General of the Monasteries because of his gross abuse of power (Charles, 1916).

The Counter-Reformation and the Catholic Inquisitions

The concept of evil, belief in Satan and the existence of witches have lingered tenaciously throughout history, all codified in the Bible, despite the occasional sanity that rational men attempted to inject into an opposing argument. For example, Exodus 22:18 states: "Thou shalt not suffer a witch to live". Leviticus 20:27 contains this sinister passage: "A man also or woman that hath a familiar spirit, or that is a wizard, shall surely be put to death: they shall stone them with stones: their blood shall be upon them". Around 400 CE, at least for a time, St Augustine of Hippo dissuaded the Church from its belief in magic, witches, witchcraft and the supernatural by claiming that only God could suspend the laws of the universe. However, the issue was reignited in 1208 by Pope Innocent III, who attacked Cathar heretics for believing that both God and Satan had supernatural powers and because, according to popular belief, the Cathars worshipped Satan (Lambert, 1998).

St Thomas Aquinas further complicated the issue by conflating sex and witchcraft, believing that the world was evil and populated by demons intent on leading the Church's flock into temptation. He believed that God existed alongside evil and demons, who "reap[ed] the sperm of men and spread it among women".[1] Aquinas's demons not only sought their own pleasure, they delighted in tempting men into sin through the Devil's instrument – women. For a period known as the Dark Ages, the early Christians required women to be veiled and controlled lest they tempt men into sins of the flesh, thereby rendering their bodies unfit to house their immortal souls (Robinson, 2003). The same demonization of women as evil temptresses is apparent in some fundamentalist Islamic countries today.

By the mid-1400s, more systematic abuse and torture of heretics and witches became widespread in Europe. Heretics were accused of entering into satanic pacts and engaging in sexual misdeeds motivated by demons. Under the extreme pressure induced by torture, the accused often concocted bizarre confessions to appease their accusers, which had the unfortunate effect of validating the original accusations and cementing the concept of witchcraft. Matters escalated in the late fifteenth century, when Pope Innocent VIII declared that German satanists were consorting with demons and were casting spells that destroyed crops and caused pregnant women to miscarry (Dixon, 2002). The pope commissioned a full report on these goings-on. The resulting volume, *Malleus maleficarum* (Hammer of witches), was a hateful, paranoid parody of scientific enquiry that reported evidence of witches having sex with demons and wreaking havoc on mankind. This work was considered the authoritative text on the crime of witchcraft. It was used to determine "whether the Belief that there are such Beings as Witches is so Essential a Part of the Catholic Faith that Obstinacy to maintain the Opposite Opinion manifestly savours of Heresy" and "If it be in Accordance with the Catholic Faith to maintain that in Order to bring about some Effect of Magic, the Devil must intimately co-operate with the Witch, or whether one without the other, this to say, the Devil without the Witch, or conversely, could produce such an Effect" (Kramer & Sprenger, 2009, p. 3).

By the early sixteenth century, there were mass outbreaks of witchcraft hysteria across Europe that resulted in mass executions. The 1580 publication of Jean Bodin's book *De la Démonomanie des Sorciers* (On the demon-mania of sorcerers) allowed children to testify against their parents, permitted the entrapment of the suspected and turned torture into a fine art (Hillerbrand, 2007; King, 1974). Shakespeare's *Macbeth* (1606) featured three witches that captured the popular characterization of these frightful creatures.

The Counter-Reformation and the Catholic Inquisitions represent another indelible blot on the Catholic Church (Dannenfeldt, 1970). Despite the Reformation and the decrees of Protestant Churches that witches did not exist (Gregory, 2012), in God's name and in the name of the faith and the Church that represented God's Kingdom on earth, God's representatives from the holy Catholic Church were again responsible for the torture and murder of thousands of people, many of whom were simple folk who did not understand the complexities of Church doctrine nor indeed the charges brought against them.

No one was immune to the wrath and judgement of the Inquisition. In 1616, Copernicus was denounced as a heretic for his theory that the sun was at the centre of the universe, as was Galileo, in 1633, for his publication of similar views. Punishments for so-called heretics varied but included execution, often by being burnt at the stake, having one's work denounced and consigned to the *Index Librorum Prohibitorum* (Index of Forbidden Books), first published in 1559, imprisonment and house arrest. The censoring body was the Sacred Congregation of the Roman Inquisition. Amazingly, the canon law under which the Index was authorized remained in effect until 1966 (Del Col, 2010). Between 51,000 and 75,000 people brought before the Roman Inquisition alone were executed during the second half of the sixteenth century. The Spanish Inquisition was particularly brutal as it was used, *inter alia*, to force the conversion of Jewish and Islamic citizens to Catholicism. The bloody pogroms against the Jews in Seville in 1391 soon spread to other regions, fuelled by the anti-Semitic preaching of fanatical priests. Synagogues were burnt, communities destroyed and thousands were forcibly converted and baptized, murdered or sold into slavery (Pérez, 2006).

All other concurrent forms of religious practice were denounced, including Protestantism, Lutheranism and Illuminism, a loose doctrine that aspired to greater authenticity and freedom in one's religious practice, unfettered by the dogma and rituals that accrued to Catholicism. Illuminists wanted to "embrace forms of spiritual life that [encouraged] free inspiration, internal religiosity, and effusions of the heart" (Pérez, 2006, p. 74) that could be equally available to all believers, not just the clergy and the elite.

The misuse of Christianity in the modern world

We may seem very far removed from the horrors of the Inquisition, and most of us hope that civilization and its religions have progressed from the gruesome years of the Counter-Reformation. Sadly, this is not so. In some countries, for example, Papua New Guinea, *sangumas* or witches are regularly physically tortured, condemned and burnt alive in broad daylight in full view of villagers. Wrongdoers are rarely apprehended or brought to justice because the police themselves also believe in witchcraft. The Papua New Guinea 'witches' of today bear an uncanny resemblance to the witches of the Middle Ages. During the day they appear human, but at night, disguised as animals, they visit graveyards in order to eat the recently buried corpses, an act which is believed to bestow upon them magical powers (Elliott, 2013).

More subtle forms of the misuse of Christian doctrine is evident in the marginalization and alienation of minority groups, such as people of colour and people from sexual minorities (lesbian, gay, bisexual and transsexual (LBGT)). These abuses express themselves in forms more 'civilized' or politically correct than the mass executions of the Middle Ages, or the primitive tribal practices of Papua New Guinea, but the import and intent of current practices bear an uncanny resemblance to both primitive totemic practices of the ancient world and the hysteria of the witch trials and demon hunters, whipped up by the Church to retain its hold on a straying flock.

Greene (2009) noted the "persistent reality of racism" (p. 699) in contemporary American society that has been enshrined in the "meritocracy myth" (Fine, 2002) – the privileging of rugged individualism, personal responsibility and equal opportunity – by white America, unable to see its "white skin privilege" (Greene, 2009, p. 699). Indeed, America shares with the UK, her dominions and Europe a shameful history of race-based oppression that has been sanctioned in culturally embedded religious beliefs from the first written records of human history. For example, black Africans were tainted with inferiority in the Old Testament. They were believed to be the descendants of Ham, son of Noah, who looked upon the naked body of his father and failed to cover him. God decreed that, as punishment for his profound disrespect of his father, Ham's son and all his descendants would be born black – the outward symbol of God's displeasure. Young (2001) argued that Ham's action represented an Oedipal rejection of paternal authority and that "the blackening and banishing of Ham's progeny [was] the retaliatory castration by the higher Father, God" (p. 25).

West (1996) exposed the historically systemic distortions of black sexuality as predatory, savage and hungry for white women, and the degradation of black bodies and black facial features that served the commercial and social purposes of the dominant white culture, allowing them to be exploited and oppressed as a race. On the other hand, the routine rape of black slave women by their white masters suggested a white fascination and desire for black female bodies, thereby creating a dilemma for white masters – desiring that which is denigrated and devalued, in fact, taboo. Freud tells us that when we desire that which is taboo, the unacceptable aspects of ourselves are split off and projected into the forbidden object of desire. This defensive manoeuvre relieves the shame and guilt about these forbidden sexual impulses and heightens the need to further devalue the source of shame and guilt, which is now external to the self. The need to discredit and destroy the taboo object is also evident in the enactment of violent assaults and exclusion from public life of gay men and women.

On a social level, these processes were played out in the irrational prohibition and criminalization of mixed racial marriages (Gaines & Leaver, 2002), and the segregation of white and black schoolchildren, which legalized an indefensible form of racial discrimination. Those who violated these prohibitions were perceived as dangerous to the social order because they exposed the inherent fallacy and artificiality of the legalized boundaries that had been drawn between black and white (Ross, 2002).

Today, the intense debate regarding same-sex marriage represents the same intrapsychic process discussed above with respect to racial minorities. Greene (2009) argued that inter-racial and same-sex relationships are embodiments of prohibited forms of desire that awaken envy in others, and which therefore require careful management in the form of restrictive legislation lest these forbidden impulses erupt and seek expression. It is only a small step in a fired-up imagination (unconscious) from a desirable black woman to a witch and from a powerful black male to a demon. Their subjugation is imperative, via formal channels such as legislation, and through informal channels, through random acts of violence, discrimination, ostracism and demonization.

Throughout its history, the Christian Church has had a problem with sex. The widespread abuse of children by Catholic priests has been a horrific scandal, both in the act itself and in the Church's failure to curtail or sanction the behaviour of abusing priests. A scathing report (*The Betrayal of Trust*) from the 2013 inquiry into child sexual abuse in the Catholic Church in Australia found that Church leadership viewed the issue as a "short-term embarrassment" rather than a gross violation of the trust of the Catholic families in their care that required a sweeping review of their culture and values to address its "sliding morality" (Schwartz & Lee, 2013). Believing that the Church was incapable of monitoring and apprehending offending priests, the committee recommended that legislation be enacted to criminalize 'grooming' a child and child endangerment. In addition, it recommended removing the statute of limitations on child sexual offences, and making it a crime to conceal child abuse.

Another atrocity involving the Catholic Church, sex and the mistreatment of its flock that has only recently come to light is the abuse perpetrated on 'fallen' young Catholic women who were sent to work as slaves in the Magdalene laundries run by the Catholic Church in Ireland. The use of the word 'slave' in this context is not hyperbole. These young women toiled for long hours in appalling conditions for years with no pay and no prospect of release. They were often abandoned by their families for the disgrace they wrought upon them by becoming pregnant out of wedlock. Most were forced to give up their infants for adoption; these babies were removed in the most brutal way from their mothers, without notice and without hope of ever tracing them. The girls were dehumanized by having their names changed by the nuns, by their letters to family never being posted and letters from family to them never being delivered. The girls were left to suffer excruciating pain during labour and childbirth; many did not survive the ordeal and died along with their newborns (Finnegan, 2001). The nuns to whose care they had been entrusted had been hardened and embittered by their own emotional and sexual deprivations and frustrations, which they projected into these 'bad' girls, whom they punished mercilessly for giving in to Satan's temptations. To its eternal shame, the Catholic Church operated these institutions from 1758 to 1966; the last laundry in Ireland was finally closed in 1996 (Ryan, 2011). In 2011, the Irish Prime Minister, Enda Kenny, under pressure from the United Nations, made a public apology to the victims of these institutions and offered financial compensation for all the years they had worked unpaid. Australia's Sisters of the Good Shepherd ran eight laundries across all states of Australia between 1940 and 1970. Girls who were wards of the state or deemed delinquent were sent to work in these establishments. The Prime Minister of the day, Kevin Rudd, similarly apologized to Australian victims in 2009 (Wheatley, 2013b).

How has religion, or rather the misuse of religion, contributed to marginalization, stigmatization and systemic abuse of minorities, the vulnerable and the unchampioned? I would argue that because the nature of the abuse being perpetrated against minorities is felt at some (unacknowledged) level within the abusing individual to be reprehensible, its legitimization, by social means, through subgroup membership and, legally, through legislation, may not provide sufficient justification for a conscience that is pressing to be heard. Religion provides the additional fortification because there is strength in numbers (i.e., the religious collective) and the views being promulgated are sanctioned by the highest authority there is – God – through His representatives on earth, the Church, thereby allowing the individual to abrogate personal responsibility for his/her views. Greene (2009) observed that "[e]very group in human history that has practised social domination or genocide against another group did so out of an evaluative framework and such frameworks were often couched in religious belief or convictions" (p. 707).

The Ku Klux Klan, an extreme right-wing, white supremacist terrorist organization, is an apt exemplar. The Klan comprises disaffected individuals who are anti-African Americans, especially those who are upwardly mobile, anti-Jewish, anti-Catholic, anti-immigration, anti-communist and anti-alcohol. Parsons (2005) described the membership as a diverse conglomeration of individuals who overtly shared only the characteristics that they are white, Protestant and Democrat. However, they are all united by a hate agenda grounded in fear of black and Jewish competition. Many have criminal records, are sadists, rapists or coercive moral reformers (Parsons, 2005). They are uncompromising in their self-righteous, judgemental attitudes. Joining the Ku Klux Klan bolsters their fragile self-esteem, legitimizes their paranoia and provides a means whereby they can project their inadequacy, rage and hate into those whom they target (Booth, 1991).

With its symbol of the Christian icon, the burning cross, the Klan blazed its hateful message across the night sky in the name of Christianity. It was lit during Klan meetings, at which time it was accompanied by prayers and the singing of hymns. It was also left as a 'calling card' in the front gardens of the thousands of African American homes that they torched in the 1950s and 1960s. The Klan in the southern states of the USA had the support of the police and the judiciary. For example, when the freedom riders arrived in Birmingham, Alabama, the police gave the Klan 15 minutes to attack them before arriving to quell the disturbance (McWhorter, 2001).

The God of war

> Is there any way of delivering mankind from the menace of war? ... [W]ith the advance of modern science, this issue has come to mean a matter of life and death for civilization as we know it; nevertheless, for all the zeal displayed, every attempt at its solution has ended in a lamentable breakdown.
>
> (Einstein, 1932, p. 199)

Freud's "Why war?" (1933b) was his response to a letter from Albert Einstein, who was involved in the establishment of the League of Nations. Einstein grasped the inherent weakness in this enterprise – it could not enforce its decrees or verdicts and if it could, would contribute to conflict rather than resolve it. He was seeking new ways of thinking about the question that he posed at the beginning of his correspondence, reproduced above. Einstein looked to Freud to shine a light on "the dark places of human will and feeling", to bring clarity to "man's instinctive life" and to propose some "educative methods ... outside the scope of politics" (Einstein, 1932, p. 199). Einstein declared that man must have within him "a lust for hatred and destruction" (Einsten, 1932, p. 201). He identified religious zeal, social factors and persecution of racial minorities as proximal causes of international conflict and civil war, but wanted to understand the "cruel and extravagant ... conflict between man and man" that appears to underpin all such conflict (Einstein, 1932, p. 201). Freud replied in a flattering manner, indicating that Einstein had answered his own questions, but volunteered to expand on those insights. Freud observed that the problem of violence is seen in the animal kingdom of which man is a part. He traced the source of power and violence in primitive human hordes – first, superior muscular strength (brute violence), and then the development of tools and weapons (violence plus intellect). Man gradually realized, argued Freud, that there was strength in numbers (*l'union fait la force*), that is, violence could be overcome by united opposition, and the rule of law, as it gradually evolved, could counter the violence of individuals. This process entails the loss of personal liberty and the exercise of personal power, so there is always an inherent tension undermining the survival of the collective. Freud identified that a "supreme agency" like the League of Nations was a possible solution but it lacked the vital condition – power – and was thus doomed to failure. He concluded his letter with a hope that men will one day become pacifists through a change in cultural attitude and a shared dread of the consequences of future wars. "Whatever fosters the growth of civilization works at the same time against war" (Freud, 1933b, p. 215). Alas! Freud's vision has not been realized.

God has always been invoked to render victory to the righteous on both sides of armed conflict; the American Civil War (1861–5) and the two world wars of the twentieth century are key modern examples. When the Allies were victorious, they were quick to praise God who gave them the victory! These examples demonstrate the psychological phenomenon of projection discussed earlier, whereby people evacuate unwanted parts of themselves into hated others. The same process is at work when we project our wishes into a deity, allowing us to believe that God sanctions or indeed assists us in the fulfilment of our wishes, thereby sparing us from confronting the thought that we might be selfishly pursuing our own ends for our own enhancement at the expense of others. One shining example of this process is the notion of the divine right of kings, which was a socio-political equivalent of the Church's dominion over the will of God via His revelations to exalted priests, bishops and popes, who were charged with interpreting these to the faithful. In both cases, the ruling classes, whether secular or religious, projected their grandiosity and narcissism into 'God' who had revealed Himself to them; they then used their claimed privileged access to God to further their own kingdoms on earth.

Holy texts of every stamp are full of human projections of rage, hate and murderous destructiveness that have been attributed to the will of God. The Hebrew scriptures recorded the following divine revelation: "Thus saith the Lord of Hosts ... [G]o and smite Amalek, and utterly destroy all that they have" (1 Samuel 15:3). Similarly, the God of the Qur'ān admonishes the angels: "I am with you ... I shall fill the hearts of the infidels with terror. So smite them on their necks and in every joint and incapacitate them. ... It was not you who killed them but God did so" (Qur'ān 8:12). These kinds of projections are still very evident in today's leaders, which in the hands of powerful politicians and leaders, can have catastrophic effects on millions of innocent people. President George W. Bush's "War on Terror" displays these characteristics. This highly emotive war cry is resonant at emotional, national and international levels, and was therefore very effective as a rallying cry of the righteous against the terrorists. The phrase had its first public outing following 11 September 2001 (9/11), when 19 members of an Islamic terrorist group, al-Qaida, hijacked four passenger planes and launched coordinated attacks on the Twin Towers of the World Trade Center in New York City and the

Pentagon in Washington, DC, killing 3,000 American citizens on their own soil. Osama bin Laden did not claim responsibility for the attacks until 2004, citing US support of Israel, the presence of American troops in Saudi Arabia and the imposition of sanctions against Iraq as the motivating reasons for the attacks. America's response was to invade Afghanistan in order to attack the terror, the Taliban, at its source. Bin Laden, who was the most hunted criminal in American history, evaded capture until May 2011, at which time he was executed by American military forces.

The power of language, and in particular sloganeering, is nowhere better demonstrated by the new vocabulary that emerged following 9/11. In addition to the "War on Terror", phrases like "Axis of Evil" (that included Afghanistan, Iraq, Iran and North Korea) and "weapons of mass destruction" (WMD) made frequent appearances in Western international media. This language had both moral and political intent. It polarized the world into those who were terrorists and those who fought terrorists. George W. Bush, a born-again Christian, is quoted as saying to the Palestinian Foreign Minister at the time, Nabil Shaath:

> I am driven with a mission from God. ... Go and fight these terrorists in Afghanistan ... and I did. Go and end the tyranny in Iraq and I did. ... And now, again, I feel God's words coming to me, "Go get the Palestinians their state and get the Israelis their security, and get peace in the Middle East". And, by God, I'm gonna do it.
>
> (MacAskill, 2005)

In a speech at about the same time, also reported by MacAskill, Bush stated "We're facing a radical ideology with unalterable objectives: to enslave whole nations and intimidate the world."

The birth of Islam: the Prophet Muhammad

> Muhammad is not the father of any man among you, but he is the messenger of Allah and the Seal of the Prophets.
>
> (Qur'ān 33:40)

Muslims believe that the prophet Muhammad was the last in the long line, beginning with Moses and including Jesus, of God's holy prophets on earth. Muhammad believed that he had been chosen by God to reform the corrupted religions of Judaism and Christianity through the explicit rejection of their foundations in magic and irrationalism. He accepted the validity of the ministries of Moses and Jesus as prophets, but rejected the imposition on Jesus of divine status as flawed and no more than a faulty belief in a disrespectful pagan magic born of ignorance and neglect of the Supreme Being. While Muhammad accepted Jesus's virgin birth and that he had performed miracles, he argued that these were evidence of divine power, not signs of divinity in Jesus.

Born in Mecca into a merchant family and a polytheistic society, Muhammad was orphaned early and was reared by his grandfather and uncle. He subsequently became a merchant and married a wealthy widow, who was herself a merchant. They had several sons, none of whom survived to adulthood, and four daughters. Muhammad lived a fairly conventional life for people of his class until 610, when, at the approximate age of 40 years, he reported experiencing visions and hearing voices. Before the 'visions' began, Muhammad regularly retreated to the mountains outside Mecca to pray. He also received regular religious counsel from an Arabian monotheist who derided paganism and the worship of idols (Lapidus, 2002). It is perhaps not surprising, therefore, that one of the strongest messages Muhammad derived from his visions was that there was only one God, a proclamation that angered his fellow merchants, who worried that this view would incur the wrath of the many pagan gods who protected their trade. Thus scorned for his beliefs, Muhammad fled Mecca with a small group of supporters and founded the first Muslim community in Medina in 622.

After Muhammad's death the year of the flight, *hijra* (Arabic, 'migration'), from Mecca to Medina became year one of the Islamic calendar to signify the 'birth' of Islam. This moment marked the end of paganism and the beginning of a society based not on kinship, as for most previous social groups dating back to totemism, but on common belief (Lapidus, 2002). The clans from Mecca who supported Muhammad and the clans, comprising pagan Arabs, of Medina, whom Muhammad recruited and converted to Islam united in one *umma* (a community of Muslims). Muhammad triumphantly reclaimed Mecca,[2] although he never returned to live there, and abolished all forms of paganism. Initially generous in victory, Muhammad subsequently won many converts. Islam quickly spread to Pakistan, Spain and north Africa.

During this period, Muhammad continued to experience visions, the most elaborate of which were encounters with Moses, Abraham and Jesus. He also reported travelling with the archangel Gabriel through heaven and hell, and approaching God's throne. Although accepting that he had been chosen by God to be the only living human to encounter both heaven and hell, Muhammad eschewed the Christian notions of saints, saviours and miracle workers. Despite his aversion to the supernatural, there are several mentions of miracles in the Qur'ān; for example, Moses turned his staff into a serpent (7:107), Jesus created birds from clay, restored vision to the blind and raised the dead (3:49).

What do we know of Muhammad's temperament and personality? Robinson (2003) distinguishes two types of biographies about Muhammad, the first of which was focused on his campaigns and has some historical veracity. Robinson noted that Arabic culture relied to a great extent on oral transmission, so it is uncertain when these oral accounts were actually written down. However, one such account – *Kitab al-Maghazi* (Book of raiding campaigns) by al-Waqidi (d. 823) – has survived intact. The second type – the so-called populist biographies – is much more questionable with respect to verisimilitude. These accounts were probably derived from storytellers. They were generously embellished with miraculous and folkloric tales, probably as a means of maintaining the interest of their audiences, and have little historical value. Unsurprisingly, these oral-turned-written accounts underwent multiple recensions with retelling according to the particular biases of the storytellers and scribes.

W. Montgomery Watt noted that Muhammad "was given to sadness, and there were long periods of silence when he was deep in thought" (Watt, 1961, p. 229). Watt also observed that Muhammad was especially fond of children, which "[p]erhaps [demonstrated] the yearning of a man who saw all his sons die as infants" (Watt, 1961, p. 230). As a statesman, Muhammad showed "courage, resoluteness, impartiality and firmness inclining to severity but tempered by generosity ... he had a charm of manner which won their affection and secured their devotion" (Watt, 1961, p. 230). Muhammad was also a social reformer who introduced a system of social security, reformed family structure and instilled the principle of land ownership – that is, the land belonged to Allah and all who developed it (Imam Shirazi, n.d.). In view of his social reform agenda, some commentators on the life of Muhammad view him as a politically savvy "historical prophet-ruler ... who claimed divine backing for completing Christ's mission as a human political project" (Nafissi, 2005, p. 413).

I was surprised to find that many accounts of Muhammad's 'visions' were reported uncritically in the scholarly literature. Many are simply a reiteration of the original myth of the origin of Islam and its holy book, the Qur'ān. Freud has almost nothing to say about them, even though he was mightily intrigued by the religious delusions of Christoph Haizmann and Daniel Schreber. Muhammad's 'visions' evince similar characteristics to the accounts of the storytellers. For example, Muslims and Jews at first coexisted amicably after Muhammad's migration to Medina. Muslims continued to observe Jewish prayer rituals that included, as demonstrations of acceptance, praying towards Jerusalem and observing the Jewish Day of Atonement. However, the rift between them grew because the Jews rejected Muhammad as a prophet in the Hebrew tradition. This increasingly overt hostility had two outcomes: first, the Jews, and then the Christians, vilified Muhammad, describing him as "the great enemy" and the "prince of darkness" (*Mahound*) (Watt, 1961, p. 230). The other consequence of the widening rift was that Muhammad's 'visions' became more specific and strident, asserting that only Islam was the true religion of Abraham, that Muslims must pray facing the *Ka'bah* (House of God in Mecca) and that they must observe the newly created fast of Ramadān instead of the Jewish Day of Atonement. And so the visions changed – from initially wanting to include the Jews and Christians in the perfection of the religion of Abraham to a vision in which Islam alone was the supreme monotheistic religion. Muhammad exiled the Jewish clans from Medina, killed some their leaders and confiscated their property. Despite this turning away from association with the Jews, Jerusalem remained very significant in Muhammad's spiritual worldview, and therefore in Islamic traditions.

I do not need to reiterate my thesis that Muhammad's visions were remarkably self-serving and concordant with the Prophet's wish to establish a unique religious identity for his followers, with himself as their leader. Unlike Haizmann and Schreber, Muhammad appears more shrewd than mad, given that many of his visions comprised policy statements from a civic leader presiding over an expanding Islamic state, but which carried greater weight because they were the word of God revealed through His Prophet. Thus, Muhammad used his visions to good effect – combining his persuasive charisma to elevate his personal wishes to the status of divine commandments in order to forestall any opposition from possible dissidents. On one occasion, it was discovered that one of Muhammad's raids on the merchant caravans had occurred during a holy period when fighting was forbidden, where-upon Muhammad had a vision revealing that, owing to the immense provocation of the Meccan pagans, Allah would be merciful in the face of this violation (Robinson, 2003). An even more telling example is the saga of the Satanic verses. Anxious about his opponents and wishing for reconciliation, Muhammad had a vision from God in the form of a poem that included three pagan goddesses who were worshipped by the Meccans. This vision achieved its aim of rapprochement, but Muhammad, likely racked with guilt about violating his previous vision that there was only one God, Allah, received a subsequent vision in which Gabriel appeared before him and convinced him that he had been mistaken, and it was Satan, not Muhammad, who had been responsible for the error.

Detractors, both Christian and Muslim, have scoffed at Muhammad's visions, believing they were a ploy used in the service of his political manipulations. Others assert that his visions were a divinely induced state. There may, however, be a third plausible explanation for Muhammad's visions – he may have suffered from the psychomotor seizures of temporal lobe epilepsy, which are now called complex partial seizures (Freemon, 1976). There are many descriptions of the nature of these visions in the Qur'ān, as well as from an astute ninth-century Muslim historian, Ibn Sa'd, who observed:

> At the moment of inspiration, anxiety pressed upon the Prophet and his countenance was troubled. He fell to the ground like an inebriate or one overcome by sleep. On the coldest day his forehead would be bedewed with large drops of perspiration. … To outward appearance inspiration descended unexpectedly, without any previous warning to the Prophet. When questioned on the subject he replied: "Inspiration cometh in one of two ways; sometimes Gabriel communicateth the Revelation to me, as one man to another and this is easy; at other times it is like the ringing of a bell, penetrating my very heart, and rending me."
>
> (in Freemon, 1976, p. 424)

Of course, all of the possibilities discussed here remain speculative. The strongest arguments against the epilepsy theory is the unusually late onset of the condition (at 40 years of age) and the lucidity of Muhammad's utterances, on which the Qur'ān was based, in the post-ictal period, which experts argue is unlikely in most epileptics, who require a period of recovery before regaining coherence.

Some sources assert that Muhammad did not plan his succession or name a successor, an act which placed the responsibility in the hands of the Muslim community because they were left "without the benefit of a prophet, a priestly caste, a hereditary monarch, or even the hope of a future savior" (Nafissi, 2005, p. 414) to guide them. Muhammad was apparently opposed to dynastic succession, promoting instead an egalitarian community-based consensus regarding succession decisions. Sources disagree, with some asserting that Muhammad appointed 12 successors beginning with his cousin and son-in-law, Ali, who eventually became the fourth Caliph (Imam Shirazi, n.d.); others stated that Muhammad named only Ali as his successor and perhaps by implication Ali's descendants. The post-Prophet Islamic era was marked by internecine fighting among Muhammad's would-be successors. The third caliph was killed during a rebellion triggered by his nepotistic rule, and Ali himself was assassinated by a member of a rival political faction. Notwithstanding these 'teething' problems, Islamic rule for the first 30 years post-Prophet was a true theo-democracy,[3] a fusion of 'church' and state, in which rulers, elected by the community, governed in obedience to the injunctions of the Qur'ān. This democratic fusion of religion and politics rested on five main principles – *ijma* (consensus), *shura* (consultation), *umma* (community), *maslaha* (public interest) and *bay'a* (pledge of allegiance to the ruler) (Lapidus, 2002). "Muhammad [translated] monotheistic values into the principles of a reformed Arabian society, and [formed] a new community with its own congregational life and ritual and legal norms, [which] made Islam a new religious community" (Lapidus, 2002, p. 28).[4]

Notwithstanding his considerable achievements, and talent as a leader and statesman, subsequent scholarship has judged Muhammad harshly, claiming that he was an imposter with a self-serving interest in propagating a form of religion that satisfied his sexual lust and his lust for power. Voltaire (1736) wrote a play about the prophet entitled *Le fanatisme, ou Mahomet le Prophète* (literally "Fanaticism, or Mahomet the Prophet"), which accuses Muhammad of brutality, superstition and fanaticism. Muhammad was also a slave trader who legalized sexual relationships (i.e., rape) between masters and slaves without the need for consent from the enslaved woman, even if she were already married (Stark, 2003). On the positive side, Muhammad also urged humane treatment of slaves, and often bought slaves for the purpose of setting them free (Holt, Lambton & Lewis, 1977).

Christians, Lutherans and Hindus have all voiced scathing criticisms of the prophet. Martin Luther described Muhammad as "a devil and first-born child of Satan" (Luther was none too Christian a character himself!). Others have called him a "wicked impostor", a "dastardly liar" and a "wilful deceiver" (Oussani, 1911). Watt (1977) cautions Westerners that their views may be prejudiced because of the extremely negative historical accounts of Muhammad written by Christians since the Crusades. This view sits in stark contrast to the current Muslim view of Muhammad. Today, he is perceived as the last of God's great prophets with a mission to spread Islam throughout the world. The period during the life of Muhammad is known to Muslims as the Islamic golden age, the return to which all subsequent ages of Islam have aspired. This is an example of a resurrective ideology, clearly based on a tunnel-visioned and somewhat fanciful view of the Prophet.

The Qur'ān, the holy book of Islam

> In the name of Allah the Most-merciful the All-merciful
> Praise be to Allah, Lord of the Worlds
> …
> the Master of the Day of Recompense.
> Thee only do we worship; Thee only do we ask for help.
> Guide us in the straight path,
> the path of those on whom Thou hast bestowed Thy favour
> not of those with whom Thou art angry and who have gone astray.

So begins the Qur'ān, which, like all holy books, contains simultaneous discourses of an omnipotent and beneficent but also a vengeful and punishing god, who favours only the obedient and righteous, thus sowing the seeds of discontent in those who are ostracized and alienated from the "favours" of the All-Merciful. The Islamic holy book bears a strong resemblance to Judaism and Christianity and contains many of the same stories and characters as those found in the Bible. For example, we may read about Adam, Abraham, Isaac and Ish'mael, Jacob, David and Goliath, Job, Jonah and Noah, among others, in both books. However, the Qur'ān has a kinder, more compassionate and forgiving turn on some of these stories compared with the Bible. For example, after the Fall of Adam, the Qur'ān [2:37–38] continues:

> Then Adam received (some) words from his Lord, so He turned to him mercifully; surely He is Oft-returning (to mercy), the Merciful. We said: Go forth from this (state) all; so surely there will come to you a guidance from Me, then whoever follows My guidance, no fear shall come upon them, nor shall they grieve.

In the Bible, the outcome of the Fall was declared in Genesis 3:17:

> And unto Adam He said, "Because thou hast hearkened unto the voice of thy wife, and hast eaten of the tree of which I commanded thee, saying, 'Thou shalt not eat of it,' cursed is the ground for thy sake; in sorrow shalt thou eat of it all the days of thy life."

The Qur'ān, like the Bible, reveres Jesus as one of God's greatest prophets, and he is described as "[the] son of Mary, illustrious in this world and the next" (Qur'ān 3:45). Islam is the youngest of the three religions and views itself as the final flowering of this long religious history (Hicks, 2006).

The word 'Islam' means submission (to the will of Allāh (God)). Islam was 'revealed' to the Prophet Muhammad in the seventh century CE in Mecca (now in Saudi Arabia). The founding mythology is that Muhammad began experiencing visions in his sleep, and as a result made spiritual retreats to a cave outside Mecca, although some sources predate these nocturnal excursions (Lapidus, 2002). It was here that the archangel Gabriel demanded that Muhammad "Read in the name of thy Lord who created", and thus began a process of recording the Qur'ān that took approximately 23 years. Historical evidence suggests that Muhammad was illiterate; the fact that he was chosen as the conduit between God and His people and assigned the task of enshrining Gabriel's dictation into a coherent text is nothing short of a miracle, which is in keeping with the centrality and importance of the miracle in the text (Vasalou, 2002). In all likelihood, the Qur'ān came into being when the Prophet conceived the idea of compiling a written scripture for the new religion, the text of which he dictated to scribes (Lapidus, 2002). The work was not completed until after the Prophet's death. Although Muslims believe that the Qur'ān is the uncorrupted word of Allah, like the Bible, there exist many variations in its texts through history (see, for example, the changing accounts of the story of Abraham, discussed in Chapter 7). This is hardly surprising given the mythology of its genesis. Endless disputes followed as to which version was authentic until, in the tenth century, Muslim scholars agreed that seven variations of the holy book were equally valid.

The word 'Qur'ān' is derived from the verb *qara'a* ('to read') but it also carries the meanings 'to recite' or 'to proclaim' (Robinson, 2003). It is commonly regarded by Muslims as the last book of divine guidance given by God to his people to sustain them until the last day, 'The Day of Judgement', in which all of humankind, both living and dead, will be brought before the divine Judge to account for themselves (Bell, 1970). Muslims believe that it supersedes both Jewish and Christian holy books. Notwithstanding the mythology of its origins and the 'magical' thinking inherent in much of its text, Islamic philosophy as articulated in the Qur'ān reveals, in places, a sensible and practical religion. Consider, for example:

> Piety does not lie in turning your face East or West: piety lies in believing in God, the last day and the angels, the Scriptures and the prophets, and disbursing your wealth out of love for God among your kin and the orphans, the wayfarers and mendicants, freeing the slaves, observing your devotional obligations, and in paying the *zakat* [alms] and fulfilling a pledge you have given, and being patient in hardship, adversity, and times of peril.
>
> (Qur'ān 2:176–177)

This passage reflects the so-called five pillars of Islam: (i) profession of faith (*shahada*) ("There is no god but God, and Muhammad is the Messenger of God"); (ii) prayer (*salat*) – Muslims pray five times a day while facing Mecca; (iii) alms (*zakat*) – giving 2.5 per cent of one's earnings to the poor, making donations and doing good works; (iv) fasting (*sawm*) during Ramadān in order to thank God for his blessings and to remember the poor and needy; and (v) pilgrimage (*hajj*) – visiting the holy city of Mecca at least once in a lifetime and praying in the Haram Mosque, built by Abraham (Esposito, 2013). The Qur'ān is also a historical document that reflects the political and social problems of the day and provides guidance with respect to law, politics, morals and religious ritual.

Because the Prophet was illiterate, he had to first listen to Gabriel, then memorize and recite the revelations to scribes who wrote down the text and assembled it into a book. Even today, Muslims willingly struggle to memorize large tracts of their holy book in honour of Muhammad's efforts to bring God's wisdom to their forebears. During Ramadān, night prayers are followed by long recitations of the Qur'ān (Robinson, 2003). The belief in the 'power' of the Qur'ān is evinced in certain superstitious practices in which particular passages (e.g., Qur'ānic Surahs 113, 114) are copied out and worn as amulets to ward off evil. Similarly, other passages are invoked to promote healing from sickness. In these usages, the Qur'ān takes on the mantle and function of a totem. We will take up the issue of what constitutes the 'true' message of the Qur'ān in the next section.

In the name of Allah: Islamic fundamentalism

> Let those fight in the way of Allah who sell the life of this world for the other. Whoso fighteth in the way of Allah, be he slain or be he victorious, on him We shall bestow a vast reward.
>
> (Qur'ān 4:74)

After the founding of Islam, there ensued hundreds of years of holy war waged between Christian crusaders who attempted to bring Christianity to the Holy Land and the Arabs and Moors, and then the Ottoman Turks who repelled them in the Middle East and the Balkans. In modern times, with the end of World War II, Western colonial empires disappeared, signalling a surge in Arab nationalism. Then, in 1967, came the Six-Day War, in which Israel effected a humiliating defeat on the collective military forces of Syria, Jordan and Egypt – Arab countries on Israel's border, whom Israel believed were about to attack. In the process, the Israelis captured the Gaza Strip and the Sinai Peninsula from Egypt, the Golan Heights from Syria and the West Bank (including East Jerusalem) of the Jordan River from Jordan, which was home to 600,000 Arabs, all highly strategic locations over which battle has been fought ever since. The war was not only a military disaster for the Arabs; psychologically, it was a devastating blow to Arab identity and morale. There followed an upsurge in Islamic fundamentalism, with the founding of the Palestinian Liberation Organization (PLO).

Fayek (2007) identified three types of militant politico-religious organizations that resulted from this upheaval in the Arab world, which were led by so-called spiritual leaders but which had primarily political intentions. The first, Hizb'Allah (the party of God), had the political aim of liberating southern Lebanon from occupation. The second, el Gihad and Hamas, had spiritual figureheads but lay leaders whose declared aims were to liberate Palestine. The third group includes the mullahs of Iran and Gama'a Islamiya, which operates in Indonesia, the Philippines,

Chechnya and elsewhere, which are essentially nationalistic organizations with no overt religious intent. Hence, while all three have manifest religious ideologies, their principal purposes are political. Armed resistance became fused or merged with a pseudo-religious mission of fighting the infidels.

With the shattering of the socio-ethnic identity and the crushing of Arab nationalism, there began a frenzied search for a new, all-encompassing identity that would restore unity and pride to Arab nations. The slogan "Islam is the solution" took hold in the Arab imagination as the potential healer of their shattered social identity. This Islamic resurgence was largely reactionary and backward looking, yearning for a return to orthodoxy and sharia law, which are in direct opposition to the central tenets of modernity, such as gender equality, egalitarian universalism (i.e., equal rights in law between all peoples, whether Muslim or non-Muslim), monogamy and the separation of church and state. Today, fundamentalist Islam presents a major obstacle to the principles of rationalism, democracy and economic progress embraced by the West, thereby placing itself on a collision course, both with the West and with Muslims wanting to embrace modernity (Nafissi, 2005). Indeed, Weber (1978) argued that Islam was a feudal, warrior religion that was essentially political at its core and could not, therefore, succeed as a religion. In tracing the history of Islam from "its original rationalizing, universalist, and democratic development of Abrahamic monotheism" to its current state of "long-term, debilitating reversals arising from the orthodoxy's attempts to mark off and safeguard the golden age's legacy against 'usurpation' by dynastic imperial states", Nafissi (2005, p. 407) notes the difficulty that Islam faces with respect to finding a way in which the fusion of religion and state in the golden age can function in the modern world. Judging from the eruption of endless civil unrest and civil wars in the Middle East (Bahrain, Egypt, Iraq, Jordan, Kuwait, Libya, Syria, Tunisia, Yemen), one can conclude that a return to the ideals of the golden age of Islam is proving elusive for today's Islamic states.

Islam: a message of love or hate?

> Surely your enemy is the one who shall be without posterity.
>
> (Qur'ān 108:3)

Some Islamic scholars argue that Islam is, at its core, a doctrine of peace and tolerance that supports a philosophy of non-violence. Hasan (2003) located the kernels of support for non-violence in the story of Adam's sons, Cain and Abel, a tale of fratricide, motivated by sibling rivalry induced by their heavenly Father, who accepted a meat offering from Abel but criticized the grain offering from Cain, whereupon Cain killed his brother in a fit of jealous rage. An interesting addition to this story in the Qur'ān is that Abel is presented as a pacifist, who purportedly said: "if thou stretchest out thy hand against me, to slay me, I will not stretch out my hand against thee, to slay thee; I fear God, the Lord of all Being" (Qur'ān 5:31–32).

In this account, Abel's act of non-violence assures him of divine forgiveness for all previous sins – a message that has clearly been misunderstood by today's Islamic extremists, who preach the opposite message – that murderous jihadists (*jihad* means 'holy war') are those who have direct access to paradise! This raises the question that if there be such a thing as a holy war in Islam, how can this be reconciled with the claimed message of non-violence? Although the derivation of the word *jihad* implied a much broader meaning – 'to struggle' – it was used to describe the battles between Muhammad and his opponents – the pagan Arab tribes of Mecca and the Jewish tribes of Medina – and gradually took on the meaning of a military struggle. Some passages in the Qur'ān give a mixed message, as for example "Fight in the way of Allah with those who fight with you, but aggress not; Allah loves not the aggressors. And slay them wherever you come upon them, and expel them from where they expelled you; persecution is more grievous than slaying" (Qur'ān 2:186–187). Yet persecution was not the cause of the holy wars post-Muhammad; expansionist and economic motives were ascendant, giving these early Islamic empires no legitimate mandate for *jihad*. Similarly, the current view among Islamic fundamentalists that any war against non-Muslims is justified is equally counter-scriptural.

In 2012, the Pew-Templeton Global Religious Futures Project asked the following question of Muslims living in one of the countries listed in Table 8.2: "Are suicide bombing and other forms of violence against civilian targets justified in order to defend Islam from its enemies?"

These statistics do not sit well with arguments that the Islamic religion is built upon love, in particular the love of God, forgiveness, compassion and tolerance, emotions which "[reflect] God's Mercy on [ourselves]". Gülen, Ünal and Haliloğlu (2004) assert that *jihad* (holy fighting in Allah's Cause) is based on a misinterpretation of the Qur'ān and that Muslims need to be re-educated in order to come to an understanding that those who practise terrorism are not 'true' Muslims. However, the Qur'ān, like the human psyche, has a dark side, which is revealed in some very dark passages, akin to the biblical wrath found in the Christian holy book, containing threats of dire punishment for unbelievers and wrongdoers that provide a scriptural foundation for those seeking a mandate for violence. Here are a few examples: "Whoever is the enemy of Allah and His angels and His apostles … so surely Allah is the enemy of the unbelievers" (Qur'ān 2:98); " Allah does not guide the unbelieving people" (Qur'ān 2:264); "O mankind! Fear your Lord. Lo! the earthquake of the Hour of Doom is a tremendous thing" (Qur'ān 22:1); "those who disbelieve will not cease to be in doubt thereof until the Hour come upon them unawares, or there come unto them the doom of a disastrous day" (Qur'ān 22:55); "Yes! Whosoever earns evil and his sin has surrounded him, they are dwellers of the Fire [i.e., hell]; they will dwell therein forever" (Qur'ān 2:81); "taste the torment [in hell] for rejecting Faith" (Qur'ān 3:106). Such passages are reminiscent of many passages from the bible.

There are also Qur'ānic verses that are specifically supportive of *jihad*: "Jihad is ordained for you [Muslims] though you dislike it, and it may be that you dislike a thing which is good for you and that you like a thing which is bad for you.

TABLE 8.2 Percentage of Muslims who agreed that suicide bombing against civilian targets is often or sometimes justified, by country

Country	Often justified (%)	Sometimes justified (%)	Total (%)
Palestinian Territories	18	22	40
Afghanistan	18	21	39
Egypt	11	18	29
Bangladesh	9	17	26
Turkey	3	12	15
Jordan	4	11	15
Pakistan	4	9	13
Indonesia	2	5	7
Iraq	3	4	7
Russia	1	3	4
Kazakhstan	<1	2	3

Source: 2012 Pew–Templeton Global Religious Futures Project, www.globalreligiousfutures.org/explorer/custom#/?countries=Worldwide&question=935&subtopic=47&year=2012&chartType=map&answer=15581&religious_affiliation=23&gender=all&age_group=all.

Allah knows but you do not know" (Qur'ān 2:216).[5] Indeed, the following verse is openly critical of those who do *not* wish to engage in *jihad*: "It is only those who believe not in Allah and the Last Day and whose hearts are in doubt that ask your leave to be exempted from Jihad. So in their doubts they waver" (Qur'ān 9:45). Those who refuse to engage are cursed as "disbelievers" whose destiny is hell: "And among them is he who says: 'Grant me leave to be exempted from Jihad and put me not into trial.' Surely, they have fallen into trial. And verily, Hell is surrounding the disbelievers" (Qur'ān 9:49). While there are many countervailing verses that exhort the practice of love and mercy, Muslims who wish to engage in *jihad* can be justified in their contention that the Qur'ān does call 'good' Muslims to *jihad*: Islamic scholars who claim otherwise are frankly disingenuous. In fact, some scholars have noted that Islam evolved into a "national Arabic warrior religion" (Weber, 1978, p. 623); the historical precedent was the Prophet Muhammad himself, whose "raiding campaigns" are recorded in a book written in about 823 (Robinson, 2003). However, we are advised that Muhammad was not a war-monger; he counselled against war and violence and the gratuitous destruction of property (Imam Shirazi, n.d.).

Factions within Islam are a major source of discord and unrest. The Shi'ite–Sunni conflict has been described as "the most deadly and unsolvable conflict in the Middle East" (Kedar, 2013). It is the basis for the boundless hostility between Saudi Arabia and Iran, and for the self-destruction of Syria, a country which, supported by Iran, has been relentlessly killing its Sunni citizens. The current overall death toll in Syria is estimated to be 191,000 dead (Aljazeera, 2014); millions have been left homeless and most have become refugees.

Sunni and Shi'a sects have been at war with each other since a disagreement over caliph (i.e., head of an Islamic state or Muslim community) succession after Muhammad's death in 632. At that time, the majority accepted that Abu Bakr,

Muhammad's father-in-law (from his last wife, Aisha), would succeed Muhammad. However, one group believed that Muhammad's wish was that Ali, his cousin and son-in-law (having married Muhammad's daughter, Fatima), should succeed him. Contrary to Fatima's wishes, Ali did not succeed Muhammad; Abu Bakr was appointed Muhammad's successor as the leader of Islam. The former group became known as the Shi'ites (from *Shi'a Ali*), while the latter group, the Sunnis, subscribed to an essentially democratic process for the election of caliphs. Ali became the fourth caliph but was assassinated in 661 by a rival faction. Shi'ites follow imams (spiritual leaders) who are Ali's descendants; they do not recognize the Umayyad caliphate or its successors. Shi'ites believe that there are 12 imams, all descendants of Fatima, the twelfth of whom will return on the Day of Judgement (Nasr, 2006).

The imamate of the Shi'a has a greater prophetic function than the caliphate of the Sunnis. Unlike Sunnis, Shi'as believe that special spiritual qualities have been bestowed upon Muhammad and his successors, including Ali and the succeeding imams who had a similar status to that of bishops and popes in the Christian Church. Imams were thought to be free from sin and human error (*ma'sūm*), and could interpret the hidden inner meaning of the teachings of Islam (Nasr, 2006).

The rift between these two factions of Islam remains unresolved to this day. Tensions between the minority Shi'a (10–25%), the majority (45–55%) of whom live in Lebanon, and the majority Sunni Muslims (>75%) across the Middle East have been identified as a significant problem for Muslims living in Lebanon (67%), Iraq (52%), Afghanistan (44%) and Iran (23%) (Pew Research Project on Religion & Public Life, 2013). For example, in Lebanon, the Hizb'Allah, in response to this endless enmity between these two Islamic factions, gained control to end the hundreds of years of oppression and marginalization of the Shi'ites (Kedar, 2013). The unabated political conflict between Sunni and Shi'a is the source of the majority of deaths in the Middle East. For example, the eight-year war (1980–8) between Iraq, under the Sunni Saddam Hussein, and Shi'ite Iran, under the Ayatollahs, resulted in over a million deaths of Muslims on both sides. The intensity of these conflicts is a great pity, given that both groups share many beliefs in common regarding the fundamental tenets of the Islamic faith – belief in one God, belief in God's Prophet, Muhammad, belief in heaven and hell and fasting during Ramadān.

On the world stage, in 2011, according to the National Counterterrorism Center (NCTC) (2011), Sunni extremists were responsible for 8,886 of the 12,533 terrorism-related deaths worldwide. They were engaged in at least 5,700 incidents, which represent 56 per cent of all attacks and 70 per cent of all fatalities. Of these, al-Qaida was responsible for at least 688 attacks that resulted in almost 2,000 deaths, while the Taliban in Afghanistan and Pakistan conducted over 800 attacks that resulted in nearly 1,900 deaths. A shocking fact that is probably little known in the general world community is that Muslims suffered between 82 and 97 per cent of terrorism-related fatalities over the five years to 2011 (NCTC, 2011). Countries with Muslim majorities such as Afghanistan suffered the largest number of fatalities (3,245 deaths in 2011) followed by Iraqis (2,958), Pakistanis (2,038), Somalis (1,013) and Nigerians (590).

The face of jihad: Osama bin Laden

> Resentment is like drinking poison and then hoping it will kill your enemies.
>
> (Nelson Mandela, cited in Sher 2013)

What can we discover in the early life of a person like Osama bin Laden that might help us to understand how he developed his fundamentalist commitment to Islam and *jihad*, his pathological hatred of the United States and his determination to wage holy war against his sworn enemy? In order to achieve any understanding of extremists like bin Laden, it is necessary, as discussed in Chapter 5, to consider their formative experiences, their adult personality and the influence of the socio-historical contexts in which they grew up, which for bin Laden included the rise of radical Islamic ideology and the USA's post-war foreign policy in the Middle East. Islam and Islamic states had suffered repeated reversals and humiliations since the golden age of the Prophet Muhammad. A further humiliation occurred after World War II, when the victorious West carved up the Middle East and installed puppet governments, dictatorships or monarchies that were beholden to the United States. Most significantly, the establishment of an independent Israeli state in 1948 on land previously occupied by the Palestinians was perhaps the pivotal event that polarized Muslims, Jews and Westerners. Thirty years later, Muslims began to express their rage by overthrowing (e.g., Iran's Shah Muhammad Reza Pavlavi in 1979) or assassinating (e.g., Egypt's Anwar Sadat in 1981) the 'American puppets' who had attempted to Westernize their countries in order to secure easy access for the USA to their oil reserves. Muslims were further empowered by the defeat of Russia in Afghanistan. These events triggered a regressive pull back to traditional religious values and the reassertion of Sharia law in some Muslim countries, which was motivated by the fear of being corrupted by the West with its materialist values and its obsession with money and sex. These factors, compounded by the power and wealth disparity between Middle Eastern Muslims and the West, enraged the more extreme (i.e., envious) among them. This backdrop of impotent rage against their perceived victimization provided fertile soil for the rise of a militant Islam (Maalouf, 2000).

Most fundamentalists/extremists, including Islamic extremists, have only one affiliation; it is thus easy from this position to polarize the world into believers and infidels. Membership of such groups restores identity, self-esteem and pride, fills an inner emptiness and solidifies and justifies all means of staving off attacks from the outside. It also provides a justifiable focus for externalizing envy, rage and hatred, which is expressed collectively against a common enemy, thereby rendering actions defensible and indeed heroic.

Born in Saudi Arabia in 1957 to a father with many wives and 52 children, Osama, the seventeenth child, became steeped in the extreme fundamentalism of Wahhabism, a Sunni sect to which his father subscribed and which arose as a reaction to the decadence of the Ottoman Empire in the eighteenth century (Allen, 2007). Although his father died in an air crash in 1966, when Osama was nine, Osama continued to live a life of both privilege and piety (Miliora, 2004). He graduated from university with a degree in economics and public administration, acquired four wives and became inducted into the Muslim Brotherhood at a time when the radical events described above were unfolding. By 22 years of age, Osama strongly identified with the *mujahideen* (freedom fighters) and their struggles against the 'godless' Soviets in Afghanistan. Victory was celebrated in the Muslim world as an event of enormous historical significance for Islam. When his mentor, Abdullah Azzam, who had established a worldwide network of Muslim militants, was assassinated in Pakistan in 1989, bin Laden stepped into his shoes, renaming the organization al-Qaida (The Base) and merging it with the Egyptian Jihad Group soon afterwards (Mishra, 2002). There followed a number of other formative experiences, including the Persian Gulf War, during which he became more stridently anti-Western and anti-American and preached the message of *khalifa*, that is, a Muslim world united under one leader. Disillusioned with a Westernized Saudi Arabia, which withdrew his citizenship of that country in 1994 as a result of his outspoken criticism of the ruling regime (Bergen, 2001), bin Laden moved first to Sudan and then to Afghanistan, recruited the Taliban as allies and emerged publicly as a terrorist leader whose aim was the return of the "traditions of the devout ancestors" and an "absolute commitment to jihad" against the United States, whom he characterized as the "greatest enemy of Islam" (Kepel, 2002, pp. 219–20). In 1998, he issued a *fatwa* (religious teaching/legal decree) to Muslims worldwide to kill Americans, both military and civilian. His *coup de maître* was the destruction of the Twin Towers[6] of the World Trade Center on 11 September 2001 (9/11).

It is almost impossible to imagine the effect that the complexities of his family life exerted upon a young bin Laden. Being one of 52 children would certainly pose great challenges for the development of an individual identity. Further, he lost his mother, or more correctly, he experienced the loss of his mother's status through divorce as a personal loss, and his father through death while still a very young child. He was inducted, perhaps indoctrinated, into extremist Wahhabi cult beliefs from a very early age, the embrace of which perhaps represented identification with his father, who was a committed Wahhabist. Such an environment is not conducive to the development of a strong sense of self or identity.

These early losses most likely engendered rage against both parents for failing to meet his needs. Rage engenders a desire for retaliation, but it is difficult to attack a more powerful opponent. Instead, the neglected child becomes in fantasy like the powerful depriver, adopts a mantle of self-sufficiency and denies any need. Because the parent is not all bad, the child develops two opposing representations that are internalized as the 'good' (giving) and the 'bad' (depriving) object. Splitting is the process that protects the good from the bad object. The good object is idealized as powerful in order that it may defend against, expel and annihilate the bad object. Splitting intensifies when the bad experience becomes overwhelming and unmanageable. The bad object is repressed (i.e., removed from consciousness) but its influence remains – it results in a rigidity of mind as an attempt to protect against annihilation anxiety. This rigidity engenders persecutory states of mind and fundamentalist thinking. People who have become overwhelmed by a bad object lose the capacity to empathize with others; instead, blaming and destructiveness replace the tender human emotions of concern and compassion. These feelings are then acted out – there is no space in the rigid mind for self-reflection or understanding; when these feelings are acted out collectively, they become terrorism (Young, 2001).

We all seek a 'holding' environment when our safety and security are threatened. So too did bin Laden. To bolster his weak and impoverished inner self, bin Laden became fused with Islam and the Arab people (Falk, 2001). Offences committed against Islam became offences committed against bin Laden himself; he experienced them as personal humiliations for which he hungered for revenge. He reacted with profound rage when Saudi Arabia turned to America for help during the Gulf War after his own offer of assistance had been rejected. His rage was compounded when Saudi Arabia allowed America to set up bases on Arab soil.

Bin Laden experienced an uncontainable murderous rage towards America and Americans, whom he characterized as "Jews and Crusaders", which we might speculate constituted the displaced, externalized form of the bad internal object (i.e., the abandoning father). Kobrin (2003) noted that "the bad influence of American culture that the Islamists vociferously deride masks their excitement of how unconsciously enthralled, tempted, and confused they are by such freedom" (p. 212). The unconscious defence of projective identification provides some relief from these intense but forbidden wishes and desires, because they are split off and projected into the hated 'evil' other, which then becomes the target of their expurgation rather than the self. This process cycles between "unending hatred and violence with moments of perverse pleasure" (Kobrin, 2003, p. 213). Interestingly, although Muslims are permitted only four wives, they overcome this restriction by divorcing the fourth wife and then remarrying or entering into temporary marriages. The Prophet Muhammad, whom all good Muslim men wish to emulate, was survived by at least nine wives and several concubines, two of whom were Jewish, one of whom was Christian and one of whom was seven years old at marriage and nine years old when the marriage was consummated! Thus, insatiable sexual desire for women is present in "devout" Islamic culture (Bouhdiba, 1998), but is hidden and regulated by tortuous legal means, as well as by the subjugation of women, who must hide their bodies and their sexuality under an array of restrictive clothing (e.g., abaya, niqab, chador, khimar, burqa and hijab). Some women also suffer female genital mutilation (FGM) (World Health Organisation, 2014) to reduce their sexual desire and pleasure and to ensure their virginity until marriage.[7]

Interestingly, bin Laden's mother was the fourth wife of his father and was hence devalued, divorced and reduced to the status of concubine, which was a source of great anger and humiliation to bin Laden, because, as her son, he felt similarly devalued. Kobrin (2003) asserts that this experience of denigration may have spawned bin Laden's persecutory and paranoid tendencies. "The paranoid mechanism of scapegoating maintains the splitting and purges the rage of the group-self, individual-self or both. Scapegoating is one of the explicit functions served by the suicide bomber, who carries the group's rage away" (Kobrin, 2003, p. 215), but more of this later. When his mother was banished from his father's harem, Osama became an orphan, filled with infantile rage and fear, determined to fight for her.

In summary, Osama bin Laden had many unresolved issues from his early life that left him embittered, envious, hateful, rageful and vengeful, feelings which he needed many primitive defences to manage. As he grew to manhood, gathered followers and increased his wealth through his own business dealings, he became so empowered and grandiose that, in the late 1990s, he issued two *fatwas* of global *jihad*, acts for which he had no legitimate authority. Already over-identified with the Prophet Muhammad to the point where he perceived himself to be his modern-day incarnation, this act demonstrated his antisocial grandiosity, malignant narcissism and omnipotence, which were reinforced with every successful attack against his enemies. Thus, the paranoid and primitive defences of his childhood evolved, in a conducive socio-political context, into paranoid, delusional thinking in an adult who had the financial and military means, single-minded determination and rage to wreak havoc on a world that had humiliated and shunned his child-self and later his adult-self (as a Saudi Arabian) and, finally, his group-identity (Islam).

In death as in life, Osama bin Laden was the personification of radical evil. It is not surprising that the reaction of the American public to the news that bin Laden was dead was somewhat akin to the reaction of fundamentalist Muslims to the downing of the Twin Towers. There was chanting and cheering in the streets and cries of "USA! USA!" In this moment, Americans had been resurrected and were again invincible.

Suicide bombing

> The Americans should expect reactions from the Muslim world that are proportionate to the injustice they inflict. ... Hostility towards America is a religious duty. We hope to be rewarded for it by God.[8]
>
> (Osama bin Laden)

The first suicide bombing occurred in Beirut in 1983 and became commonplace during the second Palestinian intifada in the 1990s. Since then, more than 95 per cent of all suicide bombing attacks conducted worldwide have been carried out by Muslim extremists (Lechner, 2007). Suicide bombers have been variously described as madmen, psychopaths and murderers on the one hand, and inadequate, marginalized, alienated and already suicidally depressed or frankly suicidal on the other. It is a supreme irony that Islam does not allow or condone suicide (Lechner, 2007). Nonetheless, applying Muhammad's strategy of self-serving rationalizations to justify behaviours that are expressly forbidden by Islam, modern–day Muhammads in radical Islamic groups distinguish between the psychologically ill suicide-completer who ends his emotional misery by ending his life (forbidden suicide), and a *shahid/shahida* (martyr), who loves Islam and life, but who has the inner strength to act in the common (Islamic) good (permitted suicide). This is clearly an effective strategy, given that this justification of a particular form of suicide and the use of religious incentives such as a promise of a place in heaven for the bombers and their families, and financial rewards and enhanced social status for the families of the *shahid/shahida*, have ensured a steady stream of recruits to the cause.

How can we explain behaviour that appears so foreign to the majority as to be utterly incomprehensible? Some (e.g., Oliver & Sternberg, 2005) argue that being imbued with extreme Islamic fundamentalism is a core characteristic of suicide bombers, particularly among the Palestinians, while others maintain that their motivations are more political and secular than religious (Pape, 2005). Pape also noted that recruitment to al-Qaida increased markedly during the US–led invasion and occupation of Iraq and concluded that nationalism rather than religion was the stronger underlying motivation for suicide bombing, although both were influential, but in different ways. While the goals of suicide bombing may be primarily political, religion is recruited in the process of resistance to demonize the occupier and to legitimate martyrdom (Stern, 2003). Statistics available from the NCTC support the former contention, that extreme Islamic fundamentalism appears to motivate the majority of suicide bombings. For example, extremist Sunni Muslim terrorists were responsible for about 70 per cent of the 12,533 deaths by suicide bombing in 2012 (NCTC, 2012). More than half of those killed were civilians, 755 of whom were children.

Perhaps a more helpful approach to understanding the mind of a suicide bomber is to analyse not only their personal characteristics in isolation, if indeed a uniform set of characteristics can be found to define them, but also the context in which suicide bombing occurs. For example, suicide bombing is most prevalent in occupied nations, particularly when those occupiers are democratic and have an overwhelmingly superior military advantage compared with the occupied nation. Suicide bombing is even more frequent if there are significant religious differences between occupier and occupied and when the occupier is America (Pape, 2005).

While social and sociological analyses assist us to understand the cognitive motivations of suicide bombers, these may not help an ordinary person to understand or, indeed, empathize and identify with a suicide bomber. To do so, one would need to lower the dissociative barrier (i.e., our wish to disavow similar feelings in ourselves) between the suicide bomber (viewed as dehumanized, barbaric) and us (viewed as human, civilized), such that we can begin to think about what motivates such horrific, abhorrent acts. Young (2001) makes the point here with respect to the 9/11 catastrophe:

> In order to commit those atrocities, the humanity of those fundamentalists would have to have undergone a long process of caricaturing, degrading and

dehumanising Americans ... creating a huge split between themselves and those people in the World Trade Center.

(Young, 2001, p. 43)

A moment's reflection will reveal that the occupier appears in the eyes of the suicide bomber in the same way that the suicide bomber appears to the occupier – as the committer of atrocities for which they have no redress except the extreme act of mass murder/suicide. The relationship between the occupier and the occupied is one of dominance, in which all aspects of the lives of the occupied are under constant surveillance and control by the occupiers, and hostile and subversive submission, with the occupied resisting, yet succumbing to, the constant humiliations attendant upon their abject subjugation (Stern, 2003). Such repeated humiliations result in a build-up of impotent rage, frustration and despair that demands expression.

Altman (2008) observed that at its extreme, humiliation becomes mortification, which signals a wish to be dead rather than endure further humiliation. This dynamic underlies the intractable nature of the conflict between Israel and Palestine, with each viewing the other as invaders and murderers, and themselves as victims. The Jews can give no quarter because they are defending against the unspeakable humiliations they have suffered during their entire history, culminating in the Holocaust, and more recently succumbing to and then retaliating against weekly Palestinian suicide bombing attacks following the collapse of the Oslo peace agreement (1993) in 2000, which signalled the second intifada (al-Aqsa). For the Palestinians, "the pain of having lost [their] ancestral lands ha[s] been a trauma for which there [i]s no cure" (Khosrokhavar, 2002, p. 110).

When threat is imminent to oneself or to one's 'in'-group, powerful emotional reactions (such as the threat of annihilation attendant upon infant helplessness) that have their genesis within the unconscious are reactivated and influence one's response to the current threat (Hinshelwood, 2002). This usually results, for the majority, in adopting stronger 'in'-group attitudes and more polarizing 'out'-group sentiments that demand harsher military suppression for the transgressors (Govrin, 2006). Hence, a positive feedback loop of ever-increasing violence becomes self-perpetuating. What possible solution can be found with respect to this obdurate clinging to a symmetrical worldview but endless war, a fight to the death, genocide or annihilation of the weaker side? The message of psychoanalysis is clear – that unless we can acknowledge the murderous rage and envy within, we are condemned to act it out, albeit in a spirit of indignant piety and righteousness that is so commonly observed in the clergy of all religions and in the leaders of warring nations.

No one believes that suicide bombing can solve the conflicts besieging the Middle East. It is not so much an effective military strategy as a desperate form of communication that is used to convey impotent rage, humiliation, shame, despair and hunger for revenge regardless of any possible consequences to the perpetrators. Altman (2008) poses a critical question: "Why is it better ... to intend to be killed than to be willing to die?" He concluded that "having the intention to die makes one immune from all traditional measures meant to dissuade or intimidate. The overwhelming military might of the occupier is disabled ...[as is] any preventive or retaliatory strategy" (Altman, 2008, p. 52). Suicide bombing epitomizes the ultimate defiance of the rule of the oppressor, placing perpetrators outside the oppressor's sphere of influence. The intention to die thus incapacitates the occupying military force and momentarily passes the mantle of power, restoring dignity and agency to the suicide bomber and to the oppressed whom s/he represents. Durkheim (1951) calls the form of suicide that has an ostensibly self-transcendent motivation "altruistic suicide". Suicide bombing is also a bizarre paradox, representing as it does a nation's willingness to destroy itself to service a goal of self-determination (Altman, 2008).

The psychology of suicide bombers

> Not equal are those believers who sit (at home) and receive no hurt, and those who strive and fight in the cause of Allah with their goods and their persons. Allah hath granted a grade higher to those who strive and fight with their goods and persons than to those who sit (at home). Unto all (in Faith) hath Allah promised good: But those who strive and fight hath He distinguished above those who sit (at home) by a special reward.
>
> (Qur'ān 4:95)

Profiling of suicide bombers does not appear to be a useful endeavour, given that the profile varies considerably. Interestingly, Israelis at first targeted Palestinian males aged between 18 and 45 years for surveillance and additional restrictions, believing them to be the main demographic for suicide bombers during the first intifada. Subsequently, the Palestinians widened the suicide bomber demographic in order to make detection more difficult. Suicide bombers now include children as young as seven who have been sold to the Taliban to become suicide bombers. Young boys are 'trained' in the madrassahs (i.e., schools for teaching Islamic ideology) in Pakistan, which serve as feeders for Taliban training camps.[9] They are told that if they carry verses of the Qur'ān with them, they will be protected from the bomb blast when they detonate the bombs strapped to their bodies. Although the use of brainwashed young boys has become almost commonplace, the use of girls is rarer. However, on 6 January 2014, a 10-year-old Afghan girl, Spogmai, was found wearing a suicide bomb vest after her brother, a Taliban commander, encouraged her to carry out a suicide mission on border police in Helmand province. The ostensible motivation for sacrificing his sister was that she had supposedly had 'illicit relations' with the police officers whom she was despatched to kill. A traumatized Spogmai decided to hand herself in to the police and begged not be returned home for fear that she would suffer atrocities at the hands of her family.[10]

There have been recent increases in the number of female suicide bombers recruited, in particular, from among widows or bereaved siblings who wish to expel their rage and grief about the loss of their loved ones in a retaliatory action against a hated enemy (Pape, 2005). Those successfully recruited are likely to have suffered not only the current profound loss of a husband or brother but earlier narcissistic injuries constituted through insufficient caregiver attention and empathy (Olsson, 2005) that leave them with fragile self-esteem, low self-confidence and undis-charged feelings of shame and anger for which narcissistic defences such as gran-diose fantasies and reactive narcissistic rage are mobilized to rectify the imbalance (Khalid & Olsson, 2006). Becoming a suicide bomber simultaneously addresses all these psychological crises.

Suicide bombers can also be found among the affluent and well educated, who may have been born and reared in a Western country or who live or have lived abroad, many married with family and professional occupations. This group is par-ticularly difficult to understand. It is possible that while they appear well adjusted and assimilated into Western society, they may feel marginalized, lonely and deval-ued at their core because of the discomfort they feel in a society whose values are alien and at odds with the values of their parents with which they grew up. To assuage these feelings, they may seek comfort from fellow countrymen at mosques and other religious gatherings where they come to the attention of radical Islamic clerics who induct them into Islamic fundamentalism that is saturated with hatred of the West. Even in a relatively benign and distant land like Australia, there are growing numbers of young men who are being recruited for martyrdom, most recently in Syria. A study of radicalized Muslim youth in Australia found that they tended to be young (<30), unmarried, socially marginalized and economically dis-advantaged, and see themselves as part of the global *umma* (Islamic nation) (Ali, 2012). Andrew Zammit, a terrorism researcher, is quoted in Olding (2013) as iden-tifying three key factors that entice Australian-born Muslims to Syria: (i) Lebanon's links to *jihad*; (ii) hostility towards Syria; and (iii) international inaction.

A recent report by journalist Rachel Olding (2013) tracked the Facebook posts of a young Turkish Muslim whose interests gradually shifted from Xbox and soccer to reporting what he had heard at seminars and from the mouths of fanatical terrorist clerics. In October 2013, he posted the following message on Facebook: "Wake up to the reality that your sisters are being killed and raped in front of there [sic] children and husbands, children being blown up by jets and helicopters, men being humiliated like dogs, then slaughtered like cattle. What will our reply be to Allah on that day?" (Olding, 2013, p. 4). He subsequently went to Syria to fight against the forces of President Bashar al-Assad. The puz-zling aspect of this story and others like it occurring in Australia is that very few of the young men being sent to Syria are in fact Syrian, nor do they have any personal connection with Syria. They say that as human beings and Muslims, they cannot sit idle in a comfortable life thousands of miles from the strife while fellow Muslims are being killed by al-Assad. The role of social media in bringing the ugliness of these conflicts into the homes of young Muslims abroad is only one way in which they become fired up with zeal. There appear to be no shortage of pan-Islamic political organizations, mosques and Islamic clerics, both local and in the ether, filling them with messages of hatred and *jihad*. Ali commented that sheikhs leading young men into *jihad* was a case of the "blind leading the blind" because the sheikhs and clerics are ill-informed, uneducated and lacking in personal self-awareness about their own motivations.

A follow-up article by Ruth Pollard (2014) reporting from Kilis, a province in south-central Turkey, found that the majority of foreign fighters arriving in Syria do not join the Free Syrian Army. They are drawn to groups, such as *Jabhat al-Nusra*, linked to al-Qaida, whose aim is to establish "a transnational Islamic state beyond the current borders ... and to shape a new Syria" (Pollard, 2014, p. 6). Figures made available by Australian Federal Police show that foreign fighters are primarily arriving from Jordan (2,089), Saudi Arabia (1,016), Tunisia (970) and Lebanon (890). There have been 366 from the UK and 100 from Australia. In all, estimates stand at 11,000 foreign fighters from 74 countries.

In an interview study of would-be suicide bombers who were apprehended before they could detonate their explosives, Khalid and Olsson (2006) reported that no severe psychopathology, such as clinical depression, schizophrenia or other psychosis, was identified among this group. However, all behaviour is context-embedded and is a complex outcome of conscious and unconscious motivations and environmental factors. Assessing for the presence of a classifiable psychiatric illness may be too blunt an instrument to identify the intrapsychic mechanisms that potentiate the murderous rage of a suicide bomber. A more nuanced analysis has been provided by Volkan (2004), who has observed the deep connection between "a hurt and victimized country and the spiritual-warrior leader who himself feels personally victimized" (p. 157). The whole country's rage, hate and desire for retribution and revenge is projected into a leader or a suicide bomber who already resonates with these very sentiments, which thus become collectively justified and amplified, ripe for extreme action. We need only recall the hateful and paranoid stances of Adolph Hitler, Joseph Stalin and Osama bin Laden to witness how such a process becomes manifest.

These hateful philosophies are generationally transmitted through a number of processes that include modelling the behaviour and beliefs of important attachment figures (see Chapter 6) like mothers and fathers, imams, teachers and older peers, religious indoctrination through saturated education programmes that exclude alternative forms of social and political analysis (i.e., brainwashing) and the deliberate formation of a strong group identity (e.g., as jihadists) that overshadows the development of individuality and self-identity (Khalid & Olsson, 2006). This process results in a merging of individual identity, pain, rage and loss with the group's identity, rage, pain and loss. Suicide bombers are trained in this way. They come to feel important, specially chosen to enact a holy mission on behalf of their people. They become, for a brief moment, "a spokesperson for the traumatized community" who can, by the ultimate act of choosing death, "reverse the shared sense of victimization and helplessness by expressing the community's rage" (Volkan, 2004, p. 159) with impunity, since their deliberate suicide places them out of reach of their oppressors.

A detailed profile of a young jihadist presented by journalist Barney Henderson (2013) provides some of the personal detail and life chronology that is frequently missing from more political or clinical biographies of suicide bombers (Erlich, 2003). This poignant account underscores the point that for some young recruits to martyrdom, their understanding of their own motivations and those of their 'handlers' is at best immature and at worst childish in its gullibility and credulity. Ajmal Amir Kasab was just 21 years old when he ended the lives of 52 random civilians and wounded another 104 people who were waiting for trains at Chhatrapati Shivaji Terminus with his AK-47 assault rifle as part of a terrorist attack on Mumbai, India on 26 November 2008. Ajmal was the sole survivor of the police counter-attack and was intensively interviewed over a four-year period before being hanged for his crimes in November 2012. Henderson traces his transformation from a poor, uneducated boy from rural Pakistan with few skills but high aspirations to a petty thief and failed burglar in Lahore, where he went to look for work, to a kitchen hand in a downmarket restaurant in Rawalpindi, to a skilled marksman for the terrorist group *Lashkar-e-Taiba* (Army of the pure) who was prepared to die on command and to take out as many people as he possibly could on his way to martyrdom.

What underpinned this radical transformation? The answer is deceptively simple – he had a chance encounter with a Muslim preacher, Shabaan Mustaq, a member of *Jamaat-ud-Dawa*, the 'education' arm of *Lashkar-e-Taiba*, whose aim was to liberate Kashmir from India. Mustaq invited Ajmal to join his organization, with promises of life transformation and training in how to use weapons if he did so. Kasab spent most of that year in intensive military training. In the training camp, he was astounded at the quality of the food, accommodation and respect he was given. During his interrogation, Kasab stated that *Chacha* ('Uncle') (chief planner of the Mumbai attacks) said that "[w]e could have anything in the world we wanted before setting out for Mumbai" (Henderson, 2013, p. 31). The young recruits, in addition to intensive military and physical fitness training, were subjected to relentless religious indoctrination beginning with daily prayer sessions at 4 a.m. that continued throughout the day. Prior to recruitment, Kasab held no firm beliefs of any kind. During interrogation, he revealed a simplistic understanding of his mission, which was "about killing and getting killed and becoming famous ... it was a very honourable and daring job", for which his family would receive riches in abundance and he would "make Allah proud" (Henderson, 2013, p. 31). He was assured that his "name would be etched in gold and every Pakistani will praise you" (Henderson, 2013, p. 31). He had no understanding of the politics of his mission related to Kashmir.

As it turned out, Kasab found his calling – he proved to be an expert marksman, which was demonstrated by the fact that most of his victims were shot through the head or chest. Kasab further stated, "My handlers always told me that this life is not important, the next life is very important. You will see that there is a glow on your face and there is scent emanating from your body when you die in the cause of jihad" (Henderson, 2013, p. 32). Kasab was escorted to the Mumbai morgue, where the nine dead bodies of his fellow jihadists lay decomposing in the oppressive heat and unsanitary conditions of a morgue without refrigeration. Kasab was shocked that there was no glow or perfume emanating from the bodies of his fellow jihadists, at which point he broke down, weeping, in a moment of realization that he had been duped. At night, in his prison cell, he could be heard "weeping like a baby and calling out for his mother" (Henderson, 2013, p. 33), although, in the days before his death, he rejected an invitation to meet with and bid farewell to his parents. In fact, he had no last requests, and his final words were: "Allah ki kasam, dobara aisi galti nahin karunga" (I swear by God, I will not commit such a mistake ever again).

Conclusions and a cautionary tale

> [A]ll men are equal, not in their gifts and talents, but in their basic human qualities.
>
> (Fromm, 1964, p. 70)

I have argued in this book that the puzzle of religion and most behaviour spawned in its name can best be accounted for and possibly advanced using psychoanalytic theory, with the support of cognitive developmental theory, neuroscience, attachment theory and social psychology. Yet there is a profound paradox in my argument, because psychoanalysis itself has been riven almost from its inception by internecine conflict, profound 'sibling' rivalries, primitive defences and cult-like behaviour. Disagreements between various schools of psychoanalysis closely resemble the religious and philosophical disputes that are so apparent in the histories of religion and philosophy. Such disputes are not amenable to rational resolution, despite efforts to find solutions in reason – hence, their enduring nature.

Interestingly, although the conflict began with Freud's successive breaks with his erstwhile acolytes (e.g., Jung, Rank, Adler, Sullivan), it was cemented by the dispute within the British Psychoanalytic Society between Anna Freud, daughter of Sigmund, and Melanie Klein, the founder of object relations theory, who, although she broke with Freud in her theoretical orientation, competed for the position of Freud's intellectual heir with his biological daughter, Anna, who remained truer to her father's theory.

André Green (2005), in commenting on all the dissidents who followed in the wake of Freud's monumental psychoanalytic theory, wondered whether subsequent adherents should "attach [themselves] to an embalmed and stiffened corpse, [thus] failing to pursue a critical evaluation of [psychoanalytic] theories as challenged by present practice" (p. 287) or continually renew, revise, radically rethink and extend the theory's concepts and tenets, and expose themselves to unfettered self-examination and self-criticism, as all psychoanalytic patients are exhorted to do. This is the very dilemma with which I have grappled in this book. Today's literalist and fundamentalist adherents of ancient religious texts and doctrines are themselves regressively and unthinkingly attached to an embalmed and stiffened corpse of primitive religious orthodoxy, formulated by men who had not the capacity for abstract or dialectical thinking, and who were informed only by their own pre-logical and magical thinking and early unresolved psychological trauma.

While the origins of religion from such shaky foundations is understandable – man's religious beliefs could not be more developed than the cognitive capacity from which they emanated – the current slavish adherence to such precepts thousands of years later seems utterly indefensible. And yet, this is the current state of affairs. Why? In this book, I have tried to argue, I hope successfully, that the answer lies within our own psychic functioning, in the realm of the powerful, primitive, pre-verbal affects that have arisen from early emotional traumata, both individual and collective, which remain unprocessed and unresolved in the absence of an empathically attuned listener (Holt, 2003). Further, our struggle to grapple with the overwhelming forces of nature and our place in cosmology constitutes the second key source of our need and desire for a Heavenly Father and for all the trappings that accrue to such a title – a house of God, a faithful flock of the chosen people, just rewards, eternal life. Black (2006) reiterates Freud's caution that our mature adult functioning is coextensive with our primitive emotional beginnings. All attempts to dissociate ourselves from the 'infant within' can have catastrophic consequences both for the individual, who reacts without awareness to events that retrigger powerful feelings of envy, hate and rage, and for the collective, into whom such feelings are projected.

Osama bin Laden and his fundamentalist followers chose to align themselves with the embalmed and stiffened corpse of the Prophet Muhammad, representing as he did an infantile wish to restore the limitless grandiose narcissism of the very young child, which is cruelly crushed over time by the inevitable disappointments of life. Osama bin Laden was consumed with murderous rage against a father who denigrated and then discarded his beloved mother, and against both parents who (unintentionally) abandoned him during his tender years. Unprocessed murderous rage enfeebles the self, leaving it vulnerable to attacks on esteem and value which can become collectivized and understood as an attack on one's affiliations, both national and religious. For Osama bin Laden, his personal rage was transmuted into the collective rage of Islam against the all-encompassing Infidel, originally his faithless parents, then America and finally his homeland, Saudi Arabia, which shamed and expelled him.

Lest this sounds like an unlikely argument to political scientists and historians who are much better versed than I in the geopolitical and economic complexities and precursors of the new wave of hatred against the West and the drive to return to fundamentalist Islamic rule in many countries, I can only repeat that all human action is contextualized and historically embedded. All such events are driven by the human psyche, and it is this component of a very complex picture with which I have been most concerned in this book. The Dalai Lama (1990) once commented:

> Human history ... is the history of human mental thought. ... Tragedy, tyranny, all the terrible wars ... have happened because of negative human thought. ... World peace must develop out of inner peace.

(pp. 102–3)

The Dalai Lama's wisdom – that we cannot change the world unless we change its inhabitants, ourselves – has been the central thesis in this book.

Despite the sombre cautions articulated in these closing paragraphs, it is incumbent upon me to end with a personally meaningful expression of optimism, not out of a Pollyanna-ish desire to deny a dire reality, but out of a sense of responsibility that I contribute to the ideal that we can one day act collectively to make our planet an equitably shared habitat for all its citizens. Many great philosophers have expressed a similar wish. The humanistic movement dates back to the fifteenth and sixteenth centuries and remained vibrant throughout the Renaissance and the Enlightenment to the present day. Its principal underlying philosophy is that "in each individual all of humanity is contained; that each man is all men, that each individual represents all of humanity ... the development of the universal is based on the fullest development of the individual" (Fromm, 1964, p. 70). The banner of humanism has been carried through the ages by some of our greatest thinkers, artists and philosophers – Manetti (*De Dignitate et Excellencia Hominis* – On the dignity and excellence of man), della Mirandola, Erasmus, Hume, Hegel, Spinoza, Goethe and Schweitzer.

Eric Fromm (1964) viewed psychoanalysis as a humanistic philosophy that constituted one of the greatest protections against religious fanaticism. It is, therefore, with his words that I choose to conclude this book.

> *Making the unconscious conscious transforms the mere idea of the universality of man into the living experience of this universality; it is the experiential realization of humanity.* To experience my unconscious means that I know myself as a human being, that I know that I carry within myself all that is human, that nothing human is alien to me, that I know and love the stranger, because I have ceased to be a stranger to myself.
>
> ...
>
> [I]n its deepest roots, psychoanalysis is part of the humanist movement which began in Europe five hundred years ago. The humanism of the Renaissance ... was the form in which modern man emancipated himself from the shackles of medieval authority. It was a protest against secular and ecclesiastic restriction of man's thought and activities ... the fanaticism of religion and nationalism, and ... the subjection of man to the idolatry of economic interests. ... It was the force that had faith in man and faith in reason, and which tried to avert the catastrophe that fanaticism and inhumanity eventually brought to Europe. [It] transcended the fanatical religious partisanship of the sixteenth century, just as today ... [it] tries to transcend the fanaticism of political partisanship. *The future of man depends on the strength of humanism in our time, and we hope that psychoanalysis will serve the idea of humanism and contribute to its strength.* [My italics]
>
> (Fromm, 1964, pp. 77 and 78)

Notes

1 http://law2.umkc.edu/faculty/projects/ftrials/salem/witchhistory.html (accessed 28 October 2014).
2 This took eight years and several wars, details of which are beyond the scope of this book.
3 Thereafter it became an inherited dynastic kingship.
4 Current Muslim scholarship does not concur that the pillars of Islam include a pledge of allegiance to the ruler. Rather, this was asserted by Muslim authors in later juristic and historical literatures. The so-called pillars are all acts of faith and worship, obviously with social implications (Ahmad Shboul, personal communication, 2014).
5 The Hadith (the report of the deeds and sayings of Muhammad) stated that this verse was narrated at a time when Muhammad was trying to motivate his reluctant people to undertake raiding campaigns on merchant caravans!
6 A psychoanalytic colleague speculated that the Twin Towers may have psychically represented the hated parental couple.
7 FGM has cultural, religious and social origins. FGM predates Islam but it has persisted as a cultural tradition that crosses religious borders. Although it is claimed that there are no explicit references to FGM in Islamic religious texts – it does not appear in the Qur'ān – there are, in fact, some Islamic texts/manuals that prescribe the practice of FGM as mandatory. For example, in *The Classic Manual of Islamic Sacred Law 'Umdat al-Salik* (Ahmad ibn Naqib al-Misri (d. 769/1368)), the following passage appears: "Circumcision is obligatory (for every male and female) by cutting off the piece of skin on the glans of the penis of the male, but circumcision of the female is by cutting out the clitoris (this is called HufaaD)" (http://answering-islam.org/Sharia/fem_circumcision.html).

   Other Islamic sources permit female circumcision "as an act of tolerance by Islamic law for pre-Islamic practices" but forbid "harmful acts" that include clitorodectomy and infibulation. Even mild forms of FGM are "disliked" and should be discouraged (www.minaret.org/fgm-pamphlet.htm). Recently, a book by Qasim Rashid, *The Wrong Kind of Muslim* (AyHa Publishing, 2013) specifically "repudiates the barbaric myth that Islam endorses FGM". There have also been many calls from Islamic scholars in the Middle East and Africa to end FGM and to declare infibulations a criminal act. Notwithstanding, according to UNICEF (2013), 125 million girls and women have endured FGM in 29 countries in Africa and the Middle East alone. The majority of Muslims in Southeast Asia who adhere to Shafii law consider FGM *wajib* (obligatory), while Sunnis and Shi'a consider it *sunnah* (recommended). A recent survey found that 90 per cent of 1,000 Malay Muslim women attending university indicated that they had undergone FGM (ABC News, "Malaysia storm over female circumcision", 7 December 2012, www.abc.net.au/news/2012–12–07/an-malaysia-debate-over-female-circumcision/4416298). In the USA, where FGM is illegal, the African Women's Health Center of the Brigham and Women's Hospital reported that 228,000 women and girls have either suffered the procedure or are at risk of FGM, a number that increased by 35 per cent between 1990 and 2000 (http://theahafoundation.org/issues/female-genital-mutilation/).
8 Interview with Osama bin Laden, *Time Magazine*, January 1999. www.rense.com/general13/duty.htm (accessed 26 December 2013).
9 www.telegraph.co.uk/news/worldnews/asia/pakistan/8964205/Parents-knew-brutal-truth-of-Pakistani-madrassah-dungeon.html (accessed 28 October 2014).
10 www.smh.com.au/world/girl-10-forced-to-wear-suicide-bomb-vest-20140107-hv7oq.html (accessed 28 October 2014).

REFERENCES

Abel, T. (1986). *Why Hitler Came to Power.* Cambridge, MA: Harvard University Press.

Adams, R. (1987). *The Virtue of Faith.* New York: Oxford University Press.

Akhtar, S. (2009). *The Damaged Core.* Lanham, MD: Jason Aronson.

Alcock J. (2005). *Animal Behavior: An Evolutionary Approach,* 8th edn. Sunderland, MA: Sinauer Associates.

Alexander, E. (2012). *Proof of Heaven. A Neurosurgeon's Journey into the Afterlife.* New York: Simon & Schuster.

Aljazeera (2014). UN says Syrian death toll more than 191,000. http://www.aljazeera.com/news/middleeast/2014/08/un-says-syrian-death-toll-more-than-191000-20148221441540572.html (accessed 23 August 2014).

Ali, J. (2012). *Islamic Revivalism Encounters the Modern World: A Study of the Tablīgh Jamā 'at.* New Delhi: Sterling Publishers.

Allen, C. (2007). *God's Terrorists: The Wahhabi Cult and the Hidden Roots of Modern Jihad.* London: Abacus.

Altman, N. (2008). On suicide bombing. *International Journal of Applied Psychoanalytic Studies,* 5:51–66.

Andersen, H. C. (1836). The Little Mermaid. In: *Fairy Tales Told for Children* (1835–1837). Champaign, IL: Project Gutenberg. Also at http://hca.gilead.org.il/li_merma.html (accessed 3 February 2015).

Andersen, H. C. (1858). The Little Match Girl. In: *New Fairy Tales.* New York: Orion Press. http://hca.gilead.org.il/li_match.html (accessed 3 February 2015).

Anon. (1924). Review of O. Pfister, *Some Applications of Psychoanalysis.* Authorized English version. New York: Dodd & Mead. *Psychoanalytic Review,* 11(2):221–3.

Anselm of Canterbury (1962, 2013). *Anselm's Basic Writings,* 2nd edn (trans. S. W. Deane). La Salle, IL: Open Court Publishing.

Anselm of Canterbury (1962, 2013). *Proslogium or Discourse on the Existence of God* (trans S. W. Deane). Medieval Sourcebook, Fordham University Center for Medieval Studies. www.fordham.edu/halsall/basis/anselm-proslogium.asp (accessed 17 September 2013).

Aquinas, St Thomas (1992). *Summa contra gentiles* (trans. A. C. Pegs). Chicago: University of Notre Dame Press.

Aquinas, St Thomas (2012). *Summa theologica*, 2nd edn (trans. Fathers of the English Dominican Province and ed. Craig Paterson). Los Angeles: Viewforth Press.

Arendt, H. (1963). *Eichmann in Jerusalem: A Report on the Banality of Evil*. London: Faber & Faber.

Arieti, S. (1976). *Creativity: The Magic Synthesis*. New York: Basic Books.

Aristotle. (1956). *Metaphysics*. New York: E.P. Dutton.

Armstrong, K. (2000). *The Battle for God: Fundamentalism in Judaism, Christianity and Islam*. New York: HarperCollins.

Asch, S.E. (1956). Studies of independence and conformity: A minority of one against a unanimous majority. *Psychological Monographs*, 70:1–70.

Ash, T. (2001). The case against the cosmological argument. www.bigissueground.com/atheistground/ash-againstcosmological.shtml (accessed 19 September 2013).

Ashbach, C. & Schermer, V.L. (1986). *Object Relations, the Self, and the Group: A Conceptual Paradigm*. London & New York: Routledge & Kegan Paul.

Atkinson, J.C. (1891). *Forty Years in a Moorland Parish: Reminiscences and Researches in Danby in Cleveland*. London: Macmillan.

Atkinson, J.W. & Birch, D. (1970). *The Dynamics of Action*. New York: Wiley.

Atran, S. (2003). Genesis of suicide terrorism. *Science*, 299(5612):1534–9.

Atran, S. (2004). *In Gods We Trust*. Oxford: Oxford University Press.

Atwood, G.E. (2010). The abyss of madness: An interview. *International Journal of Psychoanalytic Self Psychology*, 5(3):334–56.

Atwood, G.E., Stolorow, R.D. & Orange, D.M. (2011). The madness and genius of post-Cartesian philosophy: A distant mirror. *Psychoanalytic Review*, 98(3):263–85.

Auden, W.H. (1952). *The Living Thoughts of Kierkegaard*. New York: New York Review of Books.

Augustine of Hippo, St. (397–8). *Confessions* (trans. R.S. Pine-Coffin). London: Penguin Classics, 1995.

Austin, J.H. (1998). *Zen and the Brain*. Boston, MA: MIT Press.

Azam, J.P. (1995). How to pay for the peace? A theoretical framework with reference to African countries. *Public Choice*, 83:173–84.

Azari, N.P. & Slors, M. (2007). From brain imaging religious experience to explaining religion: A critique. *Archiv für Religionspsychologie*, 29: 67–85.

Azari, N.P., Missimer, J. & Seitz, R.J. (2005). Religious experience and emotion: Evidence for distinctive cognitive neural patterns. *International Journal for the Psychology of Religion*, 15(4):263–81.

Azari, N.P., Nickel, J.P., Wunderlich, G., Niedeggen, M., Hefter, H., Tellmann, L., Herzog, H., Stoerig, P., Birnbacher, D. & Seitz, R.J. (2001). Neural correlates of religious experience. *European Journal of Neuroscience*, 13:1649–52.

Bandura, A. (1965). Influence of models' reinforcement contingencies on the acquisition of imitative responses. *Journal of Personality and Social Psychology*, 1:589–95.

Bandura, A. (1977). *Social Learning Theory*. Englewood Cliffs, NJ: Prentice-Hall.

Bandura, A., Ross, D. & Ross, S.A. (1961). Transmission of aggression through imitation of aggressive models. *Journal of Abnormal and Social Psychology*, 63:575–82.

Barber, P. (1988). *Vampires, Burial and Death: Folklore and Reality*. New Haven, CT: Yale University Press.

Barbour, I.G. (2000). *When Science Meets Religion: Enemies, Strangers, or Partners?* New York: HarperCollins.

Barkway, P. & Kenny, D.T. (2009). Behaviour change. In: P. Barkway (ed.), *Psychology for Health Professions*. Sydney: Elsevier Australia, pp. 125–46.

Barlow, N. (ed) (1958). *The Autobiography of Charles Darwin 1809–1882*. London: Collins.

Barrett, J.L. (2000). Exploring the natural foundations of religion. *Trends in Cognitive Sciences*, 4(1):29–33.

Barrett, J.L. & Keil, F.C. (1996). Anthropomorphic and God concepts: Conceptualizing a non-natural entity. *Cognitive Psychology*, 3:219–47.

Bateman, A. & Fonagy, P. (2004). *Psychotherapy for Borderline Personality Disorder*. Oxford: Oxford University Press.

Bear, D., Levin, K., Blumer, D., Chetham, D. & Ryder, J. (1982). Inter-ictal behavior in hospitalized temporal lobe epileptics: Relationship to idiopathic psychiatric syndromes. *Journal of Neurology, Neurosurgery, and Psychiatry*, 45:481–8.

Behe, M.J. (1996). *Darwin's Black Box: The Biochemical Challenge to Evolution*. New York: The Free Press.

Beit-Hallahmi, B. & Argyle, M. (1997). *The Psychology of Religious Behaviour, Belief and Experience*. London: Routledge.

Bell, R. (1970). *Bell's Introduction to the Qur'ān* (revised and enlarged by W. Montgomery Watt). Edinburgh: Edinburgh University Press.

Bellah, R.N. (2011). *Religion in Human Evolution*. Cambridge, MA: Belknap Press of Harvard University Press.

Bergen, P.L. (2001). *Holy War, Inc.: Inside the Secret World of Osama bin Laden*. New York: The Free Press.

Berger, P.L. (ed.) (1999). *The Desecularization of the World: Resurgent Religion and World Politics*. Washington, DC: Ethics and Public Policy Center.

Berke, J.H. (1996). The wellsprings of fascism: Individual malice, group hatreds, and the emergence of national narcissism. *Free Associations*, 6C:334–50.

Bettelheim, B. (1976). *The Uses of Enchantment: The Meaning and Importance of Fairy Tales*. New York: Alfred A. Knopf.

Bion, W.R. (1961). *Experiences in Groups and Other Papers*. London: Tavistock.

Black, D.M. (ed.) (2006). *Psychoanalysis and Religion in the 21st Century: Competitors or Collaborators?* New York: Routledge.

Blakemore, S.-J. & Frith, C.D. (2003). Self-awareness and action. *Current Opinion in Neurobiology*, 13:219–24.

Blanke, O., Landis, T., Spinelli, L. & Seeck, M. (2004). Out-of-body experience and autoscopy of neurological origin. *Brain*, 127(2):243–58.

Blass, R.B. (2003). The puzzle of Freud's puzzle analogy: Reviving a struggle with doubt and conviction in Freud's *Moses and Monotheism*. *International Journal of Psychoanalysis*, 84:669–82.

Blass, R.B. (2006). Beyond illusion: Psychoanalysis and the question of religious truth. In: D.M. Black (ed.), *Psychoanalysis and Religion in the 21st Century: Competitors or Collaborators?* New York: Routledge, pp. 23–43.

Bollas, C. (1998). Origins of the therapeutic alliance. *Scandinavian Psychoanalytic Review*, 21:24–36.

Bomford, R. (1990). The attributes of God and the characteristics of the unconscious. *International Review of Psycho-Analysis*, 17:485–91.

Bond, R. & Smith, P.B. (1996). Culture and conformity: A meta-analysis of studies using Asch's (1952b, 1956) line judgment task. *Psychological Bulletin*, 119(1):111–37.

Booth, L. (1991). *When God Becomes a Drug*. New York: Putnam.

Bouhdiba, A. (1998). *Sexuality in Islam*. London: Saqi Books.

Bourdieu, P. (1972). *A Theory of Practice*. Cambridge: Cambridge University Press.

Bowlby, J. (1958). The nature of the child's tie to his mother. *International Journal of Psycho-Analysis*, 9:350–73.

Bowlby, J. (1960). Separation anxiety. *International Journal of Psycho-Analysis*, 41:89–113.

Bowlby, J. (1969). *Attachment and Loss: Attachment* (vol. 1). London: Hogarth Press.

Bowlby, J. (1973). *Attachment and Loss: Separation, Anxiety and Anger* (vol. 2). London: Hogarth Press.

Bowlby, J. (1988). *A Secure Base: Clinical Applications of Attachment Theory*. London: Routledge.

Boyd, R. & Richerson, P.J. (1985). *Culture and the Evolutionary Process*. Chicago: University of Chicago Press.

Boyer, P. (1996). What makes anthropomorphism natural? Intuitive ontology and cultural representations. *Journal of Religious Anthropology*, 2:1–15.

Boyer, P. (2001). *Religion Explained: The Evolutionary Origins of Religious Thought*. New York: Basic Books.

Boyer, P. & Bergstrom, B. (2008). Evolutionary perspectives on religion. *Annual Review of Anthropology*, 37:111–30.

Breuer, J. (1893). Part III, 'Theoretical'. In: Joseph Breuer & Sigmund Freud, *Studies on Hysteria (1893–1895). Standard Edition of the Complete Psychological Works of Sigmund Freud* (hereafter, *SE*), 2:183–251. London: Hogarth Press.

Britton, R. (2006). Emancipation of the super-ego. In: D.M. Black (ed.), *Psychoanalysis and Religion in the 21st Century: Competitors or Collaborators?* New York: Routledge, pp. 83–96.

Brown, D.E. (1991). *Human Universals*. New York: McGraw-Hill.

Brown, P. (1969). The diffusion of Manichaeism in the Roman Empire. *Journal of Roman Studies*, 59(1/2):92–103.

Burger, J. M. (2009). Replicating Milgram: Would people still obey today? *American Psychologist*, 64(1): 1–11.

Byrne, P. (2013). Moral arguments for the existence of God. In: E.N. Zalta (ed.), *The Stanford Encyclopedia of Philosophy* (Spring Edition). http://plato.stanford.edu/archives/spr2013/entries/moral-arguments-god (accessed 28 October 2014).

Cadzow, J. (2013). Heart and mind. *Sydney Morning Herald*, 8 June, *The Good Weekend*. www.smh.com.au/national/heart-and-mind-20130603-2nkn0.html (accessed 28 October 2014).

Caesarius of Heisterbach. (1219). *Caesarii Heisterbachensis monachi: Dialogus miraculorum* (ed. Joseph Strange), 2 vols. Cologne, Bonn & Brussels: J.M. Heberle, 1851.

Capps, W.H. (1995). *Religious Studies: The Making of a Discipline*. Minneapolis: Fortress Press.

Carr, B. (ed.). (2007). *Universe or Multiverse?* Cambridge: Cambridge University Press.

Charles, R.H. (1916). Introduction. In: *The Chronicle of John, Bishop of Nikiu*. London: Williams & Norgate.

Chomsky, N. (2000). *New Horizons in the Study of Language and Mind*. Cambridge: Cambridge University Press.

Clodd, E. (1891). *Myths and Dreams*, 2nd edn. London: Chatto & Windus.

Cohen, D. (1989). *Encyclopedia of Monsters: Bigfoot, Chinese Wildman, Nessie, Sea Ape, Werewolf and Many More*. London: Michael O'Mara.

Collins, F. (2006). *The Language of God: A Scientist Presents Evidence for Belief*. New York: Simon & Schuster.

Collins, F. (2008). The language of God: Intellectual reflections of a Christian geneticist. The Veritas Forum, Berkeley, California. www.youtube.com/watch?v=DjJAWuzno9Y (accessed 28 October 2014).

Colman, W. (1988). After the Fall: Original loss and the limits of redemption. *Free Associations*, 1:59–83.

Combe, G. (1857). *On the Relation between Science and Religion*, 4th and people's edn. Edinburgh: MacLachlan & Stewart, pp. 253–60.

Copan, P. & Craig, W.L. (2004). *Creation Out of Nothing*. Leicester: Apollos.

Craig, W.L. (1993). *Theism, Atheism and Big Bang Cosmology*. Oxford: Clarendon Press.

Craig, W.L. (1994). *Reasonable Faith*. Wheaton, IL: Crossway Books.

Cruz, L. (2013). *The Individuation of God*: The Asheville Jung Center reviews this must-own book written by Peter Todd. www.prweb.com/releases/2013/7/prweb10933509.htm (accessed 25 July 2013).

Dalai Lama. (1990). *A Policy of Kindness*. Ithaca, NY: Snow Lion Publications.

Dalton, A. (2013). Rick Warren preaches first sermon after son's suicide. *Huffington Post*, 27 July, www.huffingtonpost.com/2013/07/28/rick-warren-preaches_n_3667264.html (accessed 28 October 2014).

Danilov, V. et al. (eds) (2004). *Sovetskaia derevnia glazami VChK-OGPU-NKVD* (vol. 3). Moscow: ROSSPEN. www.holodomor.org.uk/ (accessed 13 December 2013).

Dannenfeldt, K.H. (1970). *The Church of the Renaissance and Reformation: Decline and Reform from 1300 to 1600*. St. Louis, MO: Concordia Publishing House.

Davanloo, H. (1995). *Unlocking the Unconscious: Selected Papers of Habib Davanloo*. Chichester: Wiley.

Davanloo, H. (2005). Intensive short-term dynamic psychotherapy. In: B. Sadock & V.A. Sadock (eds), *Kaplan and Sadock's Comprehensive Textbook of Psychiatry* (vol. 2). New York: Lippincott Williams Wilkins, pp. 2628–52.

Dawa-Samdup, L.K. (2000). *The Tibetan Book of the Dead, or the After Death Experiences on the Bardo Plane* (ed. and trans. W.Y. Evans-Wentz). Oxford: Oxford University Press.

Darwin C.R. (1874). *The Descent of Man and Selection in Relation to Sex*. New York: Rand, McNally & Company.

Darwin, C.R. (1876). *The Origin of Species by Means of Natural Selection, or the Preservation of Favoured Races in the Struggle for Life*, 6th edn with additions and corrections. London: John Murray. www.darwingame.org/origin%20annotated.pdf (accessed 28 October 2014).

Davis, W. (2000). Heaven's Gate: A study of religious obedience. *Nova Religio*, 3:241–67.

Dawkins, R. (1989). *The Selfish Gene*, 2nd edn. Oxford: Oxford University Press.

Dawkins, R. (2006). *The God Delusion*. Boston, MA: Houghton Mifflin.

Dawkins, R. (2013). *An Appetite for Wonder: The Making of a Scientist*. London: Bantam Press.

Dawkins, R. & Coyne, J. (2005). One side can be wrong. *Guardian*, 2 September. www.theguardian.com/science/2005/sep/01/schools.research (accessed 28 October 2014).

Deacon, T. (1997). *The Symbolic Species: The Coevolution of Language and the Human Brain*. London: Penguin.

Del Col, A. (2010). *L'Inquisizione in Italia*. Milan: Oscar Mondadori.

Dembski, W. (2003). The act of creation: Bridging transcendence and immanence. In: M.M. Zarandi (ed.), *Science and the Myth of Progress*. Bloomington, IN: World Wisdom, pp. 269–302.

De Mello Franco, O. (1998). Religious experience and psychoanalysis: From man-as-god to man-with-god. *International Journal of Psychoanalysis*, 79:113–31.

Dennett, D.C. (1987). *The Intentional Stance*. Cambridge, MA: MIT Press.

Dennett, D.C. (2006). *Breaking the Spell: Religion as a Natural Phenomenon*. New York: Viking Penguin.

Dewey, J. (1922). *Human Nature and Conduct*. New York: Henry Holt & Company.

Diamond, S. (2011). Evil deeds. *Psychology Today*, 2 May. www.psychologytoday.com/blog/evil-deeds/201105/the-violent-life-and-death-osama-bin-laden-psychological-post-mortem (accessed 10 April 2014).

Dickinson, E. (1924). *The Complete Poems of Emily Dickinson*. Boston, MA: Little, Brown & Co. www.bartleby.com/113/, 2000, Part One: Life, CXXVI, "The brain is wider than the sky".

Dixon, C.S. (2002). *The Reformation in Germany*. Oxford: Blackwell.

Dolot, M. (1985). *Execution by Hunger: The Hidden Holocaust*. New York: W.W. Norton.

Drabkin, D. (1994). A moral argument for undertaking theism. *American Philosophical Quarterly*, 31:169–75.

Durham, W.H. (1991). *Coevolution: Genes, Cultures and Human Diversity*. Stanford, CA: Stanford University Press.

Durkheim, E. (1892). *The Division of Labor in Society*. New York: The Free Press.

Durkheim, E. (1912). *The Elementary Forms of the Religious Life* (trans. C. Cosman). Oxford: Oxford University Press.

Durkheim, E. (1951). *Suicide: A Study in Sociology* (trans. John A. Spaulding & George Simson). New York: The Free Press.

Durkheim, E. (1964). *The Elementary Forms of Religious Life*. London: George Allen & Unwin.

Ehrsson, H.H. (2007). The experimental induction of out-of-body experiences. *Science*, 317(5841):1048.

Eigen, M. (1985). Aspects of omnipotence. *Psychoanalytic Review*, 72(1):49–59.

Eigen, M. (1998). *The Psychoanalytic Mystic*. Binghamton, NY: ESF.

Eigen, M. (2001). *Ecstasy*. Middletown, CT: Wesleyan University Press.

Einstein, A. (1932). Letter to Sigmund Freud, 30 July, reproduced in Freud (1933b), pp. 199–201.

Einstein, D.A. & Menzies, R.G. (2004a). Role of magical thinking in obsessive-compulsive symptoms in an undergraduate sample. *Depression and Anxiety*, 19:174–9.

Einstein, D.A. & Menzies, R.G. (2004b). The presence of magical thinking in obsessive compulsive disorder. *Behaviour Research and Therapy*, 42:539–49.

Einstein, D.A. & Menzies, R.G. (2008). Does magical thinking improve across treatment for obsessive-compulsive disorder? *Behaviour Change*, 25:149–55.

Elliott, T. (2013). Witch-hunt. *Sydney Morning Herald*, 20 April, *The Good Weekend*, pp. 16–21.

Ember, C. (1988). *Cultural Variation* (trans. D. Shanshan). Berkeley, CA: Laoning Renmin Chubanshe.

Encyclopaedia Britannica. 2010. Taboo. www.britannica.com/EBchecked/topic/579821/taboo (accessed 2 October 2014).

Erikson, E. (1959). *Identity and the Life Cycle*. New York: International University Press.

Erlich, H.S. (2003). Reflections on the terrorist mind. In: S. Varvin & V.D. Volkan (eds), *Violence or Dialogue: Psychoanalytic Insights on Terror and Terrorism*. London: International Psychoanalytical Association, pp. 146–52.

Esposito, J.L. (ed.) (2013). Pillars of Islam. In: *The Oxford Dictionary of Islam*. Oxford Islamic Studies Online. www.oxfordislamicstudies.com/article/opr/t125/e1859 (accessed 10 December 2013).

Evans-Pritchard, E. (1961). Zande clans and totems. *Man*, 61:116–21.

Falk, A. (2001). Osama bin Laden and America. *Mind and Human Interaction*, 12:161–73.

Fayek, A. (2007). The impasse between the Islamists and the West: Dreaming the same nightmare. *Annual of Psychoanalysis*, 35:273–86.

Fearon, R.M., Van Ijzendoorn, M.H., Fonagy, P., Bakermans-Kranenburg, M.J., Schuengel, C. & Bokhorst, C. (2006). In search of shared and non-shared environmental factors in security of attachment: A behavior-genetic study of the association between sensitivity and attachment security. *Developmental Psychology*, 42:1026–40.

Fenichel, O. (1938). Problems of psychoanalytic technique. *Psychoanalytic Quarterly*, 7:303–24.

Ferenczi, S. (1933). Confusion of tongues between adults and the child. In: M. Balint (ed.), *Final Contributions to the Problems and Methods of Psycho-Analysis* (trans. E. Mosbacher). London: Karnac Books, 1980, pp. 156–67.

Feuerbach, L. (1841). *The Essence of Christianity* (trans. George Eliot). London: John Chapman, 1854.

Fine, M. (2002). 2001 Carolyn Wood Sherif award address. The presence of an absence. *Psychology of Women Quarterly*, 26:9–24.

Finnegan, F. (2001). *Do Penance or Perish: Magdalen Asylums in Ireland*. Piltown, Ireland: Congrave Press.

Fiske, S.T., Harris, L.T. & Cuddy, A.J. (2004). Why ordinary people torture enemy prisoners. *Science*, 306(5701):1482–3.

Fonagy, P. (2001). The psychoanalysis of violence. Paper presented to the Dallas Society for Psychoanalytic Psychology Professional Seminar, 15 March. www.dspp.com/papers/fonagy4.htm (accessed 18 September 2013).

Fonagy, P. & Target, M. (1996a). Playing with reality: I. Theory of mind and the normal development of psychic reality. *International Journal of Psychoanalysis*, 77:217–33.

Fonagy, P. & Target, M. (1996b). Predictors of outcome in child psychoanalysis. A retrospective study of 763 cases at the Anna Freud Centre. *Journal of the American Psychoanalytic Association*, 44(1):27–77.

Fonagy, P. & Target, M. (1997). Attachment and reflective function: Their role in self-organization. *Development and Psychopathology*, 9:679–700.

Fonagy, P. & Target, M. (2002). Early intervention and the development of self-regulation. *Psychoanalytic Inquiry*, 22(3): 307–35.

Foulkes, S.H. (1946). On group analysis. *International Journal of Psycho-Analysis*, 27:46–51.

Fox, J. (2004). The rise of religious nationalism and conflict: Ethnic conflict and revolutionary wars, 1945–2001. *Journal of Peace Research*, 41:715–31.

Frankel, J. (2002). Exploring Ferenczi's concept of identification with the aggressor: Its role in trauma, everyday life, and the therapeutic relationship. *Psychoanalytic Dialogues*, 12(1):101–39.

Frazer, J.G. (1910a). *Totemism and Exogamy* (vol. 3). New York: Cosimo Publications, 2009.

Frazer, J.G. (1910b). *Totemism and Exogamy* (vol. 4). New York: Cosimo Publications, 2009.

Freemon, F.R. (1976). A differential diagnosis of the inspirational spells of Muhammad the Prophet of Islam. *Epilepsia*, 17:423–7.

Freud, A. (1936). *The Ego and the Mechanisms of Defense*. In: *The Writings of Anna Freud* (vol. 2). New York: International Universities Press, 8 vols, 1966–80.

Freud, S. (1893). Frau Emmy von N. In: *Studies on Hysteria. SE*, 2:48–105. London: Hogarth Press, 1955.

Freud, S. (1900). *The Interpretation of Dreams. SE*, 4, 5. London: Hogarth Press, 1953.

Freud, S. (1901). *The Psychopathology of Everyday Life: Forgetting, Slips of the Tongue, Bungled Actions, Superstitions and Errors. SE*, 6. London: Hogarth Press, 1960.

Freud, S. (1907). Obsessive actions and religious practices. *SE*, 9:115–27. London: Hogarth Press, 1959.

Freud, S. (1909). *Notes upon a Case of Obsessional Neurosis. SE*, 10:151–320. London: Hogarth Press, 1955.

Freud, S. (1910). Leonardo da Vinci and a memory of his childhood. *SE*, 11:57–138. London: Hogarth Press, 1957.

Freud, S. (1911a). Psycho-analytic notes on an autobiographical account of a case of paranoia (dementia paranoides). *SE*, 12:1–82. London: Hogarth Press, 1958.

Freud, S. (1911b). Formulations on the two principles of mental functioning. *SE*, 12:213–26. London: Hogarth Press, 1958.

Freud, S. (1913a). *Totem and Taboo: Some Points of Agreement between the Mental Lives of Savages and Neurotics* [1912–13]. *SE*, 13:v, 2–162. London: Hogarth Press, 1955.

Freud, S. (1913b). The disposition to obsessional neurosis: A contribution to the problem of choice of neurosis. *SE*, 12:311–26. London: Hogarth Press, 1958.

Freud, S. (1915). Thoughts for the times on war and death. *SE*, 14:273–300. London: Hogarth Press, 1957.

Freud, S. (1915–17). *Introductory Lectures on Psycho-Analysis*. *SE*, 15, 16. London: Hogarth Press, 1963.

Freud, S. (1917). *Introductory Lectures on Psycho-Analysis*. *SE*, 16: 241–463. London: Hogarth Press.

Freud, S. (1918). *From the History of an Infantile Neurosis*. *SE*, 17:1–124. London: Hogarth Press, 1955.

Freud, S. (1921). *Group Psychology and the Analysis of the Ego*. *SE*, 18:65–144. London: Hogarth Press, 1955.

Freud, S. (1923a). A seventeenth-century demonological neurosis. *SE*, 19:67–106. London: Hogarth Press, 1961.

Freud, S. (1923b). *The Ego and the Id*. *SE*, 19:1–66. London: Hogarth Press, 1961.

Freud, S. (1926). *The Question of Lay Analysis*. *SE*, 20:177–258. London: Hogarth Press, 1959.

Freud, S. (1927). *The Future of an Illusion*. *SE*, 21:1–56. London: Hogarth Press, 1961.

Freud, S. (1930). *Civilization and its Discontents*. *SE*, 21:57–146. London: Hogarth Press, 1961.

Freud, S. (1933a). *New Introductory Lectures on Psycho-Analysis*. *SE*, 22:1–182. London: Hogarth Press, 1964.

Freud, S. (1933b). Why war? *SE*, 22:195–216. London: Hogarth Press, 1964.

Freud, S. (1933c). Dreams and occultism. In: *New Introductory Lectures on Psycho-Analysis*. *SE*, 22:31–56. London: Hogarth Press, 1964.

Freud, S. (1935). Postscript. In: *An Autobiographical Study* [1925]. *SE*, 20:71–6. London: Hogarth Press, 1959.

Freud, S. (1939). *Moses and Monotheism*. *SE*, 23:1–138. London: Hogarth Press, 1964.

Friedland, R. (2001). Religious nationalism and the problem of collective representation. *American Review of Sociology*, 27:125–52.

Friedland, R. (2005). Drag kings at the totem ball: The erotics of collective representation in Emile Durkheim and Sigmund Freud. In: J.C. Alexander & P. Smith (eds), *The Cambridge Companion to Durkheim*. Cambridge: Cambridge University Press, pp. 239–73.

Friedman, R.E. (2003). *The Bible with Sources Revealed*. New York: HarperCollins.

Frith, C. (2004). The pathology of experience. *Brain*, 127(2):239–42.

Fromm, E. (1942). *Fear of Freedom*. London: Routledge.

Fromm, E. (1964). Humanism and psychoanalysis. *Contemporary Psychoanalysis*, 1(1):69–79.

Fromm, E. & Narváez, F. (1968). The Oedipus complex: Comments on "The case of little Hans". *Contemporary Psychoanalysis*, 4(2):178–87.

Gadamer, H.-G. (1975). *Truth and Method*. New York: Crossword.

Gaines, P. & Leaver, M. (2002). Interracial relationships. In: R. Goodwin & D. Cramer (eds), *Inappropriate Relationships: The Unconventional, the Disapproved and the Forbidden*. Hillsdale, NJ: Erlbaum, pp. 65–78.

Galanter, M. (2013). Charismatic groups and cults: A psychological and social analysis. In: K. I. Pargament, J. J. Exline & J. W. Jones (eds), *APA Handbook of Psychology, Religion, and Spirituality (Vol 1): Context, Theory, and Research*. Washington, DC: American Psychological Association, pp. 729–40.

Garson, J. (2013). Modal logic. In: E.N. Zalta (ed.), *The Stanford Encyclopedia of Philosophy* (Spring 2013 Edition). http://plato.stanford.edu/archives/spr2013/entries/logic-modal/ (accessed 28 October 2014).

Gay, P. (1987). *A Godless Jew: Freud, Atheism and the Making of Psychoanalysis*. New Haven, CT: Yale University Press.

Gentile, J. (2010). Weeds on the ruins: Agency, compromise formation, and the quest for intersubjective truth. *Psychoanalytic Dialogues*, 20(1):88–109.

Gibson, J. (ed.). (2001). *Thomas Hardy: The Complete Poems*. New York: Palgrave.

Giménez-Dasí, M., Guerrero, S. & Harris, P.L. (2005). Intimations of immortality and omniscience in early childhood. *European Journal of Developmental Psychology*, 2:285–97.

Gintis, H. (2000). Strong reciprocity and human sociality. *Journal of Theoretical Biology*, 206:169–79.

Girard, R. (2011). *Sacrifice*. East Lansing: Michigan State University Press.

Goldhagen, D.J. (1996). *Hitler's Willing Executioners: Ordinary Germans and the Holocaust*. New York: Little, Brown & Co.

Golding, R. (1982). Freud, psychoanalysis and sociology: Some observations on the sociological analysis of the individual. *British Journal of Sociology*, 33(4):545–62.

Gorski, P.S. & Türkmen-Dervişoğlu, G. (2013). Religion, nationalism, and violence: An integrated approach. *Annual Review of Sociology*, 39:193–210.

Gorsuch, R.L. (1988). Psychology of religion. *Annual Review of Psychology*, 39:201–21.

Govrin, A. (2006). When the underdog schema dominates the we-ness schema: The case of radical leftist Jewish-Israelis. *Psychoanalytic Review*, 93(4):623–54.

Green, A. (2005). *On Private Madness*. London: Karnac Books.

Greene, B. (2009). The use and misuse of religious beliefs in dividing and conquering between socially marginalized groups: The same-sex marriage debate. *American Psychologist*, 64(8):698–709.

Greene, J.C. (1959). Darwin and religion. *Proceedings of the American Philosophical Society*, 103(5):716–25.

Greenfield, S. (2000). *The Private Life of the Brain*. New York: John Wiley & Sons.

Gregory, B.S. (2012). *The Unintended Reformation: How a Religious Revolution Secularized Society*. Cambridge, MA: Harvard University Press.

Grijalva, E., Harms, D., Newman, D.A., Fraley, R.C. & Gaddis, B.H. (2014). Narcissism and leadership: Does it work to be a jerk? *Personnel Psychology*. doi: 10.1111/peps.12072.

Grossman, D. (1995). *On Killing: The Psychological Cost of Learning to Kill in War and Society*. Boston, MA: Little, Brown & Co.

Guibert of Nogent. (1115). *Autobiographie* (ed. and trans. Edmond-René Labande). Paris: Société d'Édition Les Belles Lettres, 1981.

Guiley, R.E. (1989). *The Encyclopedia of Witches and Witchcraft*. New York & Oxford: Facts on File.

Guizzardi, L. (2007). Children of the totem: Children under the law. Notes on the filiation bond in Emile Durkheim. *Durkheimian Studies*, 13:61–84.

Gülen, M.F., Ünal, M. & Haliloğlu, N. (2004). *Toward a Global Civilization of Love and Tolerance*. Somerset, NJ: The Light.

Haney, C. & Zimbardo, P.G. (1998). The past and future of U.S. prison policy twenty-five years after the Stanford prison experiment. *American Psychologist*, 53(7):709–27.

Haney, C., Banks, W.C. & Zimbardo, P.G. (1973). Study of prisoners and guards in a simulated prison. *Naval Research Reviews*, 9:1–17. Washington, DC: Office of Naval Research.

Harris, S. (2004). *The End of Faith*. London: W.W. Norton.

Harris, S. (2006). *The Moral Landscape*. London: Transworld Publishers.

Harris, S. (2008). *Letter to a Christian Nation*. New York: Vintage Books.

Harris, S. (2009). The strange case of Francis Collins. http://www.samharris.org/site/full_text/the-strange-case-of-francis-collins (accessed 3 February 2015).

Hart, D.B. (2009). *Atheist Delusions: The Christian Revolution and its Fashionable Enemies*. New Haven, CT: Yale University Press.

Hasan, Z. (2003). Islamic non-violence. *Star Magazine*, Bangladesh, 7 February. https://sites.google.com/site/liberalislamnet/nonviolence (accessed 28 October 2014).

Haslam, S.A., Reicher, S.D. & Platow, M.J. (2011). *The New Psychology of Leadership*. New York: Psychology Press.

Hauser, M.D. (2006). *Moral Minds: How Nature Designed Our Universal Sense of Right and Wrong*. New York: HarperCollins.

Heidegger, M. (1927). *Being and Time*. Oxford: Blackwell, 1962.

Henderson, B. (2013). The mind of a terrorist. *Sydney Morning Herald*, 11 May, *The Good Weekend*, pp. 30–4.

Heydrich, L. & Blanke, O. (2013). Distinct illusory own-body perceptions caused by damage to posterior insula and extrastriate cortex. *Brain*, 136(3):790–803.

Hicks, J. (2006). *The New Frontier of Religion and Science*. New York: Palgrave Macmillan.

Hillerbrand, H.J. (2007). *The Division of Christendom: Christianity in the Sixteenth Century*. Louisville, KY: Westminster John Knox.

Hinde, R.A. (1999). *Why Gods Persist: A Scientific Approach to Religion*. London & New York: Routledge.

Hinshelwood, R.D. (1991). *A Dictionary of Kleinian Thought*. London: Free Association Books.

Hinshelwood, R.D. (2002). Psychological defense and nuclear war. In: C. Covington, P. Williams, J. Arundale & J. Knox (eds), *Terrorism and War: Unconscious Dynamics of Political Violence*. London: Karnac Books, pp. 249–61.

Hitchens, C. (2007). *God is not Great: The Case against Religion*. London: Atlantic Books.

Holt, P.M., Lambton, S. & Lewis, B. (1977). *The Cambridge History of Islam*. Cambridge: Cambridge University Press.

Holt, R.R. (2003). *Primary Process Thinking: Theory, Measurement, and Research*. Madison, CT: International Universities Press.

Hume, D. (1757). *The Natural History of Religion* (with an Introduction by John M. Robertson). London: A. & H. Bradlaugh Bonner, 1889.

Hume, D. (1779). *Dialogues Concerning Natural Religion*. London: Penguin Classics, 1990.

Huntington, A.P. (1993). The clash of civilizations? *Foreign Affairs*, 72(3):22–50.

Huxley, A. (2004). *The Doors of Perception and Heaven and Hell*. New York: HarperCollins.

Huxley, T. (1913). *Life and Letters of Thomas Huxley* (ed. L. Huxley). London: Macmillan.

Hypatia (n.d.). Return to the Temple of Serapis. http://penelope.uchicago.edu/~grout/encyclopaedia_romana/greece/paganism/hypatia.html (accessed 24 September 2013).

Imam Shirazi (n.d.). A brief biography of Prophet Muhammad. http://imamshirazi.com/prophet-biography.html (accessed 10 December 2013).

Internet Encyclopaedia of Philosophy (IEP) (2013). Western concepts of God. www.iep.utm.edu/god-west/ (accessed 16 September 2013).

Ivey, D. (2010). The vampire myth and Christianity. Rollins College, Winter Park, FL, Masters of Liberal Studies Theses. Paper 16. Rollins Scholarship Online. http://scholarship.rollins.edu/mls/16/ (accessed 28 September 2013).

Jackson, K.D. (1992). *Cambodia, 1975–1978: Rendezvous with Death*. Princeton, NJ: Princeton University Press.

Jacoby, M. (1985). *The Longing for Paradise: Psychological Perspectives on an Archetype*. Boston, MA: Sigo.

James, W. (1902). *The Varieties of Religious Experience: A Study in Human Nature. Being the Gifford Lectures on Natural Religion Delivered at Edinburgh in 1901–1902*. New York: Modern Library.

Janis, I.L. (1972). *Victims of Groupthink: A Psychological Study of Foreign-Policy Decisions and Fiascoes*. Boston, MA: Houghton Mifflin.

Jansen, E.R. (2002). *The Book of Hindu Imagery: Gods, Manifestations and their Meanings*. New Delhi: New Age Books.

John, Bishop of Nikiu. (1916). *The Chronicle* (trans. from Zotenberg's Ethiopic text R.H. Charles). London: Williams & Norgate.

Johnson, J.G., Cohen, P., Brown, J., Smailes, E.M. & Bernstein, D.P. (1999). Childhood maltreatment increases risk for personality disorders during early adulthood. *Archives of General Psychiatry*, 56:600–5.

Johnson, P. (1987). *A History of the Modern World: From 1917 to the 1980s.* London: Weidenfeld & Nicolson.

Johnson, R., Kanewske, L.C. & Barak, M. (2014). Death row confinement and the meaning of last words. *Laws*, 3:141–52. doi:10.3390/laws3010141.

Jones, E. (1910). *On the Nightmare.* London: Hogarth Press and the Institute of Psycho-Analysis, 1931.

Jones, J.W. (2002). *Terror and Transformation: The Ambiguity of Religion in Psychoanalytic Perspective.* Hove, UK: Brunner-Routledge.

Joyce, R. (2001). *The Myth of Morality.* Cambridge: Cambridge University Press.

Jung, C.G. (1921). *Psychological Types.* Collected Works of C.G. Jung (ed. and trans. G. Adler & R.F.C. Hull) (hereafter *CW*) (vol. 6). Princeton, NJ: Princeton University Press, 1971.

Jung, C.G. (1929). Freud and Jung: Contrasts. *CW* (vol. 4). Princeton, NJ: Princeton University Press, pp. 33–40.

Jung, C.G. (1933). *Man in Search of a Soul.* London: Routledge, 2001.

Jung, C.G. (1963). *Memories, Dreams, Reflections.* London: Fontana, 1983.

Jung, C.G. (1970). *Psychology and Religion: West and East. CW* (vol. 11). Princeton, NJ: Princeton University Press.

Jung, C.G. (1976). The spiritual problem of modern man. In: J. Campbell (ed.), *The Portable Jung.* London: Penguin, pp. 456–79.

Jung, C.G. (1977). *The Symbolic Life: Miscellaneous Writings. CW* (vol. 18). Princeton, NJ: Princeton University Press.

Jung, C.G. (1979). *Aion. Researches into the Phenomenology of the Self. CW* (vol. 9.ii). Princeton, NJ: Princeton University Press.

Kakar, S. (1991). *The Analyst and the Mystic. Psychoanalytic Reflections on Religion and Mysticism.* Chicago: University of Chicago Press.

Kant, I. (1781). *Critique of Pure Reason* (trans. and ed. P. Gruyer & A.W. Wood). Cambridge: Cambridge University Press, 1998. Also at www.gutenberg.org/files/4280/4280-h/4280-h.htm (trans. J.M.D. Meiklejohn) (accessed 18 September 2013).

Kaplan, B.J. (2007). *Divided by Faith: Religious Conflict and the Practice of Toleration in Early Modern Europe.* Cambridge, MA: Belknap Press of Harvard University Press.

Katz, L.D. (ed.) (2000). *Evolutionary Origins of Morality: Cross-Disciplinary Perspectives.* Thorverton, UK: Imprint Academic.

Keats, J. (1884). *The Poetical Works of John Keats* (ed. Francis T. Palgrave). London: Macmillan.

Kedar, M. (2013). The most deadly Middle East conflict is Shia vs. Sunni. www.israelnationalnews.com/Articles/Article.aspx/14132#.UsjbAPuwSuk (accessed 4 January 2014).

Keil, F.C. (1989). *Concepts, Kinds and Cognitive Development.* Cambridge, MA: MIT Press.

Kenny, A. (1979). *The God of the Philosophers.* Oxford: Oxford University Press.

Kenny, D.T. (2012). Foreword. In P. Todd, *The Individuation of God: Integrating Science and Religion.* Asheville, NC: Chiron, pp. xii–xvi.

Kenny, D.T. (2013). *Bringing up Baby: The Psychoanalytic Infant Comes of Age.* London: Karnac Books.

Kenny, D.T. (2014). *From Id to Intersubjectivity: Talking about the Talking Cure with Master Clinicians.* London: Karnac Books.

Kent, S.A. (1994). Misattribution and social control in the Children of God. *Journal of Religion and Health*, 33:29–43.

Kepel, G. (2002). *Jihad: The Trail of Political Islam.* Cambridge, MA: Harvard University Press.

Khalid, U. & Olsson, P. (2006). Suicide bombing: A psychodynamic view. *Journal of the American Academy of Psychoanalysis*, 34:523–30.

Khosrokhavar, F. (2002). *Suicide Bombers: Allah's New Martyrs*. London: Pluto Press.

Kierkegaard, S. (1843). *Either/Or: A Fragment of Life*. Princeton, NJ: Princeton University Press, 1941.

Kierkegaard, S. (1849). *The Sickness unto Death*. Princeton, NJ: Princeton University Press, 1941.

King, P.T. (1974). *The Ideology of Order: A Comparative Analysis of Jean Bodin and Thomas Hobbes*. London: George Allen & Unwin.

Kirkpatrick, L.A. (2005). *Attachment, Evolution, and the Psychology of Religion*. New York: Guilford.

Kirshner, L.A. (2004). *Having a Life: Self-pathology after Lacan*. Hillsdale, NJ: Analytic Press.

Kitayama, S. (2014). Mapping mindsets. *Observer*, 26:10. www.psychologicalscience.org/index.php/publications/observer/2013/december-13/mapping-mindsets.html (accessed 14 January 2014).

Kitayama, S. & Uskul, A.K. (2011). Culture, mind, and the brain: Current evidence and future directions. *Annual Review of Psychology*, 62:419–49.

Klein, M. (1948). *The Importance of Symbol-Formation in the Development of the Ego: Contributions to Psycho-Analysis*. London: Hogarth Press.

Klein, M. (1975). *Envy and Gratitude and Other Works 1946–1963*. International Psycho-Analytic Library 104. London: Hogarth Press and the Institute of Psycho-Analysis.

Kobrin, N.H. (2003). Psychoanalytic notes on Osama bin Laden and his jihad against the Jews and Crusaders. *Annual of Psychoanalysis*, 31:211–21.

Kohlberg, L. (1984). *Essays in Moral Development: The Psychology of Moral Development* (vol. 2). New York: Harper & Row.

Kovel, J. (1990). Beyond *The Future of an Illusion*: Further reflections on Freud and religion. *Psychoanalytic Review*, 77(1):69–87.

Kramer, H. & Sprenger, J. (2009). *Malleus maleficarum* (trans. Montague Summers). Digidreads.com Publishing.

Krebs, D.L. (2008). Morality: An evolutionary account. *Perspectives in Psychological Science*, 3(3):149–72.

Krebs, D.L. & Denton, K. (2006). Explanatory limitations of cognitive-developmental approaches to morality. *Psychological Review*, 113:672–5.

Krishan, Y. (1986). Buddhism and the caste system. *Journal of the International Association of Buddhist Studies*, 9(1):71–84.

Kroll, J. & Bachrach, B. (1982). Medieval visions and contemporary hallucinations. *Psychological Medicine*, 12:709–21.

Küng, H. (1986). Religion: The final taboo? *Origins*, 16(2):26–32.

Kurtines, W.M., Gewirtz, J.L. & Bandura, A. (1991). Social cognitive theory of moral thought and action. In: W.M. Kurtines & J.L. Gewirtz (eds), *Handbook of Moral Behavior and Development* (vol. 1). Hillsdale, NJ: Erlbaum, pp. 54–104.

Lacan, J. (1998). *The Seminar of Jacques Lacan: The Four Fundamental Concepts of Psychoanalysis* (Book XI) (ed. J.-A. Miller, trans. Alan Sheridan). New York: W.W. Norton.

Lachmann, F. (2010). Addendum: Afterthoughts on Little Hans and the universality of the Oedipus complex. *Psychoanalytic Inquiry*, 30(6):557–62.

Lakoff, G. & Johnson, M. (1980). *Metaphors We Live By*. Chicago: University of Chicago Press.

Lambert, M.D. (1998). *The Cathars*. Oxford: Blackwell.

Langone, M. (2001). An investigation of a reputedly psychologically abusive group that targets college students. Report for the Danielsen Institute. Boston, MA: Boston University.

Lapidus, I.M. (2002). *A History of Islamic Societies*, 2nd edn. Cambridge: Cambridge University Press.

Lauritzen, B. (2006). *The Invention of God: The Natural Origins of Mythology and Religion*, 2nd edn. StreetWrite, Earth360.com.

Lawson, E.T. & McCauley, R.N. (1990). *Rethinking Religion: Connecting Cognition and Culture*. Cambridge: Cambridge University Press.

Lawson, J. (1910). *Modern Greek Folklore and Ancient Greek Religion: A Study in Survivals*. Cambridge: Cambridge University Press.

Lechner, A. (2007). Changing tack: The ever-changing profile of the suicide bomber. *Intersect: The Journal of International Security*, March.

Lee, H.W., Hong, S.B., Seo, D.W., Tae, W.S. & Hong, S.C. (2000). Mapping of functional organization in human visual cortex: electrical cortical stimulation. *Neurology*, 54:849–54.

Leen-Feldner, E.W., Feldner, M.T., Knapp, A., Bunaciu, L., Blumenthal, H. & Amstadter, A.B. (2013). Offspring psychological and biological correlates of parental posttraumatic stress: Review of the literature and research agenda. *Clinical Psychology Review*. doi: http://dx.doi.org/10.1016/j.cpr.2013.09.001.

Lefkowitz, M. (2003) *Greek Gods, Human Lives: What We Can Learn from Myths*. New Haven, CT: Yale University Press.

Lemma, A. & Patrick, M. (eds). (2010). *Off the Couch: Contemporary Psychoanalytic Perspectives*. London: Routledge.

Lenggenhager, B., Tadi, T., Metzinger, T. & Blanke, O. (2007). Video ergo sum: Manipulating bodily self-consciousness. *Science*, 317(5841):1096–9.

Lévi-Strauss, C. (1963). *Structural Anthropology* (trans. Claire Jacobson & Brooke Grundfest Schoepf). New York: Doubleday Anchor Books, 1967.

Lévi-Strauss, C. (1966). *The Savage Mind*: Chicago: University of Chicago Press.

Lévy-Bruhl, L. (1910). *Les Fonctions Mentales dans les Sociétés Inférieures* (trans. Lilian A. Clare as *How Natives Think*, London: G. Allen & Unwin, 1926). Paris: Presses Universitaires de France.

Lock, M. (1995). *Encounters with Ageing: Mythologies of Menopause in Japan and North America*. California: University of California Press.

Ludin, J. (2009). La parola elusa. *Psicoanalisi*, 13(2):5–18.

Maalouf, A. (2000). *In the Name of Identity: Violence and the Need to Belong* (trans. Barbara Bray). New York: Arcade Publishing.

MacAskill, E. (2005). George Bush: "God told me to end the tyranny in Iraq". *Guardian*, 7 October.

Mackay, C. (1841). *Memoirs of Extraordinary Popular Delusions and the Madness of Crowds*, rev. edn. London: R. Bentley, 1852, 3 vols.

McWhorter, D. (2001). *Carry Me Home: Birmingham, Alabama, The Climactic Battle of the Civil Rights Revolution*. New York: Simon & Schuster.

Malinowski, B. (1927). *Sex and Repression in Savage Society*. London: Kegan Paul, Trench & Tubner.

Marcy, G., Butler, R.P., Fischer, D.A., Vogt, S.S., Wright, J.T., Tinney, C.G. & Jones, H.R.A. (2005). Observed properties of exoplanets: Masses, orbits, and metallicities. *Astrophysics, Progress of Theoretical Physics Supplement*, 158:1–19.

Marx, K. (1843). *Correspondence of 1843*. Cited in: E. Kamenka, *Ethical Foundations of Marxism*. London: Routledge & Kegan Paul, 1962. www.marxists.org/archive/kamenka/1962/ethical-foundations/ch02.htm (accessed 28 October 2014).

Masuzawa, T. (1988). *In Search of Dreamtime: The Quest for the Origin of Religion*. Chicago: University of Chicago Press.

de Mayo, T.B. (2007). *The Demonology of William of Auvergne: By Fire and Sword*. Lewiston, NY: Edwin Mellen Press.

Mead, M. (1930). An ethnologist's footnote to "Totem and Taboo". *Psychoanalytic Review*, 17(3):297–304.

Meissner, W. W. (1984). *Psychoanalysis and Religious Experience.* New Haven, CT: Yale University Press.

Meissner, W. W. (2009). The God question in psychoanalysis. *Psychoanalytic Psychology*, 26:210–33.

Mendelsohn, D. (2006). *The Lost: A Search for Six of Six Million.* New York: HarperCollins.

Meyer, S. C. (2013). *Darwin's Doubt: The Explosive Origin of Animal Life and the Case for Intelligent Design.* New York: HarperOne.

Mildefort, H. C. (1972). *Witch Hunting in Southwestern Germany 1562–1684: The Social and Intellectual Foundations.* Stanford, CA: Stanford University Press.

Milgram, S. (1963). Behavioral study of obedience. *Journal of Abnormal and Social Psychology*, 67:371–8.

Milgram, S. (1965a). Liberating effects of group pressure. *Journal of Personality and Social Psychology*, 1:127–34.

Milgram, S. (1965b). Some conditions of obedience and disobedience to authority. *Human Relations*, 18:57–76.

Milgram, S. (1974). *Obedience to Authority: An Experimental View.* New York: Harper & Row.

Miliora, M. T. (2004). The psychology and ideology of an Islamic terrorist leader: Usama bin Laden. *International Journal of Applied Psychoanalytic Studies*, 1:121–39.

Miller, G. (2007). Out-of-body experiences enter the laboratory. *Science*, 317(5841):1020–1.

Mishra, P. (2002). The Afghan tragedy. *New York Review of Books*, 17 January, pp. 43–9.

Mobley, G. (2013). Review of De La Torre, M.A. & Hernandez, A. (2011). *The Quest for the Historical Satan.* Minneapolis: Fortress. *Theology Today*, 70(2):238–9.

Moore, B. & Fine, B. (eds). (1990). *Psychoanalytic Terms and Concepts.* New York: American Psychoanalytic Association.

Moore, R. I. (2006). *The Formation of a Persecuting Society: Power and Deviance in Western Europe, 1050–1250.* Oxford: Basil Blackwell.

Moreland, J. P. & Craig, W. L. (2003). *Philosophical Foundations for a Christian Worldview.* Downers Grove, IL: InterVarsity Press.

Nafissi, M. (2005). Reformation, Islam, and democracy: Evolutionary and antievolutionary reform in Abrahamic religions. *Comparative Studies of South Asia, Africa and the Middle East*, 25(2):407–37.

Nagel, T. (1979). What is it like to be a bat? In: *Mortal Questions.* Cambridge: Cambridge University Press, pp. 165–80.

Nasr, V. (2006). *The Shia Revival.* New York: W. W. Norton.

National Counterterrorism Center (NCTC) (2011). Report on Terrorism. www.fas.org/irp/threat/nctc2011.pdf (accessed 13 January 2015).

National Counterterrorism Center (NCTC) (2012). www.state.gov/j/ct/rls/crt/2011/195555.htm (accessed 1 April 2014).

Neiwert, D. A. (1999) *In God's Country: The Patriot Movement and the Pacific Northwest.* Pullman, WA: Washington State University Press.

Neville, F. G. & Reicher, S. D. (2013). The experience of collective participation: shared identity, relatedness and emotionality. In: J. Drury & C. Stott (eds), *Crowds in the 21st Century: Perspectives from Contemporary Social Science.* London: Routledge, pp. 377–96.

Newberg, A., Alavi, A., Baime, M., Pourdehnad, M. J., Santanna, J. & d'Aquili, E. (2001). The measurement of regional cerebral blood flow during the complex cognitive task of meditation: A preliminary SPECT study. *Psychiatry Research*, 106:113–22.

Newberg, A.B. & d'Aquili, E. (2001). *Why God Won't Go Away: Brain Science and the Biology of Belief.* New York: Ballantine Books.

Newton, I. (1687). *Principia.* London: Apud Guil. & Joh. Innys, 1726.

Nichols, S. (2002). Norms with feeling: Towards a psychological account of moral judgment. *Cognition,* 84:221–36.

Nietzsche, F. (1882). *The Gay Science* (trans. and commentary W. Kaufman). New York: Vintage Books, 1974.

Nietzsche, F. (1886). *Beyond Good and Evil.* New York: Penguin, 1973.

Nietzsche, F. (1908). *Ecce Homo.* New York: Vintage, 1967.

Oesterdiekhoff, G.W. (2009). *Mental Growth of Humankind in History.* Norderstedt, Germany: Books on Demand.

Oesterdiekhoff, G.W. (2012). Was pre-modern man a child? The quintessence of the psychometric and developmental approaches. *Intelligence,* 40(5):470–8.

Olding, R. (2013). A blinding fervour: The devout Australian Muslims ready to give their lives in Syria. *Sydney Morning Herald,* 7 December, News Review, p. 4.

Oliver, A.M. & Sternberg, P. (2005). *The Road to Martyrs' Square: A Journey into the World of the Suicide Bomber.* Oxford: Oxford University Press.

Olsson, P. (2005). *Malignant Pied Pipers of our Time: A Psychological Study of Destructive Cult Leaders from the Rev. Jim Jones to Osama bin Laden.* Baltimore, MD: Publish America.

O'Neil, M.K. & Akhtar, S. (eds). (2009). *On Freud's "The Future of an Illusion".* London: Karnac Books.

Onians, R.B. (1954). *The Origins of European Thought about the Body, the Soul, the World, Time and Fate.* Cambridge: Cambridge University Press.

Otloh of St Emmeram. (1070). *Liber de temptatione cuiusdam monachi: Untersuchung, kritische Edition und Übersetzung* (ed. and trans. Sabine Gäbe). Berne: Peter Lang, 1999.

Otsuka, K., Sakai, A. & Dening, T. (2004). Haizmann's madness: The concept of bizarreness and the diagnosis of schizophrenia. *History of Psychiatry,* 15(1):73–82.

Otto, R. (1917). *The Idea of the Holy* (trans. J.W. Harvey). New York: Oxford University Press, 1958.

Oussani, G. (1911). Mohammed and Mohammedanism. In: *The Catholic Encyclopedia.* New York: Robert Appleton Company. www.newadvent.org/cathen/10424a.htm (accessed 17 January 2014).

Palmer, M. (1997). *Freud and Jung on Religion.* London: Routledge.

Pape, R.A. (2005). *Dying to Win: The Strategic Logic of Suicide Terrorism.* New York: Random House.

Parsons, E.F. (2005). Midnight rangers: Costume and performance in the reconstruction-era Ku Klux Klan. *Journal of American History,* 92(3):811–36.

Parsons, W. (2010). On mapping the psychology and religion movement: Psychology as religion in modern spirituality. *Pastoral Psychology,* 59:15–25.

PDM Task Force. (2006). *Psychodynamic Diagnostic Manual.* Silver Spring, MD: Alliance of Psychoanalytic Organizations.

Pérez, L. (2006). *The Spanish Inquisition.* London: Profile Books.

Peter Lombard (2008). *The Sentences. Book 2: On Creation* (trans. Giulio Silano). Toronto: Pontifical Institute of Mediaeval Studies. Available at The Franciscan Archive, n.d. www.franciscan-archive.org/lombardus/II-Sent.html (accessed 3 October 2013).

Peter the Venerable. (1988). *Petri Cluniacensis Abbatis: De miraculis libri duo* (ed. and commentary Denise Bouthillier). *Corpus Christianorum. Continuatio Mediaevalis* (vol. 83). Turnhout: Brepols.

Peters, K.E. (2010). Zygon and the future of religion-and-science. *Zygon,* 45(2):432–6.

Pew Research Center Forum on Religion & Public Life. (2011a). The future of the global Muslim population. www.pewforum.org/2011/01/27/the-future-of-the-global-muslim-population/ (accessed 8 November 2013).

Pew Research Center Forum on Religion & Public Life (2011b). Government restrictions index. www.pewforum.org/2011/08/09/rising-restrictions-on-religion-gri/ (accessed 8 November 2013).

Pew Research Project on Religion & Public Life. (2013). Many Sunnis and Shias worry about religious conflict: Concern especially high among Muslims in Lebanon. www.pewforum.org/2013/11/07/many-sunnis-and-shias-worry-about-religious-conflict/ (accessed 18 November 2013).

Pew-Templeton Global Religious Futures Project. (2010). Pew-Templeton Religious Futures Project: Explore the data. www.globalreligiousfutures.org/explorer#/?subtopic=76&countries=Worldwide&index=SHI&chartType=scatter&year=2011 (accessed 13 September 2013).

Pew-Templeton Global Religious Futures Project (2012). http://www.globalreligiousfutures.org/explorer/about (accessed 18 September 2013).

Pfister, O. (1923). *Some Applications of Psychoanalysis* (authorized English version). New York: Dodd & Mead.

Piaget, J. (1927). The child's first year. *British Journal of Psychology*, 18:97–120.

Piaget J. (1932). *The Moral Judgment of the Child*. London: Routledge & Kegan Paul.

Piaget, J. (1936). *The Origins of Intelligence in Children*. New York: W.W. Norton, 1963.

Piaget, J. (1947). *The Psychology of Intelligence*. Oxford: Armand Colin.

Piaget, J. (1954). *The Construction of Reality in the Child* (trans. M. Cook). New York: Basic Books.

Piaget, J. (1967). *Biologie et Connaissance*. Paris: Gallimard.

Piaget, J., Tomlinson, J. & Tomlinson, A. (1929). *The Child's Conception of the World*. London: Routledge & Paul.

Pickering, W.S.F. (1984). *Durkheim's Sociology of Religion: Themes and Theories*. London: Routledge & Kegan Paul.

Picq, L. (1989). *Beyond the Horizon: Five Years with the Khmer Rouge*. New York: St. Martin's Press.

Plantinga, A. (1965). *The Ontological Argument from St. Anselm to Contemporary Philosophers*. Garden City, NY: Doubleday.

Plantinga, A. (1974). *God, Freedom, and Evil*. New York: Harper & Row.

Plantinga, A. (2000). *Warranted Christian Belief*. Oxford: Oxford University Press.

Plato. (1949). *Timaeus*. New York: Liberal Arts Press.

Pojman, L.J. (2003). Faith, hope, and doubt. In: L.J. Pojman (ed.), *Philosophy of Religion: An Anthology*. Belmont, CA: Wadsworth Thomson Publisher, pp. 436–46.

Polkinghorne, J.C. (2003). *Belief in God in an Age of Science*. New Haven, CT: Yale University Press.

Pollard, R. (2014). The Syrian storm. *Sydney Morning Herald*, 4–5 January, News Review, pp. 6–7.

Pribram, K.R. (2004). Consciousness reassessed. *Mind and Matter*, 2(1):7–35.

Puri, B.K., Lekh, S.K., Nijran, K.S., Bagary, M.S. & Richardson, A.J. (2001). SPECT neuroimaging in schizophrenia with religious delusions. *International Journal of Psychophysiology*, 40:143–8.

Pyper, H.S. (1997). The selfish text: The Bible and memetics. The Bible into Culture Colloquium, Sheffield, 9–12 April. www.lycaeum.org/~sputnik/Memetics/bible.html (accessed 6 August 2013).

Radcliffe-Brown, A. (1952). *Structure and Function in Primitive Society*. Glencoe, IL: The Free Press.

Rank, O. (1914). *The Myth of the Birth of the Hero.* The Journal of Nervous and Mental Disease Monographs 18. New York: The Journal of Nervous and Mental Disease Publishing Company.

Rashid, Q. (2013). *The Wrong Kind of Muslim.* London: AyHa Publishing.

Richert, R.A. & Harris, P.L. (2006). The ghost in my body: Children's developing concept of the soul. *Journal of Cognition and Culture*, 6:409–27.

Rieffer, B.-A.J. (2003). Religion and nationalism: Understanding the consequences of a complex relationship. *Ethnicities*, 3:215–42.

Riffert, F.G. (2002). On non-substantialism in psychology – convergences between Whitehead's process philosophy and Piaget's genetic structuralism. *International Journal for Field-Being*, 21(1), Article 2.

Rizzuto, A. (1979). *The Birth of the Living God. A Psychoanalytic Study.* Chicago: University of Chicago Press.

Robinson, N. (2003). *Discovering the Qur'ān: A Contemporary Approach to a Veiled Text*, 2nd edn. London: SCM Press.

Ross, J. (2002). The sexualization of difference: A comparison of mixed-race and same-gender marriage. *Harvard Civil Rights–Civil Liberties Law Review*, 37:255–88.

Roughgarden, J. (2006). *Evolution and Christian Faith: Reflections of an Evolutionary Biologist.* Washington, DC: Island Press.

Russell, B. (1957). Why I am not a Christian. In: Edwards (ed.), *Why I am not a Christian and Other Essays on Religion and Related Subjects.* London: George Allen & Unwin Ltd. http://schutt.org/files/documents/russell-why_i_am_not_a_christian.pdf (accessed 18 September 2013).

Ruys, J. (2012). Sensitive spirits: Changing depictions of demonic emotions in the twelfth and thirteenth centuries. *Digital Philology*, 1(2):184–209.

Ryan, C. (2011). Irish Church's forgotten victims take case to U.N. *The New York Times*, 25 May.

Saad-Ghorayeb, A. (2002). *Hizbu'llah: Politics and Religion.* London: Pluto.

Schachter, S. & Singer, J. (1962). Cognitive, social, and physiological determinants of emotional state. *Psychological Review*, 69:379–99.

Scharf, B.R. (1970). Durkheimian and Freudian theories of religion: The case of Judaism. *British Journal of Sociology*, 21(2):151–63.

Schatzman, M. (1973). *Soul Murder: Persecution in the Family.* New York: Random House.

Schmidt, W. (1931). *The Origin and Growth of Religion* (trans. H.J. Rose). London: Methuen.

Schoenfeld, C.G. (1962). God the Father – and Mother: Study and extension of Freud's conception of God as an exalted father. *American Imago*, 19:213–34.

Schönpflug, U. (ed.) (2009). *Cultural Transmission: Psychological, Developmental, Social, and Methodological Aspects.* Cambridge: Cambridge University Press.

Schwab, M.E. (1977). A study of reported hallucinations in a south eastern country. *Health and Society*, 4:344–55.

Schwartz, B. & Lee, J. (2013). Inquiry into child sex abuse slams Catholics, recommends sweeping change. www.smh.com.au/national/inquiry-into-child-sex-abuse-slams-catholics-recommends-sweeping-change-20131113-2xfdg.html (accessed 24 December 2013).

Schwartz, R.M. (1997). *The Curse of Cain: The Violent Legacy of Monotheism.* Chicago & London: University of Chicago Press.

Sher, M.L. (2013). Don't drink poison (12 December). www.huffingtonpost.com/margery-leveen-sher/dont-drink-poison_b_4408347.html (accessed 13 December 2013).

Shilling, C. (2005). Embodiment, emotions, and the foundations of social order: Durkheim's enduring contribution. In: J.C. Alexander & P. Smith (eds), *The Cambridge Companion to Durkheim.* Cambridge: Cambridge University Press, pp. 211–38.

Shtulman, A. (2008). Variation in the anthropomorphization of supernatural beings and its implications for cognitive theories of religion. *Journal of Experimental Psychology. Learning, Memory, and Cognition*, 34(5):1123–38.

Sidgwick, H., Johnson, A., Myers, F.W.H., Podmore, F. & Sidgwick, E.M. (1894). Report on the census of hallucinations. *Proceedings of the Society for Psychical Research*, 10:25–422.

Siegel, A.B. (2005). Children's dreams and nightmares: Emerging trends in research. *Dreaming*, 15(3):147–54.

Silver, A. & Ursini, J. (1993). *The Vampire Film: From Nosferatu to Bram Stoker's Dracula*. New York: Limelight.

Simonds, P. (1974). *The Social Primates*. New York: Harper Row.

Skelton, R. (ed.). (2006). *The Edinburgh International Encyclopaedia of Psychoanalysis*. Edinburgh: Edinburgh University Press.

Smith, A.D. (2003). *Chosen Peoples: Sacred Sources of National Identity*. Oxford: Oxford University Press.

Smith, J.H. & Handelman, S. (eds) (1990). *Psychoanalysis and Religion*. Baltimore & London: Johns Hopkins University Press.

Smythe, T. (2011). A critique of recent criticisms of Freud on religious belief. *Open Journal of Philosophy*, 1:11–15.

Socrates Scholasticus. (2001). *The Ecclesiastical History*. Chapter 15: Of Hypatia the female philosopher, p. 165. www.aren.org/prison/documents/religion/Church%20Fathers/The%20Ecclesiastical%20History.pdf (accessed 24 September 2013).

Sosis, R. (2003). Why aren't we all Hutterites? Costly signaling theory and religious behavior. *Human Nature*, 14:91–127.

Sperber, D. (1996). *Explaining Culture: A Naturalistic Approach*. Oxford: Blackwell.

Spezzano, C. & Gargiulo, G.J. (eds). (1997). *Soul on the Couch: Spirituality, Religion, and Morality in Contemporary Psychoanalysis*. Hillsdale, NJ: Analytic Press.

Stacey, R.D. (2003). *Complexity and Group Process: A Radically Social Understanding of Individuals*. Hove, UK & New York: Brunner-Routledge.

Stark, R. (2003). *For the Glory of God: How Monotheism Led to Reformations, Science, Witch-Hunts, and the End of Slavery*. Princeton, NJ: Princeton University Press.

Steels, L. (2009). Is sociality a crucial prerequisite for the emergence of language? In: R. Botha & C. Knight (eds), *The Prehistory of Language*. Oxford: Oxford University Press, pp. 36–57.

Stern, J. (2003). *Terror in the Name of God: Why Religious Militants Kill*. New York: HarperCollins.

Stoker, B. (1897). *Dracula*. TR Wheeler eBooks.

Stolorow, R.D. (2007). *Trauma and Human Existence*. New York: Routledge.

Stolorow, R.D. & Atwood, G.E. (1996). The intersubjective perspective. *Psychoanalytic Review*, 83(2):181–94.

Stolorow, R.D. & Atwood, G.E. (2013). The tragic and the metaphysical in philosophy and psychoanalysis. *Psychoanalytic Review*, 100(3):405–21.

Strachey, J. (1930). Editor's introduction to *Civilization and its Discontents*. SE, 21:59–63. London: Hogarth Press.

Summers, M. (2005). *Vampires and Vampirism*. Mineola, NY: Dover Publication.

Swinburne, R. (1992). *Revelation: From Metaphor to Analogy*. Oxford: Clarendon Press.

Swinburne, R. (1996). *Is There a God?* Oxford: Oxford University Press.

Symington, N. (1994). *Emotion and Spirit: Questioning the Claims of Psychoanalysis and Religion*. London: Cassell.

Tajfel, H. (1978). Inter-individual and inter-group behaviour. In: H. Tajfel (ed.), *Differentiation between Groups: Studies in the Social Psychology of Intergroup Relations*. London: Academic Press, pp. 27–60.

Todd, P. (2012). *The Individuation of God: Integrating Science and Religion*. Asheville, NC: Chiron.

Trinkaus, E. & Shipman, P. (1993). *The Neanderthals: Changing the Image of Mankind*. New York: Knopf.

Turner, M.E. & Pratkanis, A.R. (1998). Twenty-five years of groupthink theory and research: Lessons from the evaluation of a theory. *Organizational Behavior and Human Decision Processes*, 73:105–15.

Tyerman, C. (2006). *God's War: A New History of the Crusades*. Cambridge, MA: Belknap Press of Harvard University Press.

UNICEF. (2013). *Female Genital Mutilation/Cutting: A Statistical Overview and Exploration of the Dynamics of Change*. New York: UNICEF.

Vasalou, S. (2002). The miraculous eloquence of the Qur'ān: General trajectories and individual approaches. *Journal of Qur'a⁻nic Studies*, 4(2):23–53.

Vasquez, K., Keltner, D., Edenbach, D.H. & Banaszynski, T.L. (2001). Cultural variation and similarity in moral rhetorics: Voices from the Philippines and United States. *Journal of Cross-Cultural Psychology*, 32:93–120.

Volkan, V. (2004). *Bind Trust: Large Groups and their Leaders in Times of Crises and Terror*. Charlottesville, VA: Pitchstone Press.

Voltaire. (1736). *Mahomet*. In: *The Works of Voltaire: The Dramatic Works of Voltaire* (vol. 8.ii) (ed. and trans. T. Smollett, J. Morley, W.F. Fleming & O.H.G. Leigh). Akron, OH: Werner, 1905, pp. 5–86.

Voltaire. (1765). *Questions sur les Miracles*. In: *Oeuvres Complètes de Voltaire*, ed. Louis Moland (vol. 25). Paris: Garnier, 1877–85, pp. 357–450.

Voltaire. (1767). Letter to Frederick II of Prussia, 6 April. http://en.wikiquote.org/wiki/Voltaire (accessed 16 November 2013).

Ward, T.D. (1994). Structured imagination: The role of category structure in exemplar generation. *Cognitive Psychology*, 27:1–40.

Warren, R. (1997). *The Purpose-Driven Life: What on Earth am I Here For?* Grand Rapids, MI: Zondervan.

Watt, W.M. (1961). *Muhammad: Prophet and Statesman*. Oxford: Oxford University Press.

Watt, W.M. (1977). Muhammad. In: *The Cambridge History of Islam* (vol. 1). Cambridge: Cambridge University Press, pp. 30–56. Cambridge Histories Online. http://dx.doi.org/10.1017/CHOL9780521219464.004 (accessed 19 January 2014).

Watts, A.L., Lilienfeld, S.O., Smith, S.F., Miller, J.D., Campbell, W.K., Waldman, I.D., Rubenzer, S.J. & Faschingbauer, T.J. (2013). The double-edged sword of grandiose narcissism: Implications for successful and unsuccessful leadership among U.S. Presidents. *Psychological Science*, online 8 October. doi: 10.1177/0956797613491970.

Webber, A.J. (2011). *The Doppelgänger: Double Visions in German Literature*. Oxford: Oxford University Press.

Weber, M. (1978). *Economy and Society*. Berkeley, CA: University of California Press.

Wei, H.-L. (1968). Categories of totemism in ancient China. *Chung Yang Yen Chiu Yuan Min Tsu Hsueh Yen Chiu So Chi K'an/Bulletin of the Institute of Ethnology Academia Sinica*, 25:1–34.

West, C. (1996). Cornel West on heterosexism and transformation: An interview. *Harvard Educational Review*, 66:356–67.

Westphal, M. (1998). *Suspicion and Faith: The Religious Uses of Modern Atheism*. New York: Fordham University Press.

Wheatley, J. (2013a). An arch-atheist reveals his poetic soul. *Sun Herald*, 15 September, Extra, p. 31.

Wheatley, J. (2013b). The slaves of Magdalen. *Sydney Morning Herald*, 21 December, *The Good Weekend*, pp. 28–31.

Whitsett, D. & Kent, S.A. (2003). Cults and families. *Families in Society*, 84(4):491–502.

William of Auvergne (*c.* 1230). *De universo. Guilielmi Alverni Episcopi Parisiensis: Opera omnia* (vol. 1). Facsimile. Frankfurt-am-Main: Minerva, 1963, pp. 593–1074.

Wilson, K. (1985). The history of the word 'vampire'. *Journal of the History of Ideas*, 46(4):577–81.

Wilson, R.A. (1966). *Feminine Forever*. New York: M. Evans.

Winnicott, D.W. (1953). Transitional objects and transitional phenomenon: A study of the first not-me possession. *International Journal of Psycho-Analysis*, 34:89–97.

Winnicott, D.W. (1965). Morals and education. In: *The Maturational Processes and the Facilitating Environment*. New York: International Universities Press, pp. 93–105. (Originally published 1963.)

Winnicott, D.W. (1969). The use of an object. *International Journal of Psycho-Analysis*, 50:711–16.

Winseman, A.L. (2004). Eternal destinations: Americans believe in heaven, hell. Religion and Social Trends, 25 May. Princeton, NJ: The Gallup Organization.

Wittgenstein, L. (1921). *Tractatus Logico-Philosophicus*. London: Routledge, 1974.

Wolpert, K. (2006). *Six Impossible Things before Breakfast: The Evolutionary Origins of Belief*. New York: W.W. Norton.

World Health Organization. (2014). Female genital mutilation. www.who.int/mediacentre/factsheets/fs241/en/ (accessed 30 March 2014).

Wundt, W.M. (1906). *Völkerpsychologie: Sprache, Mythus und Sitte*. Leipzig: Wilhelm Engelmann

Wundt, W.M. (1916). *Elements of Folk Psychology: Outlines of a Psychological History of the Development of Mankind*. London: George Allen & Unwin.

Xingliang, H. (2003). The origin of totems. Institute of Nationality Studies, Chinese Academy of Social Sciences. http://bic.cass.cn/english/infoShow/Arcitle_Show_Forum2_Show.a sp?ID=259&Title=The+Humanities+Study&strNavigation=Home%3EForum&BigCl assID=4&SmallClassID=8 (accessed 29 November 2013).

Yalom, I.D. (1989). *Love's Executioner and Other Tales of Psychotherapy*. London: Bloomsbury.

Yau, J. & Smetana, J.G. (2003). Conceptions of moral, social-conventional, and personal events among Chinese pre-schoolers in Hong Kong. *Child Development*, 74:647–58.

Young, R.M. (2001). Fundamentalism and terrorism. *Free Associations*, 9:24–57.

Yu, C.K.-C. (2013). Obsessive-compulsive distress and its dynamic associations with schizotypy, borderline personality, and dreaming. *Dreaming*, 23(1):46–63.

Zilboorg, G. (1939). The fundamental conflict with psycho-analysis. *International Journal of Psycho-Analysis*, 20:480–92.

Zimbardo, P. (2007). *The Lucifer Effect: Understanding How Good People Turn Evil*. New York: Random House.

Zubrzycki, G. (2006). *The Crosses of Auschwitz: Nationalism and Religion in Post-Communist Poland*. Chicago: University of Chicago Press.

Zuckerman, S. (1932). *The Social Life of Monkeys and Apes*. New York: Harcourt & Brace.

INDEX

Page numbers with 't' are tables.

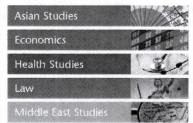

CPSIA information can be obtained at www.ICGtesting.com
Printed in the USA
LVOW10s1158130316

478975LV00007B/72/P